REVIE

REVERED AND REVILED

The Authorised Biography by
RICHARD SUTCLIFFE

GREAT NORTHERN

For Annie

Great Northern Books
PO Box 213, Ilkley, LS29 9WS
www.greatnorthernbooks.co.uk

ISBN: 978-1905080-78-6

Design and layout: David Burrill

Printed and bound in the UK by CPI Mackays, Chatham ME5 8TD

CIP Data
A catalogue for this book is available from the British Library

CONTENTS

Foreword

by Kevin Keegan

'Who was the best manager you played under?' is a question often asked of former footballers. My answer never wavers - Bill Shankly, with Don Revie coming in a very close second. And as someone who loved Shanks like a father, I can think of no higher accolade to pay a man who was not only my international manager with England for three years but also, later in life, a very dear friend. I still treasure the memories of the hours we spent together after Don had moved to Marbella, where we would play a lot of golf and pass many a happy evening socialising with our families. Don had retired from football by then, but the fierce competitive streak and will-to-win that had characterised his great Leeds United team were alive and well. We were, in fact, quite a formidable pair on the golf course, willing to take on all-comers with the added spice of a little bet on the side to keep things interesting. Two Irish lads were our regular opponents, and Don would mischievously get to work on the pair from the moment we stepped on to the first tee. Speaking just loud enough for them to hear, he would lean towards me and say, 'Chip, chip, chip, Kevin... keep chipping away'. The mantra would then be repeated as we made our way around the course, all the time unsettling the two Irish lads who were wondering what the hell Don was on about. I must admit I wasn't certain myself but the upshot was that we would invariably win. Eventually, and after countless rounds between the four of us, curiosity got the better of the two lads and they asked Don about the significance of his 'chip, chip, chip...' comment. He explained it simply by telling us to imagine a block of granite, and then asked what would be the best way to break it up. Before anyone could answer, he added, with a glint in his eye, 'I find chipping away at the granite is far more effective than attempting to blast it apart in one go'. And that was what Don had been doing, making sure we kept chipping away at the two Irish lads during the round. It was a simple psychological trick he had learned very early as a football manager and one he had never forgotten.

Mind, the Irish lads did eventually exact a revenge of sorts. After we had trounced them in Spain for the umpteenth time, they demanded a rematch on home soil and insisted on paying for everything – flights to Ireland, hotels, you name it. Don and I started well, winning the first two matches only for the Irish lads to then introduce a professional called Paddy McGuirk to their team. I was quite relaxed about it but Don was not happy. He kept saying, 'You can't beat a pro, Kevin, it is simply not possible'. He was right, of course, though we did take that third match to the 16th hole before we lost. But, despite putting up a brave effort when the odds had been stacked firmly against us, Don was absolutely gutted to lose, proving how even a happy retirement could not dilute his renowned competitive instinct.

That will-to-win is, of course, something that anyone fortunate enough to have seen Don's Leeds United side play will know all about. They were ruthless and a team that, at Liverpool, we were always desperate to beat. To say we hated Leeds in those days would be a bit strong, but there was no denying the two clubs were bitter rivals on the pitch. Don and Bill Shankly had been good friends for many years, as had some of the lads. But come the day of a game between the two teams, all that meant nothing. We were both chasing the same prizes and a win over Leeds would often make all the difference, hence the huge rivalry. Leeds were a difficult team to play against, as not only were they very physical but also tremendously talented. We had many hard tussles over the years so, when I found out Don had been appointed England manager in 1974, it is fair to say I was not overly thrilled at the news. To those of us who played for Liverpool, he was part of the enemy and yet here I was, suddenly, on the same side as him. I felt it might be a hard adjustment to make. Those fears were allayed, however, from the moment I joined up with an England squad under Don for the first time. I warmed to him straight away. I could see everything was geared towards building a strong team spirit, hence the introduction of the bingo sessions and the putting competitions that would later become a stick that the critics used to beat Don. Some players didn't like them, I accept that. To me, it seemed something of a north-south divide as I doubt some of the southern lads such as Stan Bowles and Alan Hudson had even heard of bingo, never mind played it. But, on the whole, most of the squad responded well to what was only ever intended to be a pleasant way of passing the time when 20-odd players were cooped up in the same hotel.

It was a similar story with the infamous dossiers Don and his coaching staff prepared for us ahead of internationals. History has since shown that Don was ahead of his time, with in-depth analysis of the opposition having since become the rule in football rather than the exception. Plus, it is important to remember that football in the 1970s was not like it is now when what seems like every league in the world can be watched on television from the comfort of your own armchair. Back then, we would be hard pressed to know more than a couple of the East German side. Or even, for that matter, Brazil. So, to have their strengths and weaknesses laid out in front of us was useful. I would say 75 per cent of the England players bought in to the dossiers idea but the other quarter didn't. And, unfortunately for Don, the press picked up on the 25 per cent and ridiculed him as a result.

Like any football manager, Don's fate was always going to be decided by results. And in his three years with England, we didn't get the necessary results. But I still firmly believe that had he stayed in the job longer then England would have been successful under Don Revie. Unfortunately, the way he left to take up a job offer with the United Arab Emirates tainted Don in the eyes of the public. But, I have to say the image many still have of Don to this day could not be more wide of the mark. I had to laugh, for instance, at how the film *The Damned United* depicted him as a dour and miserable figure. It was so, so wrong. The people behind the film were, no doubt, trying to pretend they knew all about Don and his character. To me, though, all they ended up doing was proving the exact opposite.

Certainly, the Don I got to know was a warm and kind man, who enjoyed simple pleasures and loved his family. He was also a loyal friend, even insisting on coming along to support me when playing golf in Marbella after the onset of motor neurone disease had left him unable to walk around the course. Don would put a few quid on me and then drive round in a buggy, offering encouragement all the way round. That is the man I remember and why I feel the time has come for the story of the real Don Revie to be told.

Kevin Keegan, 2010.

Introduction

Elland Road, May 1988

The face was unmistakeable, as was the adoration and affection felt towards the man emerging hesitantly from the tunnel at Elland Road. His 'sons', the boys he turned into men while transforming Leeds United into one of Europe's most feared football teams, were all there, some having travelled hundreds of miles for what was always going to be a poignant occasion. All were determined to pay tribute to a very special man on what, deep down, they knew would be the last reunion of the old gang in his presence. Many were blinking back tears, a mixture of sadness at the cruel hand fate had played their old boss and pride at his determination not to give in to the unforgiving motor neurone disease. The 'Keep Fighting' sign he had once hung on the Leeds United dressing room wall as a mantra to inspire his players was clearly something Don Revie had not forgotten as he bravely fought an incurable condition that robs its victims of their mobility and leaves healthy minds trapped in wasted bodies.

Confined to a wheelchair, he was back in Leeds for a benefit game being held in his honour where the proceeds were being split between research into motor neurone and the Leeds City Council children's charity 'Give a Life'. It had taken an almighty effort on Revie's part to travel down from his home in Scotland but there was no way he was going to, in his eyes at least, let anyone down.

Standing 60 yards away from where Revie was taking the acclaim of the Elland Road crowd for one last time, I was transfixed by not only the commotion near the tunnel but also what was happening all around me. The Gelderd End, long since established as the lifeblood of the Leeds United support, had by now become my second 'home' during the winter months. This being the 1980s, the fare on offer in the Second Division was not up to much but this was more than made up for by the passion that poured down from what, to this then teenage fan, seemed a vast terrace. Nine days before Leeds were due to take on a Revie All-Stars XI in the name of charity, another disappointing league season at Elland Road had come to an end with a 1-0 win over Crystal Palace. John Sheridan scored the only goal for the home side from the penalty spot but the abiding memory of the afternoon was several thousand supporters remaining behind on the Gelderd End and ignoring repeated requests over the PA system to leave. Instead, they demanded the team reappear to take one last bow despite promotion having proved beyond the club once again. It was almost an hour after the final whistle before we started to drift off home, Billy Bremner's team having finally emerged from the dressing room.

For Don Revie's final return on May 11, 1988, the Gelderd End was less busy and the atmosphere less frenetic than when league points had been at stake. But the love and admiration felt by all those around me, as the man who had built Leeds United almost from scratch a little over a quarter-of-a-century earlier was pushed down the tunnel, was unmistakeable. Seeing the man they revered in a wheelchair initially came as a shock to some but, soon, the chant 'there's only one Don Revie' was filling the air. Even the lustiest rendition of the club anthem, Marching On Together, during the season just passed could not compete in terms of the emotion and passion evident as his name was sung. It was a special moment and one that gave me a new understanding of just what Don Revie meant to Leeds United.

I had nearly not attended the game, as back then the wages of a paper boy from Keighley were sufficient to stretch as far as a fortnightly trip to Elland Road and a programme but little else. As I looked mournfully into my coin jar at home the previous night, it seemed the chance of seeing Kevin Keegan and English football's new bright prospect Paul Gascoigne take on Leeds in an All-Stars XI would pass me by. That was, however, until my late father stepped in. He had given me a love of football, though much to his disappointment I had - with the careless indifference sons often show to the feelings of fathers - chosen to support Leeds and not his beloved Burnley. Dad didn't care much for Leeds after having spent one particularly harrowing afternoon at Elland Road in 1974 fearing for his life as the Clarets beat the soon-to-be-crowned league champions 4-1. Supporting rival teams did mean, though, there was plenty of banter at home, hence him asking on the eve of that benefit game in 1988: "I suppose you're going to watch Dirty Leeds tomorrow?" I was expecting my negative reply to elicit a flippant response of 'come to your senses at last, eh?' Instead, Dad adopted the sort of expression that only usually came out when I brought home one of my less than impressive school reports. "What do you mean you're not going," said my now deadly serious Dad. "It's for Don Revie, isn't it? That man built your football club so the least you can do is go along and thank him because, without Don Revie, Leeds United would be nothing." And with that, he handed over the fiver needed for the train fare and admission.

Dad's words had taken on extra resonance as the desperately ill Revie made that final, fleeting appearance at Elland Road. Being born just three days before the ill-fated 1973 FA Cup final against Sunderland, I had been too young to watch his great side. Don't get me wrong, I knew my history with certain dates, places and games firmly entrenched in the mind along with utterly useless trivia such as which player had once been nick-named 'Jasper' by his team-mates due to looking like the comedian Jasper Carrott. (Kevin Hird, for those who are interested…) But until I witnessed, first hand, the love that both his ex-players and the club's supporters had for Don Revie, I never truly understood what it was like to be part of the Leeds United family.

Don Revie died a little over a year after his farewell to Elland Road, in an Edinburgh hospital. The date was May 26, 1989, one that every football fan in England remembers for the most dramatic finale to a season of all time as Michael Thomas won the league title for Arsenal with the final kick in the final minute of the final game. Those dramatic events at Anfield, as George Graham's Gunners pipped Liverpool to the championship courtesy of a 2-0 win, meant the ubiquitous obituaries that follow the death of a famous football figure were that bit harder to find in the following morning's newspapers. Jeff Powell, in the *Daily Mail*, paid a warm tribute, writing: "A friend of mine died yesterday, a big, loveable bear of a man." Elsewhere, however, any mention of Revie's death at the premature age of 61 invariably focused on his perceived crimes rather than his many successes in the game. Even in death, it seemed there was to be no escape from the accusations that he had, single-handedly, introduced the dark arts to English football by creating the most mean-spirited and cynical team of all time. And as if that wasn't bad enough for his long-time detractors, he had then walked out on the England job in 1977 to take up a lucrative post in the Middle East.

In Leeds, few were surprised at the vitriol bubbling just below the surface following the death of Don Revie. The city had long since resigned itself to history being unforgiving when remembering both Revie and the team he built, expecting – and receiving - little more than acerbic criticism. Never mind that he had turned a football club that was the very epitome of 'moribund' into a true power for a decade. Or that in doing so, he had jettisoned a remarkable 27 players in two years to change the ethos from getting by to getting ahead. No, Leodensians knew the nation would never regard Revie as anything but the King of the Damned. A spirit of defiance sprang up, as Leeds closed ranks around the man who had brought unparalleled success to the city's football club. In 1994, five years after his death, this manifested itself at Blackburn Rovers when Leeds were the visitors. Sir Matt Busby, Revie's great friend and one-time mentor, had passed away and a minute's silence was being held at every ground in the country. At all but one, it was impeccably observed with Ewood Park being the odd one out as hundreds of away supporters chanted 'there's only one Don Revie' throughout. The condemnation was swift and deserved, not least because the timing dragged Revie's name through the dirt along with that of the club. But it was also not a surprise to anyone with an understanding of what Revie meant to Leeds United. Where, those who took part in the protest at Blackburn were asking, was the minute's silence for our manager? Or the black armbands? And why has a man who built one of the greatest teams English football has seen been all but airbrushed from history?

The chanting at Ewood Park may have been dismissed around the country as typical of the chip-on-shoulder attitude normally associated with Yorkshire folk. But in the West Riding the resentment felt over Revie's absence from the pantheon of managerial greats had long since been a source of frustration. No-one in 1994 had a quarrel with Bill Shankly, Sir Matt Busby, Jock Stein, Brian Clough and Bill Nicholson being included, just as they don't today that Sir Alex Ferguson and Arsene Wenger have since joined the list of truly great post-war managers. All have done sterling jobs for their respective clubs and been very successful. But, as the people of Leeds will never tire of pointing out, so did Revie. His omission continues to rankle, especially when his achievements are compared to those who are lauded for their success. Just like Clough with Nottingham Forest, Revie transformed a provincial club with little footballing pedigree into one of Europe's finest. He did so, in much the same way as Ferguson would do 30 years later at Old Trafford, by developing a group of youngsters into a formidable team while taking a fatherly interest in all aspects of his players' lives. And as if that was not enough to earn Revie deserved recognition for his achievements, he was lecturing his Leeds players on the importance of diet and preparation long before Wenger had even started his playing career, never mind crossed the English Channel to revolutionise Arsenal. All this plus the fact Leeds, in 10 years from 1965, did not finish outside the top four of the old First Division and also reached four FA Cup finals, four European finals and a League Cup final makes Revie's exclusion from the list of greats even harder to take.

Instead, it seems the only time football cares to remember Don Revie and his team is for their alleged crimes. The manipulating of referees, the cynicism, the time-wasting and, above all, the downright dirty play. All are regularly listed on the charge sheet when Revie's Leeds United are in the dock.

Now, anyone who has watched the infamous 1970 FA Cup final replay against Chelsea – a game that, when assessed several years later by then Premier League referee David Elleray prompted him to say he would have dished out six red cards and 20 yellows – will concede that boundaries were sometimes crossed by United in the pursuit of success. What Revie's critics refuse to acknowledge, however, is the mitigating circumstances of the time, with hard men such as Ron 'Chopper' Harris - the Chelsea defender who was guilty of committing by far the worst foul of that 1970 bloodbath at Old Trafford when scything down Eddie Gray early on - and Tommy Smith allowed to flourish in the English game. No team could, during an era when the first horrific tackle was regarded as a 'freebie' providing it was committed early enough, hope to prosper without being able to fight fire with fire. Likewise, no team could expect to be as successful as Leeds were during the 1960s and 70s without having some exceptional players, and it is here that the critics do Revie perhaps the biggest disservice of all. In the immediate years that followed promotion to the old First Division in 1964, his side was overly cautious. Once Leeds were ahead, Revie ordered his players to protect what they had by suffocating the opposition, ensuring the game ended 1-0. It was not a popular tactic with opposition fans or the media, though in future years Jose Mourinho would use a similar 'protect what we have got' attitude to good effect as Chelsea claimed back-to-back Premier League titles. George Graham also did the same when Arsenal won the league in 1989 and 1991. Eventually, though, Revie handed his players free rein, allowing Leeds to suddenly display every bit as much skill as their more fashionable contemporaries. In back-to-back games as winter turned to spring in 1972, a 5-1 thrashing of a Manchester United side featuring George Best and Bobby Charlton was followed by a 7-0 demolition of Southampton that was captured by the *Match of the Day* cameras. So enraptured was commentator Barry Davies with one particular extravagant keep-ball sequence featuring back-heels and intricate passing, he said: "Leeds are putting on a show and poor old Southampton just don't know what day it is. It's almost cruel." The words were born of admiration but, predictably, Revie's detractors quickly rounded on Leeds for the 'unacceptable' manner in which they had humiliated fellow professionals. It seemed no matter what Leeds did, they would never win over their critics. Little, it seems, has changed with the 2009 release of the film *The Damned United* casting Revie and his team as villains to a whole new generation. Not only was his one-dimensional portrayal as a miserable, dour northerner wildly at odds with the Revie that family, friends and ex-players remember, but his managerial achievements compared to those of Brian Clough, the true subject of the film, were effectively written out of history. As if to illustrate the chasm between the charismatic Clough and his sullen predecessor at Elland Road, the director chooses to roll the credits just after the cinema audience has been told that, while Clough won two European Cups, Revie 'failed as England manager'. And just in case anyone had still missed the point, the caption then read: 'He went to the United Arab Emirates where his career ended among allegations of financial misdealings, leaving him in the soccer wilderness.'

To those in Leeds who lived through the era, the black and white description of Clough v Revie brought just a resigned shake of the head. They had heard it all before. The allegations of venality and corruption that first emerged in the aftermath of his abdication from the top job in English football had already earned him the nickname 'Don Readies'. It was a moniker he was never able to shake off. Revie, much to the regret of those closest to him, chose not to sue over the accusations - unlike his captain Billy Bremner, who won a £100,000 settlement from *The People* after the Sunday newspaper claimed he had asked Wolves to go easy in a game that, ultimately, cost Leeds the title in 1972. It means the stigma will never really go away, even though the allegations themselves have rarely been challenged. Revie is, by no means, the only big name figure in football to become embroiled in financial scandal. Brian Clough was once alleged to have received illegal payments from transfers, the High Court once being told how he 'likes a bung'. Clough was later charged by the Football Association with misconduct, only for the matter to be dropped because of his ill-health. However, unlike Revie, Clough's memory is not irreparably tainted – as the two men's depictions in the film *The Damned United* vividly illustrated.

It is a similar story with Revie's England days. His decision to walk out on his country to take up a lucrative post with the United Arab Emirates brought vilification. Mistakes were undoubtedly made. Selling the story to one newspaper was always going to lead to criticism, especially as the first his employers at the Football Association knew about his leaving was when reading it in the *Daily Mail*. Even Revie admitted later in life that it had been a mistake, not least as it led to the rest of Fleet Street picking through his past in search of scandal. What was lost in the furore, though, was that Revie had firmly believed he was on the verge of being sacked. England's results had been poor and a 2-0 defeat by Italy in Rome meant a second consecutive World Cup finals seemed likely to take place without the Three Lions. So, when Revie heard from a trusted and well-connected friend that Bobby Robson had been approached by the FA about becoming England's next manager, he decided to seize the initiative. His subsequent move to the Middle East was clumsily handled, not least Revie being absent from a friendly in Brazil because he was in Dubai holding talks with the UAE FA. But was what Revie did any different to Bobby Robson securing a job with PSV Eindhoven ahead of leading England into Italia '90? Likewise, Sven Goran Eriksson was caught negotiating a possible switch to Chelsea when still in charge of the national team and yet English football did not turn its back on the Swede as it had done with Revie more than a quarter of a century earlier. Times had changed and for the better, with the public no longer expecting the England football manager to have a similar moral code to the Pope.

Any discussion of Revie has to begin with accepting he was a complex man. He was an insecure obsessive who fretted over the smallest variables. But he also loved nothing more than to relax at home or on the golf course with his wife Elsie and their two children, Duncan and Kim. He was someone who put inordinate importance on accumulating personal wealth but gave his time freely for charities. And he was a deeply religious man who prayed nightly, but also a big advocate of Sunday football. Perhaps the biggest anomaly, though, was that, as a footballer, Revie had been a wonderfully gifted individual who epitomised the beautiful game. And yet, once in management, the team he built became synonymous with brutality and a suffocating 'win-at-all-costs' mentality that, in some quarters, is blamed for ushering in a miserable era for English football. Such condemnation means the considerable feats Revie achieved as a player are often overlooked. His most successful time came with Manchester City where he perfected what became known as the 'Revie Plan'. Based around the system Hungary had used to shatter forever England's image of superiority in 1953 at Wembley, it involved Revie playing as a deep-lying centre-forward. It was a scheming role perfectly suited to his considerable passing skills. Defenders brought up to believe the opposition number 9 would pound towards goal through the centre were left confused by the revolutionary new tactic. Revie made great use of the space afforded him by the system to pull the strings of City's gifted attack. The tactic had initially brought scorn from the less enlightened commentators and pressmen of the day, especially when its grand unveiling ended in a 5-0 defeat to Preston. But Revie, a powerfully built player who glided around the pitch, and City soon ironed out early problems. International honours followed but it was the FA Cup where the 'Revie Plan' made the most telling impact as the club reached back-to-back finals. City lost the 1955 final to Newcastle United after playing more than 70 minutes with 10 men after Jimmy Meadows was carried off with a knee injury, Revie's consolation coming when named Footballer of the Year just a few days later. Twelve months later, he had a Cup winners' medal to go with such a notable personal accolade as Birmingham City were beaten at Wembley. Revie was hailed for his match-winning performance. Had he not been so successful in management, the 1956 Cup final may well have been his epitaph in the newspapers of May 27, 1989. Instead, of course, it was the charge sheet of his Leeds United team that many focused on.

The intervening years have brought no rehabilitation for Don Revie and his image. The 20th anniversary of his death in May, 2009, received scant acknowledgement outside West Yorkshire, where fresh calls were made to erect a statue in Leeds. The Gelderd End had already been renamed the 'Revie Stand', and a minor road situated near Elland Road bore his name. But many supporters and civic leaders felt the time had finally come to mark Revie's achievements properly and the new statue is set to be unveiled in Autumn, 2011. Leeds, it seems, has finally woken up to the debt the city owes to Revie. It is to the eternal shame of the city that the benefit game held in his honour in May, 1988, was watched by a crowd of just 7,305. More than 25,000 fans had been present the previous September when Revie, then walking with the aid of a stick, had taken a bow before the home game with Manchester City, the team he had performed so magnificently for as a player. So, to see the South Stand and Lowfields Road side of Elland Road closed for the benefit game came as a big shock and disappointment to everyone who had made the effort to attend. One of those angry at what he saw as a huge snub was Gary Edwards, such a dedicated fan of the club he has missed just one Leeds game – a friendly in Toronto - since January, 1968. Gary was so incensed by the apparent lack of gratitude from his home city that he went out and had Don Revie's name tattooed on his arm the following morning. Thankfully, those who did show up to pay tribute to Leeds United's greatest manager in 1988 more than made up for the absentees with the reception they provided as Don Revie emerged from the tunnel for one last time. Those present knew exactly the debt Leeds United owed Don Revie. Perhaps the biggest testimony of all, however, came early in the new millennium when the attempts of Peter Ridsdale and David O'Leary to recapture the glories of the past proved so ruinous that their gluttonous spending spree almost killed the club that Don built.

Chapter 1

Early Days

Middlesbrough is a town that has never enjoyed the best of reputations. Just ask the viewers of Channel 4's *Location, Location, Location*, who not so long ago deemed it the 'worst place to live in the UK'. Or the compilers of the less than scientific top ten lists of 'Crap Towns' who invariably have Middlesbrough rubbing shoulders with a variety of rundown seaside resorts, Lancashire mill towns and former mining communities. Those who view Teesside as not only grim but also grimy would, they insist, never live in a town that, since the Industrial Revolution, has been synonymous with pollution. Followers of the local football team are even called 'smoggies' by rivals from the North East; four Sunderland fans even going so far as turning up one year wearing full protective suits and gas masks. Even the Boro fans had to laugh at the sheer cheek of that one. Denigrating Middlesbrough is not a new phenomenon, either, with JB Priestley describing it in *English Journey* as 'more like a vast, dingy conjuring trick than a reasonable town'. Then, just in case the reader hadn't got the point, Bradford-born Priestley dismissed what he understood to be the locals' two chief passions by insisting Middlesbrough 'is a dismal town, even with beer and football'.

Don Revie was born into this bleak and cheerless landscape on July 10, 1927. That the family was poor is not in doubt; Revie's dad, Donald senior, was a joiner but often out of work at a time of acute unemployment across the country. His mother took in washing from the more affluent families in Middlesbrough, often getting her son and his elder sisters, Joyce and Jean, to collect bundles of clothes. Later in life, Revie did not dwell on his early years, though in candid moments he would open up. Daughter Kim, one of Revie's two children, recalls: "He would tell us how hard it was. There was no money around and it was difficult. He could still laugh about it, though. I used to pull his leg by starting to hum the theme tune from the Hovis advert that used to be on television and ask him if he had to push his bike up a steep hill like the lad in it. Dad would just laugh and say, 'We couldn't afford a bike'."

Revie, clearly a fan of the Monty Python sketch 'Four Yorkshiremen' where a quartet of Tykes try to out-do each other as to how hard their life is, grew up during the Great Depression that followed the Stock Market crash in America.

Life was difficult for nearly every family in Britain, not just those in Middlesbrough. Unemployment soared, as did poverty levels, and the Revies were among tens of thousands of families who struggled to make ends meet. What made the life of a boy who would go on to become one of football's most famous figures particularly sad, though, was his mother's cancer. Her death hit the then 12-year-old Revie hard, and with his Dad struggling to find work it was a bleak time for the family – as, following his marriage to Elsie in 1949, he would sometimes recall to brother-in-law David Duncan. "Don's dad was left to look after three children on his own," says David. "It was a frugal set-up and, Don said, very hard times for the family. His Dad would often have to go out looking for sticks to put on the fire to try and keep the house warm because there was no money coming in. The Great Depression was on and there was little or no work around for anyone."

The premature loss of his mother would be something that the amateur psychologists would, in later years, seize upon as a major factor behind his apparent insecurity. Much would also be made of his impoverished childhood with many insisting it to be a major factor in Revie's attitude towards money. Brian Glanville, one of the finest sportswriters of his or any generation, covered the England football team during Revie's three-year reign as manager from 1974. He recalls a complex man, forever to be tainted in the eyes of English football by his decision to quit as England manager to take up a lucrative contract in the Middle East. "I found Don quite a strange man," says the *Sunday Times* football correspondent. "And I always had the impression he was someone who had this daily fear of waking up poor again. It meant money became something of an obsession to him." Brian Clough, also a son of Middlesbrough, had a similar foreboding and, as a result, would rarely turn down an offer of paid work from the media or advertising executives. The two were polar opposites in terms of personality and destined to clash bitterly as top-flight managers in the 1970s. But it seems accruing money was seen by both Clough and Revie as a way of ensuring they never again experienced the hardships of their respective childhoods.

A route of escape from the troubles at home in Bell Street came via football. After being taken to Ayresome Park at the age of six as a rare treat by his father, Revie had quickly fallen in love with the game that would, eventually, take him away from life on the breadline in Middlesbrough. He could often be seen kicking a ball of rags around the streets near the family home; a real football being beyond the reach of the Revie budget in his formative years. Practising for hours, he was picked for the Archibald Elementary School team and impressed across a variety of positions. Outside school, he also indulged his love for football with Newport Boys' Club. Soon, however, the iron-will to succeed that would later characterise his professional career meant Revie had his eye on a switch to Middlesbrough Swifts, a club with strong links to Football League side Leicester City. His chance came the day after the two teams had met in a league game, as Swifts manager Bill Sanderson recalled in 1974 when speaking to the *Yorkshire Post*. He said: "I first met Don on a Sunday morning when we were having a team meeting to analyse the previous day's game. I was telling our full back, Danny Campbell, that he had been taken for a 'ta-ta' by the Newport Boys' Club winger. I told him, 'I wish I had that lad with us'. I then heard this squeaky voice pipe up from the back of the room, 'I am here, Mr Sanderson'. It was young Revie, who had sneaked into our meeting. He said, 'I want to be a footballer and want to sign for the Swifts', so I went to see the Newport warden, Bob Beilby, and agreed a five-bob registration fee'." Once happily settled at his new club, Revie's football education really began. Sanderson, an engine driver by day, put great store by the whole being greater than the sum of its parts. The Swifts were run along those lines, with teamwork being everything, and far more important than individual brilliance. Whether there were any prima donnas in Middlesbrough during the early years of the Second World War is doubtful. But if there had been, they would never have got anywhere near the Swifts team. Sanderson was also a deep thinker on football and introduced Revie not only to team-talks, dossiers and post-match de-briefs, but also the use of visual aids to illustrate tactics. Friday nights would be spent analysing forthcoming opposition at a team meeting in Sanderson's cramped kitchen on Keith Road, while Sunday mornings invariably saw the manager outline on a blackboard what had gone right and wrong the previous day. Such enlightened thinking for the era had a profound effect on Revie, as he later revealed to his brother-in-law. David Duncan recalls: "The manager, in particular, made a big impression on Don, who would say several times that he took things from those days into his own management career. It was the little things and the simple ideas that Don liked, such as having a blackboard to explain things. They also had a team-talk. At most professional clubs, never mind the amateurs, a team-talk would consist of telling everyone the team and that would be it. At Middlesbrough Swifts, Don said they would talk about the other team and how to stop them."

Such thinking would be apparent in the approach of Leeds United during his first few years as manager, a determination to stop the opposition being the overwhelming priority. This was especially the case if Leeds had scored the opening – and, thanks to Revie's negating tactics, invariably only - goal of the game. Under the innovative thinking of Sanderson, Middlesbrough Swifts enjoyed a successful couple of years and notice was starting to be taken of their star player. Middlesbrough, the club whose players Revie had idolised from an early age, were interested but, in the end, the link-up between Swifts and Leicester City proved to be decisive. Revie signed in August, 1944. Alan Peacock, also a native of Middlesbrough, was signed by Revie for Leeds United in 1964 to score the goals that would just three months later clinch promotion. The pair had initially got to know each other at celebrity golf days across the north of England and become good friends. Peacock, an England international whose injury when playing for Leeds in 1965 allowed a young West Ham striker by the name of Geoff Hurst to sneak into the England squad for the following year's World Cup finals, recalls: "I was ten years younger than Don but we had many chats over the years about growing up in the same town and it was clear Middlesbrough had been his first love. Like a lot of lads in those days, he idolised Wilf Mannion and would talk about him a lot. But, because Middlesbrough Swifts were effectively a nursery club for Leicester City, he signed for them rather than the club he had supported as a boy." Revie realised his football skills had provided the means of escape from what seemed destined to be an impoverished life. Once a father himself to Kim and her elder brother Duncan, he made sure both children appreciated the value of a good education and the chances it would provide for them in later life.

In Leicester City, Revie was joining a club that had flirted with success in the 1920s, finishing just a point behind champions Sheffield Wednesday in the final full season of the decade after having chalked up a record victory of 10-0 over Portsmouth. Any hopes of building on such a notable double soon floundered, though they did reach the FA Cup semi-finals in 1934 before bowing out 4-1 to Portsmouth. Leicester would go one better and get to Wembley during Revie's time but his move to Filbert Street proved, considering the success he later enjoyed as a player and manager, more important for the influence two figures started to exert on his career. First, Leicester's Septimus Smith, who in 1936 had made his solitary England appearance, took the teenager under his wing. Key lessons were drummed into the keen-to-learn Revie, as was the need for dedication and strong fitness.

Revie's first team debut in the war-time league came just a week after he had signed for Leicester. But it would be another two years, and after the end of the Second World War, before his Football League bow came at home to

Manchester City on the opening day of the 1946-47 season. It proved an inauspicious start. Leicester, who had been relegated from Division One in 1939, lost 3-0. Despite that, Revie soon started to replicate the form he had shown for the reserves. Brian Glanville was still at school but vividly recalls the first time he saw Revie play. "I was a mad, keen Arsenal fan as a boy and first saw Revie play for Leicester reserves in the Combination Cup," recalls the *Sunday Times* football correspondent. "Leicester won and Revie had a great game. It was not long before he was in their first team and he made such an impression that when, at a later date, I went down to watch the Arsenal third team train at Hendon, I remember one of the players saying 'I want to play like that Revie'."

Less than three months after making his League debut, Revie's progress was dramatically halted when his right ankle was broken in three places during a challenge with Tottenham's Welsh international Ronnie Burgess. Revie initially thought it nothing worse than a serious sprain, but grew suspicious when no-one would look him in the eye once in hospital. Eventually, Leicester manager Johnny Duncan delivered the bad news. The specialists feared he would never play again. He was still a teenager, yet Revie's career appeared to be over and he spent the next few days in hospital contemplating what now seemed a bleak future. A return to Middlesbrough seemed his best option only for Duncan, who would follow Bill Sanderson and Sep Smith in becoming a huge influence on the youngster's life, to snap Revie out of his melancholy mood. Together, they would ensure Revie returned and, thanks to the unstinting support of his manager, he did just that to confound the doctors by taking to a football field just 19 weeks later. Confidence restored after one particularly robust challenge, Revie soon justified the manager's faith that he could return better than ever.

That Johnny Duncan should become such a father figure to Revie came as no surprise to anyone who knew the Scot. He had started his playing career at Raith Rovers before moving south to Leicester on the same day as his brother Tommy. He scored six goals in one famous 7-0 win over Port Vale on Christmas Day, 1924, a joint record he still holds with Arthur Chandler, who did the same for the Foxes almost four years later against Portsmouth. Tommy tragically died of a burst stomach ulcer in 1939, meaning Johnny became a surrogate father to his brother's five children – one of whom, Elsie, Don Revie would later marry.

Johnny, who during his career had also been known by the nickname 'Tokey', had been appointed Leicester manager in 1946 and quickly identified

Revie as the man to build his team around. He had already proved to be fiercely protective over the Middlesbrough-born youngster, as Johnny's nephew David Duncan recalls: "There was one day when Don accepted a lift home off my cousin after Leicester had played at Birmingham. We were about halfway home when the car ran out of petrol. My uncle, who was not yet manager of Leicester, was furious and tore into us. He was particularly upset that the Leicester team bus had gone past after we broke down and all the players were waving at Don. He didn't think we should have embarrassed him like that. We also got back very late as petrol was rationed then and it took us ages to scrounge some. Don took it in his stride but it showed how protective my uncle was of him, even then."

Once installed as manager at Filbert Street, Johnny Duncan's influence grew with Revie being particularly impressed at how he was able to make even the youngest members of his squad feel to be a vital cog in the Leicester machine – a lesson Revie absorbed and put to good use in his own managerial career.

With Revie now fully fit, Leicester kicked off the 1947-48 season confident of pushing for promotion only to have to settle for a ninth place finish. The club fared even worse in the league the following year, becoming embroiled in a relegation battle that lasted until the final day. Thankfully for Johnny Duncan and his players, the FA Cup proved much more to their liking. In a season that witnessed one of the biggest upsets of all time when Sunderland became the first top-flight club to lose to non-League opposition on Yeovil Town's notorious slope, the rank outsiders from Leicester beat Birmingham City and Preston North End to set up a trip to Luton Town that yielded ten goals and the need for a replay back at Filbert Street. Once again, the two defences struggled as Leicester went through to the last eight with a thrilling 5-3 triumph. Brentford were then dispatched before Leicester's name was paired with Portsmouth in the semi-finals.

Pompey were on their way to the first of two back-to-back league title successes, while Leicester seemed on course to drop into Division Three for the first time. On the face of it, the match was no contest. Those inside Highbury for the semi-final who thought the outcome a foregone conclusion were, though, to be left stunned as Leicester, with Revie in outstanding form, took a 2-1 lead. The Cup run had relied heavily on the scouting reports of Sep Smith, one of four brothers to play in the Football League. Smith, who grew up in County Durham, had joined Leicester in 1929 and, five years later, faced siblings Jack and Willie in the 1934 FA Cup semi-final defeat to Portsmouth. It was the only time three brothers had played in the same semi-final, but still

Sep was envious as Jack and Willie walked out at Wembley before facing Manchester City. He was determined that, this time, Leicester would exact some form of revenge and the Portsmouth squad's strengths and weaknesses were analysed in detail. One of his acute observations was how goalkeeper Ernie Butler liked to palm the ball over the head of an opponent when challenged before reclaiming possession. Revie, who had followed Bill Sanderson's instructions at Middlesbrough Swifts to the letter, took note and decided to hold back when the ball flew towards the goalkeeper at Highbury just in case Butler repeated the trick. His patience was rewarded during the second-half when Butler, who would be Portsmouth's only ever-present in their back-to-back league title successes, flicked the ball over Leicester's Jack Lee and Revie was on hand to score. Revie's future brother-in-law David Duncan recalls: "It was a great day for Leicester and a great day for Don, who had been the lynchpin of that victory. Portsmouth were the best club in the land at the time so for a Second Division team to knock them out of the Cup in the semi-finals was a sensation."

Revie, just 21, was suddenly big news and much was expected of him at Wembley in the final against Wolves. Unfortunately for Revie, he never made it. Instead, fate stepped in to dash any dreams of a Cup winners' medal. As Leicester went in search of the points needed to secure their Second Division status, Revie suffered the second serious injury of his fledgling career – though, this time, it almost had fatal consequences. David Duncan recalls: "Leicester were playing at Plymouth when Don's nose started to bleed. He had broken it. The injury was not thought to be too serious but soon the blood was haemorrhaging out of his nose. Even then, he didn't go to hospital in Plymouth and, instead, it was decided he should wait until the team returned to Leicester. Unfortunately, it was a long trip home from Plymouth in 1949 and when he finally got to hospital the doctors said he had only just made it in time. There was none of the medical expertise of today and another hour could have proved fatal."

Once the bleeding had been stopped, Revie was left to bemoan his bad luck as a first – and, he feared, maybe only – chance of playing at Wembley had been snatched away. He was still too weak to travel to north London for the final, so listened to the match on radio back in Leicester. What he heard did little to lift his spirits. Even the future Queen's ignorance of Cup final etiquette, Princess Elizabeth committing the cardinal sin of wearing Leicester blue when being introduced to the two teams, could not prevent Wolves from winning 3-1. Missing out on the final left Revie crushed – "he felt his chance had gone", says David Duncan – and his spirits were hardly raised a few days later when it emerged that, but for the untimely nosebleed, he would have been selected for England's end-of-season tour to Stockholm, Oslo and Paris. The semblance of a smile did return to his face a week after the Wembley defeat when Leicester's final day draw against Cardiff City was enough to keep the club up and, instead, condemn Nottingham Forest to relegation. But, as the summer got under way, Revie still cut a dejected figure.

Chapter 2

A Perfect Match

Missing the FA Cup final may have seemed like the end of the world to 21-year-old Don Revie but 1949 would soon become a year synonymous with a much happier occasion and one that proved to be the making of him as a man. He got married. Revie had met Elsie Duncan, the niece of Leicester City manager Johnny Duncan, in the summer of 1946 when on holiday in Scotland with her cousin Dave. She was one of five siblings and a keen football fan. Her father, Tommy, had played professionally with Raith Rovers before moving south to join Leicester with his brother Johnny. Tommy would later go on to play for Bristol Rovers and Halifax Town. Two other members of the Duncan clan had also gone on to play for Scotland. When Elsie met the man who would later become her husband, Revie was already an accomplished player at Filbert Street and displaying the confidence that would later set him apart as the heartbeat of Manchester City's Cup-winning side. Off the field, however, it was a different story with Revie's peers describing a 'shy' man who was not comfortable with the limelight. The life of a professional footballer in the immediate post-war years may have been a very different world to the pampered lifestyles enjoyed by today's much-feted stars but, even so, Revie's early days at Leicester were the very epitome of austerity.

Having left Middlesbrough in August, 1944, to pursue a career in football, he had, after speaking to his father, agreed to continue his apprenticeship as a bricklayer. Leicester were comfortable with the arrangement, especially as it was a trade that – with much of the country needing to be rebuilt after almost five years of war – meant he could not be called up by the army once of the requisite age. Digs were found by the club just 100 yards from Filbert Street and Revie started attending a local youth club on Hazel Street with Dave Duncan, the son of Johnny Duncan. The Duncans were soon having a major influence on the life of the young Revie.

Following the death of Tommy from a burst stomach ulcer, Johnny, known within the family as 'Uncle Jock', had immediately become a surrogate father to his brother's five children. The two boys, David and John, remained in Leicester, while their mother and sisters Jenny, Agnes and Elsie were looked after by Tommy's family in the Scottish town of Lochgelly, Fife, where they ran the general store. David, the fourth youngest Duncan sibling and then only seven-years-old, recalls: "There was no welfare system in those days so my Uncle Jock stepped in to look after us. He and Dad had both signed for Leicester City on the same day and after playing for a few other clubs, my Dad moved back to help run the pub with my uncle. After he died, it was a difficult time for everyone." Despite the War, the Duncans, though separated by hundreds of miles, remained close-knit and it was into this tight family unit that Revie wandered soon after signing for Leicester. Through Johnny, who would soon be his manager at Filbert Street, he moved digs to a house on Danvers Street in the city. He was straight opposite where Tommy's widow and her two young sons were living. David, a mad keen football fan, could not believe his luck. "I was 15 and my brother 12 or 13 so we were completely in awe of this professional footballer that had moved in over the road," he says. "Don was a few years older than us but through my uncle and cousin Dave, we got to know him and before long he was like a big brother to us. He was very friendly. If we had any problems, Don would do what he could to help. After a game on a Saturday, he would catch the bus back to Danvers Street and come round our house with my cousin Dave. We would get a bottle of Tizer from the shop and then play Monopoly all night, which I am sure is something the professional footballers of today don't do."

Revie felt comfortable in his new surroundings and, along with Johnny's son Dave, decided to spend part of his summer holidays in Lochgelly, where he put his building skills to good use by working on the Duncan family's general store. It was on this trip that he met Elsie, then training to be a teacher after completing her studies at school in Cowdenbeath. Before long, she was making regular trips to the Midlands. In October, 1949, the couple were married in Leicester. Revie's heartbreak at missing the Cup final five months earlier was forgotten, though it would not be long before he was starting to feel restless at the lack of progress being made by a club he had joined five years before. Appointed captain the previous summer, Revie was disappointed with Leicester's form after having only just avoided relegation to Division Three in the season that culminated in the trip to Wembley. That, coupled with Johnny Duncan having stepped down as manager in the same month as Revie's wedding, meant a change of scenery was required.

Arsenal were the first to make an approach but Revie felt the move was not right, just as he did when Manchester City showed interest a couple of weeks later. The transfer saga dragged on. By November, and just as it seemed he would stay at Filbert Street, he made the surprising decision to join Hull City - a club who had never played in the top flight - in a £19,000 deal. It seemed a strange choice for someone who had been courted by some of English football's biggest names, a bit like opting to sign for Reading today ahead of Manchester United or Chelsea. The big attraction of switching to East Yorkshire was manager Raich Carter. As an inside-forward with Sunderland and Derby County, Carter had been the only player to win FA Cup winners' medals either side of World War Two and been hailed for his tactical awareness when playing alongside Stanley Matthews for England. He had been appointed player-manager at Boothferry Park in 1948 and led Hull to the Division Three (North) title a year later. Revie had caught Carter's eye in an early-season game against Leicester and was seen by the Tigers manager as his ideal replacement in the team. For his part, Revie wanted to learn at close quarters just what had made Carter such a special player. Revie's brother-in-law David says: "Don considered Arsenal, who were then one of the most glamorous clubs around, but the move just did not feel right. The thought of playing for Hull did appeal because of Raich Carter. Before the War, many felt Raich to be the best player in the country and Don felt he could learn a lot from him. And he did."

Initially, the portents were good for Revie. He relished being in the same side as Carter. He found the Hull player-manager, a fellow native of the North East, an inspirational figure with his tendency never to demand the ball unless better-placed than a team-mate, something Revie quickly adopted into his own game. Results, though, were not as expected with Revie's admiration for Carter not shared by all his team-mates. Paddy Fagan, who joined Hull in 1951 from Transport FC in his native Dublin before being reunited with Revie at Manchester City two years later, said: "Raich was the man who brought me to England and I got on well with him, as did Don. But a few of the other lads didn't. He had been a great player but the problem was he always loved reminding us of that. It caused a bit of resentment among the lads. He also didn't pay too much attention to the defence, preferring his wingmen to stay forward and not help out too much."

Hull finished seventh in Division Two at the end of Revie's first season only to slip back to tenth the following year. Things were not working out on the field and neither Revie nor the fans were happy. Andy Davidson, who still holds Hull's record for most league appearances with 520, had joined the groundstaff at Boothferry Park in 1947. He said: "When Don signed, there was a real sense of excitement because he had been an important player for Leicester. It was a real coup for Raich because Hull had only just been promoted to the Second Division. The fans were really happy because they thought Don would be a younger version of Raich, which was unfair. Raich had been one of the best players this country had ever seen. Don was a fine player in his own right but the fans never really took to him at Hull."

Davidson, who had left Scotland at the age of 14 to sign for Hull, did not make his Tigers debut until the season after Revie had left the club. But he was a regular member of the squad that travelled to every game and, in the days before substitutes, found himself as the unofficial 12th man. During his time on the road with the team, Davidson got to know Revie well and he believes Hull's lack of funds was a major factor in explaining why the signing did not work out as planned. "Don was a fine player," he says. "His passing was second to none and I also never saw anyone more comfortable when controlling the ball. But the problem was Don was not a hard player, which was pretty ironic when you consider the team he built at Leeds, and the rest of the team were unable to offer the protection he needed. Because of his ability, the opposition would target Don. If Raich had been given the money to bring in a couple of blood-and-guts tacklers to play alongside him then I believe City would have been a lot more successful. It was a shame from Hull's point of view that Don had to move to realise his potential."

By the summer of 1951 and with Hull's hopes of a second promotion in quick succession having stalled, Revie was yearning for the top flight but saw little chance of his dreams being realised in the East Riding. Brother-in-law David recalls: "Don felt Hull just did not have the work ethic to be successful. There was one time in training when Don approached a South African called Alf Ackerman and said, 'You aren't doing much today, Alf'. To which the reply was, 'I am working my eyes, Don'. He thought that attitude was holding Hull back and then once Raich Carter left, he felt it was time to go as well."

Others, however, felt influences closer to home were behind the transfer request that was submitted early in the 1951-52 season. Paddy Fagan, whose move to Hull had come just a few weeks earlier, said: "I always felt his missus was the one pushing him. Don was always money-orientated so I wasn't that surprised to hear he wanted to leave, but I also think his missus ruled the roost and was ambitious on his behalf. She came from a football background and was always at Don, telling him what he had done wrong in a game and what he could improve. I felt sorry for him because the last thing you want after a bad game is to go home to more criticism. I think his missus thought his career would be better suited away from Hull."

Whether or not Elsie was the driving force behind the subsequent move to Manchester City in October 1951 in a deal worth £25,000, there is no denying the move proved the making of Revie as a footballer.

Chapter 3

Top Flight At Last

When Don Revie signed for Manchester City in October 1951, he was 24 years old and the first flushes of youth as a footballer were well behind him. A career once brimming with potential was starting to drift after a largely undistinguished stint at Hull City. With his mentor Raich Carter having left Boothferry Park and Hull struggling in the lower reaches of the Second Division, Revie had stopped enjoying his football. A change was needed. It came in the form of Manchester City, the club who had flirted with the idea of signing Revie a couple of years earlier. The Blues had just won promotion back to the top flight at the first attempt thanks to the 60-goal trio of Johnny Hart, George Smith and Dennis Westcott. They were a club on the up and Revie, mindful his career was in danger of stagnating, was interested. Here was a club with ambitions to match his own, a point vividly illustrated just two weeks before Revie joined when City paid £25,000 to sign Sunderland inside forward Ivor Broadis.

Fred Eyre, the best-selling author of the cult football book *Kicked Into Touch* that went on to sell more than a million copies, is heavily involved today with the Manchester City Ex-Players' Association. He became an apprentice at Maine Road towards the end of the 1950s but was just a fan when Revie arrived. He recalls: "Even then, City were a big club who always used to sign at least one big player every summer. We had signed Bert Trautmann in 1949, Welsh international Roy Paul from Swansea Town a couple of years before Don arrived and then Ivor Broadis who went on to become England's inside forward. But because City didn't have the money to sign 11 of these, they also had to bring in what they could from elsewhere. They got the best that was available and Don fitted into that category. He came from Hull City in the Second Division but he still had a reasonable name in the game. It was a good signing."

Unlike when Revie had joined Hull from Leicester two years earlier, the switch to Manchester did not prove to be a protracted affair once the clubs had agreed a fee of £25,000, which included the £12,000 part-exchange of full-back Ernie Phillips. Revie may not have been a stellar signing along the lines of Broadis or Roy Paul, who had cost £19,500 from Luton. But the fee still represented a sizeable outlay at a time when the British record transfer fee stood at £34,500, paid by Sheffield Wednesday just seven months earlier to Notts County for Jackie Sewell.

The move to Manchester was not just a step up in terms of division, it also represented a major advance in terms of Revie's new surroundings. Hull's Boothferry Park had only opened in 1946 so was the Football League's newest ground. It had also already hosted its record crowd of 55,019 when the Tigers were beaten by Manchester United in the FA Cup sixth round on February 26, 1949. Maine Road, though, was in a different league. In the immediate post-war years, it had been the busiest ground in the country due to Manchester United having moved in as tenants while a bomb-damaged Old Trafford was re-built. A record 2,250,000 spectators attended games at Maine Road in the 1945-46 season. With United paying rent plus a share of their gate receipts, City were able to plough some of the huge profits back into Maine Road. The Platt Lane End had seats installed to take the overall seating capacity to 18,500, more than any other ground in the country and three times what Revie had been used to at Hull's Boothferry Park.

John McTavish spent eight years with Manchester City after moving from Glasgow in June, 1952. He recalls: "Maine Road was probably the best ground in the country when I signed. The Kippax terrace that ran down one side just seemed to go on for ever when I looked up at it from the pitch. There was one time I played for City against Tottenham Hotspur in the FA Cup and there were more than 80,000 people inside Maine Road. I had never seen anything like it."

Revie settled quickly in Manchester with Elsie, the couple moving into a house within walking distance of Maine Road. Elsie, as she had in Hull, quickly found work as a teacher and they were very happy with life. Unfortunately, on the pitch, it was a different story with both City and Revie struggling for much of his first season. Results were, at best, average and the club finished in the lower half of the table. With United, now back at Old Trafford, winning the league title, a 15th place finish with 39 points and a third round exit in the FA Cup to Wolverhampton Wanderers was a big disappointment for City. So was the dramatic dip in crowds during those miserable final few weeks of the season.

Worse, however, was to follow in the 1952-53 campaign as City flirted with relegation throughout. A 6-0 defeat in the spring against a Cardiff City side that had not scored for ten weeks suggested, with six games to go, that the drop was inevitable only for a late rally that included a 5-0 hammering of FA Cup finalists Blackpool to keep the club up by a point. Instead, Stoke City were the fall-guys in 21st place. The FA Cup offered little respite from the misery enveloping City, Luton Town cantering to a 5-1 fourth round replay triumph at Kenilworth Road. Revie's own form mirrored that of the club. As had been the case at Hull when player manager Raich Carter filled the role the younger man preferred, Revie was played further forward and left isolated due to his obvious lack of pace. Passing skills and creativity were his big strengths but neither were utilised in those early seasons at Maine Road. A bigger problem for manager Les McDowall, however, was that his robust defence and skilful forward line were unable to function as a team, a quandary that many felt he would never be able to solve.

Despite his on-field troubles, Revie was enjoying life in Manchester and had formed strong friendships with several of his team-mates, including Ken Barnes and Bert Trautmann. Johnny Williamson, who had joined City from school and would later conceive what became known as the 'Revie Plan', was another who would stay in regular contact long after their playing careers were over. He recalls: "I had never met Don before he joined City, though I had seen him play a couple of times. The first thing that struck me was what a decent, family man he was. He was a couple of years older than me but we got on great from the start. Don settled very quickly off the pitch. He and Elsie bought a house about a mile or so from the ground. He would often walk to the match."

Revie was, like his new team-mates, struggling for form with just five goals in his first season being followed by a similarly disappointing return in 1952-53. But, in a taster as to how he would later build the family atmosphere that helped Leeds United to success, he still found time to offer encouragement and support to the younger members of the squad. Glasgow-born John McTavish was just 20 when he joined City from Scottish Junior League side, Dalry Thistle. "Don took me under his wing," he says. "At the weekend, and particularly on a Sunday night, he would invite me round to his house to play cards. Elsie was from Scotland so I think she realised what it was like for someone to be so far away from home. I never forgot how kind the Revies were to me. Without them, I don't know if I could have settled so well. It was the same when it came to making my debut against Middlesbrough. I had looked up to Wilf Mannion all my life so to play against him was a bit daunting. But Don made sure I was calm before the game and that I was not overawed."

On the field, the 1953-54 season was a much happier affair for Revie. With Ivor Broadis having been sold to Newcastle United, where he would join up with Jackie Milburn, Len White and Ivor Allchurch, the deeper role Revie craved was vacant. It was felt at Maine Road that Broadis' off-the-cuff approach and Revie's more measured, tactical approach had negated each other's form. That it was Broadis who was the one to leave in a £20,000 transfer surprised many, but Revie was determined to prove wrong those suggesting City had sold the wrong player.

Suddenly, his career began to blossom and recognition came in October with a call-up to the Football League XI to face the League of Ireland. Revie, who had always craved international honours, excelled by netting a hat-trick in a 9-1 victory. Buoyed by the experience, he returned to Maine Road full of confidence. England 'B' team honours followed in March, 1954, as England took on Scotland at Roker Park, while only injury put paid to hopes of a call-up to the senior side before the end of the season. Revie's improved form was not exactly mirrored in City's results, though they did improve their league position slightly from 20th to 17th with a tally of 37 points.

Nevertheless, it meant 1953-54 had been another disappointing campaign and the rumblings of discontent about Les McDowall's management grew. Away from the first team, however, there was much more encouraging news with the reserves having won their own league in style. And they did so by adopting a tactic that would, within 12 months, turn Revie into the Footballer of the Year.

Chapter 4

The Revie Plan

The end of an era, the wake-up call for a blinkered England and the moment the seeds of Don Revie finally realising his potential as a top player were sown. November 25, 1953, is a date forever enshrined in the history of English football. It was the day Hungary inflicted a defeat of such devastating proportions that nothing could ever be the same again. England, the mother country of football, had never lost at home to a team from outside the British Isles. But it was not so much the 6-3 defeat on that never-to-be-forgotten day which proved the biggest shock as the manner of the footballing lesson handed out by the Hungarians.

By forsaking the traditional 'W' shaped formation for more of a 'U' shape, Hungary shattered the illusion for good that the country who had introduced football to the world knew best. Faced with the unusual sight of the opposition number '9', Nandor Hidegkuti, being employed in a revolutionary 'deep-lying' centre-forward role behind a two-pronged attack of Ferenc Puskas and Sander Kocsis, England simply could not cope. The plan had been honed en route to Hungary winning the 1952 Olympics and involved the right-half, Jozsef Bozsik, surging forward in attack along with effervescent wingers, Laszlo Budai and Zoltan Czibor. To bring balance, left-half Jozsef Zakarias was ordered to stay deeper alongside centre-half Mihaly Lantos.

Such was the confusion caused by the formation and the rapid movement of the Hungarians, Billy Wright and his team-mates were left chasing shadows. The manner in which Puskas left Wright so mesmerised for one goal even saw the England captain being likened to 'a fire engine going to the wrong fire' by Geoffrey Green, the legendary football correspondent of *The Times*. England's humbling, they could muster just five shots to the visitors' 35, was such that the Wembley crowd rose to salute the Hungarians at the final whistle. One man who had not been surprised by the manner of the visitors' performance was future *Sunday Times* football correspondent, Brian Glanville. He had been afforded a glimpse of the Hungarians earlier the same year on a trip to Rome. "It was the inaugural game at the Stadio Olimpico and Hungary tore Italy apart 3-0," recalls Glanville. "They were sensational and I forecast then that England would have huge trouble against the Hungarians in November. They were light years in advance of everyone else, yet English football continued to arrogantly think it led the world. That defeat at Wembley shattered such thinking."

Back in Manchester, Johnny Williamson, who despite having made his first team debut in 1950 as a 20 year old was still considered a mainstay of City's reserve side, sat mesmerised in front of the television. Like everyone else at Maine Road, he was stunned by the footage of the Hungarians' comprehensive victory. The following day at training, the City players spoke of little else before getting down to work once the manager and his coaching staff had arrived to dispatch the team on their usual laps of the pitch. The conversation had returned to more mundane matters by the time training ended but Williamson could not get Hungary's innovative system out of his mind. He recalls: "It was a sensation and nothing like it had been seen before. It is difficult for anyone born since then to appreciate just what happened that day in 1953. It was ground-breaking. But, typically, English football continued to bury its head in the sand and carry on as before with the regimented system that saw number '5' mark number '9', '2' mark '11', '3' mark '7' and so on. Even though Billy Wright had come out looking for Hungary's number '9' that day at Wembley and not been able to find him." Despite the indifference of those in charge of English football, Williamson, a well-built player for whom pace was never his greatest asset, continued to mull over the events of November 25. Could the system be adapted to the English game? And would it make him more effective as a player?

His chance to find out came not too long after Hungary's demolition job at Wembley. Williamson recalls: "Frank Swift was appointed as reserve team coach at City and he moved me to centre-forward, which I didn't like the sound of as there was no way I fancied getting the battering you used to get back then. So, I thought 'why not try this deep-lying centre forward idea and see how it goes?' My thinking was that because I was not the fastest, if I came away from the defender it would probably confuse him. It also meant I could take the ball off Ken Barnes at right-half in plenty of space. In the end, I decided to try it out."

With Williamson sporting the number '9' shirt but filling the deep-lying role played so brilliantly at Wembley by Nandor Hidegkuti and Ken Barnes aping Jozsef Bozsik's game, the City reserves launched their grand experiment in front of just a few thousands fans. Williamson recalls: "The key was that both my role and Ken's had to work – there would be no point me playing deeper if there wasn't someone fulfilling the other role. You had to have two players on the same wavelength and, fortunately, we were. The first time we tried it, the opposition centre-half just didn't know what to do, whether to stay or go. If he stuck rigidly to '5' marking '9' then it left a huge gap at centre-half to exploit, allowing the inside-forward to sneak through. Ken would take advantage of that time after time in the weeks that followed by playing little Joe Hayes in. And if the centre-half decided to stay where he was, I had plenty of space to play in because, back then, centre-halves didn't have the brains to shout to their attacker 'come back and mark him'. It just wasn't the done thing – attackers attacked and defenders defended. The other thing in our favour was wingers used to take on the full-backs who, as a result, had to stay out on the flank. They wouldn't come in to the centre to cover for where the centre-half should have been. It was a simple plan, yet so effective."

Soon, results started to pick up but, with reserve team games being played on a Saturday at the same time as the senior side and the scouting of such fixtures by opposition teams still years away, the tactic remained under the radar. Johnny Williamson again: "We went on a run of 20-odd games where we just kept winning. The other reserve teams didn't have a clue how to cope with it. As we kept winning, the first team manager started to take notice and, eventually, he got us to use the system in a practice game among ourselves in training. It was right at the end of the season. Don Revie also came to watch me a few times in the reserves and liked what he saw. I was certain the first team could play the same way with Don filling my role but I wasn't sure if the manager felt the same."

Revie, however, was adamant the new tactic could work. Paddy Fagan, who by now had been reunited with Revie after the pair's earlier spell together at Hull City, recalls: "Don went to the manager and convinced him that the plan would work. Les McDowall had been a defender so, basically, didn't have a clue what the forwards should do so I think he was swayed by what Don said."

Whether Revie's intervention played a part or not, McDowall spent the summer mulling over the idea before seeking the board's approval. Consent was duly given, the belief of the directors being that, after three disappointing seasons that had seen the team finish 15th, 20th and 17th, anything fresh was worth a try.

Mindful that better players in the First Division might be more capable of reacting to the tactic than their reserve team counterparts, McDowall called his squad back for pre-season training two weeks early. Revie, whose wife Elsie had just given birth to son Duncan, was not amused as the early return would eat into his annual family holiday. But he was also pragmatic enough to appreciate that the tactic, with McDowall insisting he be the fulcrum of the remodelled side, could be the spark his career needed.

Sworn to secrecy for fear of the plan leaking out, the City players spent mornings and afternoons on the training pitch in the late weeks of summer fine-tuning the new system. So much so that, by the time of the opening day trip to Preston North End, hopes were high of a successful season. Ninety minutes later, however, McDowall's plans seemed in tatters. Preston had won 5-0. City had been destroyed and football reporter Archie Ledbrooke declared in the following Monday's *Daily Mirror*: 'I kill this plan.'

McDowall, though, would not be swayed and during the traditional Monday morning inquest into the weekend game he stressed that the team would continue to play the same way. Two days later, Sheffield United were the visitors to Maine Road but this time there would be a crucial tweak to the starting line-up. Ken Barnes, so successful as Johnny Williamson's foil in the reserves the previous season, was drafted in to replace the injured John McTavish. Williamson recalls: "I wasn't at Preston because, in those days, the reserves played on a Saturday as well. We were at home. But I was not overly surprised to learn it hadn't worked because it needed a player like Ken Barnes. Without him, it couldn't function because the inside-forward chosen instead could not play like Ken. At the meeting the following Monday, Don spoke up to say the system needed Ken to play to make it work. The manager listened and Ken was in the team against Sheffield United the following Wednesday. We won 5-2 and, after that, the team went on a little run so everyone was happy."

McTavish remains philosophical about lasting just one game before being replaced by Barnes. "I pulled my thigh muscle against Preston so Ken Barnes came in after that and did very well," he says. "It meant I was out of the side, which was frustrating but that is how it can be in football. I did get back in later after teaching myself to kick left-footed even though my right was the stronger. It meant I was able to stand in for Roy Paul at left-half."

Twelve points from the next seven games was proof that City, with the energetic Barnes and thoughtful Revie working in tandem, had overcome any teething problems and soon word was spreading via the newspapers. *Manchester Evening News* journalist Eric Thornton, in his 1970 book *Leeds United and Don Revie*, claimed to have been the first to name City's new tactic the 'Revie Plan', though others would later make similar boasts. Either way, it was a moniker that stuck. With Revie at its heart, such a tag was perhaps unsurprising – though the man himself was said to be embarrassed by the credit coming his way. Johnny Williamson, the reserve team forward who had initially brought the Hungarians' system to Manchester, recalls: "It was the newspapers who dreamed up the Revie Plan. Don was the centre-forward but a bit embarrassed by it all. He used to tell me 'no matter what they say, Johnny, we both know where it came from'. He was not the sort of man to get caught up by headlines. It wasn't exactly rocket science, just simple thinking. Football is a simple game, no matter what they say today."

Revie may have been awkward that someone else's idea was being touted as his own, but what was not in doubt was how integral he had become to its success. Paddy Fagan had played with Revie at Hull so, once reunited at City, could appreciate just how much his team-mate's game had developed. "He hadn't changed much as a person and clearly still thought he was a very good player. But what had changed was he was in a team with a lot of other good players. Don always wanted possession, every time I got it he would be shouting, 'Give me the ball'. Because he was such a good player, I usually did. Put it this way, if I had two people to pass to and one was Don, I would pass it to him. I knew he would not lose it and that, more often than not, he would do something special with it."

Johnny Williamson is another who subscribes to the theory that playing alongside better players brought the best out of Revie. "When Don arrived, I could see he was a good player. But what he had at City was better players than the ones he had been with at Leicester or Hull. Having Ken Barnes was crucial, as his presence in the team allowed Don to flourish at Maine Road."

City's momentum slowed as the season moved into winter but there was no doubting the club's credentials as a side capable of challenging for honours once again. Brian Glanville, who had witnessed Hungary's new system in Rome seven months before England's 6-3 humbling at Wembley, recognised straight away where the Revie Plan's inspiration had come from. He says: "Revie was fulfilling the deep-lying centre-forward role that the Hungarians had favoured. But, still, English football had not caught up and he was able to prosper."

Opposition teams would spend so much time worrying about what they were likely to face come Saturday afternoon that many were beaten before emerging from the tunnel. And the one they all feared most was Revie. Colin Grainger, a future team-mate of Revie's at Leeds and Sunderland, started his career at Wrexham before moving to newly-promoted Sheffield United in 1953. He recalls: "Don was at the heart of everything Manchester City did. He was such a good passer of the ball that the Revie Plan suited him perfectly. Don was a big man but not the quickest so a role that gave him so much space was ideal. In those days, teams just went out and played. There were no tactics as such, and no-one ever sat around and thought about how we should play. Even when the Revie Plan was proving successful, I can't remember ever having a team meeting to discuss how to counter it. That's just not how it was when I was a player."

Some opposing teams did try to come up with their own plan to counter City and Revie, as Jack Overfield recalls from his time at Leeds United. "Revie had been sold to Sunderland by the time we were promoted to the First Division but Manchester City were still using his plan," recalls the winger who made 163 appearances for Leeds. "Our tactic was not to mark the man filling the 'Revie role' but instead make sure the wingers were marked. That way, the man in the middle could stick to the plan of spraying the ball out to the wing where we would be waiting."

That the Revie Plan lasted long enough to be used against Leeds in the late 1950s is testament to how innovative it had been in the first place. Such longevity would, according to the original instigator in Manchester City reserves, be impossible today. Johnny Williamson insists: "Football is hyped to death these days and if someone tries something basic like a new corner routine then it will be on Sky Sports within minutes. Then, Sky and the newspapers will spend the next few days picking it to pieces to make sure everyone knows all about it. There was none of that when I was a player, which meant the opposition didn't know either what to expect or how to counter what they did find. I would say it took the rest of football about six years to catch up and work out how to deal with the Revie Plan. I remember we played Tottenham one year and Bill Nicholson said to his attackers 'get hold of Barnesy'. It was the first time anyone had got to grips with the system."

As 1954 turned into 1955, however, plans to combat the Revie Plan were some way in the distance. City, after an encouraging first half of the Division One season, were about to turn their attentions to the FA Cup. For Revie, memories of six years earlier when an unfortunate nosebleed meant he missed Leicester City's defeat to Wolverhampton Wanderers in the final were still fresh. He was determined to earn another chance to step out at Wembley. Johnny Williamson recalls: "The Cup was 'the' competition back then and everyone dreamed about playing in the final. Don had not really got over missing out in 1949 and it was definitely an inspiration to him. There were a lot of great players who had retired without ever getting to a Cup final and Don didn't want to be another one."

A third round draw that paired City with a Derby County side destined to be relegated in May brought a comfortable 3-1 win. Manchester United were then beaten 2-0 at Maine Road before City travelled to Luton Town in the fifth round as revenge was exacted for their exit two years earlier with another 2-0 triumph. Second Division Birmingham City were then put out in the last eight to earn a semi-final tie against Sunderland, who along with City were one of the six or seven sides still harbouring genuine hopes of lifting the First Division title.

A week before the semi-final, inside-forward Johnny Hart, father of former Portsmouth manager Paul, broke his leg during a league game against Huddersfield Town. Three days earlier, City had signed Bobby Johnstone for £25,000 from Hibernian so at least their preparations for the game at Villa Park were not too badly disrupted by the loss of Hart. Manager Les McDowall's pursuit of Johnstone had seemed an unnecessary luxury with City playing so well but in the semi-final it was the debutant and Revie who combined to create the only goal of the game for Roy Clarke.

Booking a first trip to Wembley in 22 years should have given City's title bid a lift but, instead, just one point from the next three games meant their challenge was all but over. Worse was to follow when Clarke, the hero of the semi-final, had to be stretchered off after sustaining a knee injury, before Johnstone and Revie also picked up worrying knocks. City eventually finished seventh, six points behind champions Chelsea, but any lingering feelings of disappointment were soon swept away by thoughts of the impending trip to Wembley. There was one row at Maine Road during the build-up when the players' wives were handed tickets that were far from the best available to the club. Revie and captain Roy Paul complained successfully to the board, who swapped the tickets for a better standard. Compared to the ructions going on behind the scenes at opponents Newcastle, it was a minor spat. Manager Duggie Livingstone had dropped Jackie Milburn for the final only for the board to intervene and reinstate 'Wor Jackie'. Livingstone, who had led Belgium to the World Cup finals the previous year, never regained his stature at St James' Park and left the club the following season.

Cup final day was, typically, warm and sunny in 1955 but this did not prevent Revie and his City team-mates emerging from the tunnel ahead of kick-off sporting new sky-blue track-suits over short-sleeved team shirts. The Newcastle players, in contrast, were stripped for action and it was those clad in black and white stripes who caught the opposition cold. It took Newcastle less than a minute to go in front, Jackie Milburn being left all alone by a statuesque defence to head a corner into the net.

If City were culpable for the opening goal, they were unfortunate just 17 minutes later when full-back Jimmy Meadows injured his knee and had to leave the pitch. With the use of substitutes still a decade away from being made legal, City were down to 10 men – much to the frustration of John McTavish. He recalls: "I was 12th man for the 1955 final so would have been able to get on and help the team if subs had been allowed. Jimmy suffered the injury, ironically, because the Wembley pitch was so good. In the weeks leading up to the final, we had been playing on really hard surfaces because there had not been much rain. It meant you could not allow the ball to bounce as it would go straight over your head. Poor Jimmy was trying to turn quickly but was injured as a result."

City were up against it and had goalkeeper Bert Trautmann to thank for keeping them in the final with a string of fine saves. Despite being on the back foot due to Newcastle's numerical advantage, City did snatch an equaliser just before the break through a Bobby Johnstone header. The half-time whistle blew moments later but any hopes of City going on to lift the Cup were dashed when Newcastle netted twice in nine second-half minutes through Bobby Mitchell and George Hannah. Paddy Fagan, who had worked tirelessly throughout the 90 minutes, remembers the gut-wrenching sense of disappointment in the City dressing room after the final whistle. "When playing on a pitch the size of Wembley, being a man down is just too much. To lose Jimmy like that so early was really unlucky and, in the end, we tired. I still believe that is the only reason Newcastle won the Cup that year. The best team doesn't always win and that was my feeling at Wembley. Everyone was so disappointed."

The season may have ended in frustration, but there was no doubting Revie's career was finally blossoming. His England debut had come in October against Northern Ireland in Belfast, the first of six caps Revie would eventually win. One of five debutants as Walter Winterbottom looked to remodel his side following their defeat to Uruguay in the World Cup quarter-finals, he had scored along with fellow new boy Johnny Haynes in a 2-0 victory. Two further appearances followed before the end of the 1954-55 season. He scored again in a 7-2 win over Scotland and was then in the England side beaten 1-0 by France in Paris. As pleasing as this international recognition was, however, by far the clearest gauge as to how far he had progressed came shortly after the Cup final defeat when he was named Footballer of the Year by the Football Writers' Association. It was an award City team-mate Johnny Williamson felt was fully justified. "The publicity that came with the new system definitely helped," he says, "but there was no doubt in my mind that Don had been the best player in the country that season. He was the centre of everything at Manchester City, while he also did well for England. Don fully deserved to be Footballer of the Year and I know he was very proud of the award."

Basking in the glow of such a prestigious award and having earned huge praise for his part in England's 7-2 demolition of Scotland, Revie could have been forgiven for heading off into the summer of 1955 feeling he had finally cracked it. Unfortunately, any momentum built up was brought to a shuddering halt by a close season dispute with City manager Les McDowall. With son Duncan due to celebrate his first birthday in July, Revie wanted to take his family on holiday to Blackpool. Permission was sought from club trainer Laurie Barnett on the understanding he would return for training a fortnight earlier than the rest of the squad. Approval was, Revie later claimed, granted. But just to make sure, he reminded Barnett of the arrangement a couple of weeks before his holiday was due to start. Barnett told him to go and see manager McDowall, who ordered Revie to commute from the seaside each day to train as usual with his team-mates. Revie refused and went on holiday, making sure he maintained a rigorous training regime of his own on the beach. McDowall's response was to suspend Revie, a move that cost the player £27 in wages – a princely sum in 1955. The furore would eventually blow over, though not the ill-feeling and, once the season got underway, Revie was no longer first-choice. Johnny Williamson recalls: "There was a lot of trouble over Don's holiday and I, personally, thought it was daft on the manager's part. Don was a very good trainer and had promised to train while he was away. Don thought the holiday had been agreed so was surprised when the manager went back on it. McDowall ended up cutting his nose off to spite his face by dropping Don and, sadly, no-one won."

Relations between Revie and McDowall never truly recovered from the row, even though it would be another 15 months before there was to be a permanent parting of the ways. The upshot was Revie playing just half of the 42 league games in 1955-56 as McDowall instead preferred Bobby Johnstone.

Despite the disruption caused to his pre-season, Revie was still in the thoughts of England manager Walter Winterbottom. He netted a hat-trick in the opening friendly of the season as Denmark were beaten 5-1 in Copenhagen, an admirable performance in a Sunday game that saw England agree not to select more than one player from each club so as not to weaken the full league programme going on back home that weekend. Unsurprisingly, Revie retained his place against Wales in October but the 2-1 defeat at Ninian Park would prove to be his last international appearance for 12 months as the lack of first team opportunities at Maine Road saw him slip out of the reckoning.

McDowall's insistence on picking Johnstone ahead of Revie was, it must be said, partly justified by City going on to enjoy another encouraging campaign. By no means as free-flowing as the previous year despite scoring more goals, McDowall's side owed many of their victories to the agility of Bert Trautmann in goal. After having fought for Germany during the Second World War, he had been captured by the Allies and shipped to Britain where he was imprisoned in a POW camp in Ashton-in-Makerfield, near Wigan. It was here that his interest in football developed and, once released after the War, Trautmann combined farm work with playing for local side St Helens Town. An impressive series of displays soon caught the attention of several Football League clubs and it was City who signed the German in 1949. Uproar followed with season-ticket holders threatening a boycott and hundreds of letters arriving at Maine Road imploring the club to cancel the signing. Trautmann eventually won the supporters over, however, and went on to make 545 appearances for the club with the 1955-56 season being comfortably his most memorable.

By then, even the most anti-German among City's support had been won over by his bravery and agility. Along with the impressive form in the league that would see Trautmann follow Revie in being named Footballer of the Year come May, he also proved a heroic figure in the FA Cup as City disposed of Blackpool (2-1), Southend United (1-0), Liverpool (2-1 after a replay) and Everton (2-1) en route to beating Spurs 1-0 in the semi-final to book a return trip to Wembley. Their opponents in the final were Birmingham City.

Revie was still on the periphery after playing just once during the run to the final, though a fine display in a 4-2 win at Portsmouth on the final day of the Division One season had given manager Les McDowall plenty to ponder ahead of naming his Wembley line-up. Even so, Revie was fearing the worst. It was here, however, that the fates intervened on his behalf as Billy Spurdle, City's right winger, was suddenly struck down by an attack of boils. Bobby Johnstone, who had taken over Revie's role of deep-lying centre-forward, was also troubled by a calf strain. McDowall had a couple of big decisions to make, as illustrated by the City manager opting not to name his team until lunchtime on the day of the game. John McTavish, who had been 12th man at Wembley a year earlier, looked set to finally get his chance. "Bobby was only 75-80 per cent fit because of his calf and I was down to play," recalls McTavish. "But then Bobby was declared fit. I did get to walk on the Wembley turf but it was still a major disappointment. Don was also sweating over whether he would be selected, though that was down to the manager and not injury."

Eventually, McDowall revealed his decision. Bobby Johnstone would move to the flank in place of boils victim Billy Spurdle, allowing Revie to slot in at centre-forward. Any lingering doubts McDowall may have had were banished within three minutes as City went ahead with Revie at the heart of a sweeping move that began just outside their own penalty area. After collecting a pass from Bill Leivers, another who had been an injury doubt ahead of kick-off, Revie spread play to Roy Clarke before racing 50 yards to collect the return and pull the ball back for an unmarked Joe Hayes to score. Birmingham, the overwhelming pre-match favourites to lift the Cup, were stunned but it did not take too long for Arthur Turner's side to hit back – Welsh international Noel Kinsey equalising in the 15th minute.

There had been no further score by half-time but Revie was not happy and determined to take positive action. Lifelong friend and City reserve team player Johnny Williamson recalls: "By half-time, Birmingham had got on top so Don pulled Ken Barnes across as they left the field and said, 'Where have you been?' Ken said he had been told by the manager to stick close to Birmingham's Peter Murphy. The role was alien to him and restricted his attacking threat, but Ken was doing what he had been told by the manager. Don listened and then said, 'Forget what he said, Barnesy, let's you and me get back to what we do best and win this Cup'. Ken agreed and we went on to win 3-1 through goals from John Dyson and Bobby Johnstone. The funny thing is I don't think the manager even noticed the change during the second-half."

With City 3-1 up and just over half-an-hour still on the clock, the story of the 1956 final seemed to have been written. The Cup did, indeed, return to Manchester but only after a remarkable show of bravery and courage from Bert Trautmann. After performing a typically heroic save at the feet of Peter Murphy with 15 minutes still to go, the German goalkeeper was knocked unconscious. After treatment from trainer Laurie Barnett, he eventually got to his feet before insisting on soldiering on despite the pain. It was only later that X-rays revealed the German had broken his neck in the challenge. John McTavish, again City's 12th man at Wembley for a second year, recalls: "We could see during the final minutes of the game that Bert was hurt but no-one had any idea how seriously. Not even Bert. He eventually had to have two steel pins put through his skull but it was typical of Bert to play on. I have seen a lot of good goalkeepers over the years but Bert was the bravest. He was also an important part of the Revie Plan. Bert had played handball back home in Germany so it meant he could throw the ball out to Don more accurately than he could kick it to anyone else."

The news of Trautmann's injury understandably attracted most of the headlines the following day, but in football terms the most notable aspect of the 1956 Cup final had been the vindication of Revie's selection. Named Man of the Match, Revie had been instrumental in City winning the Cup for a third time.

Even with his 29th birthday fast approaching, Revie's standing as a key player at Maine Road had surely been restored. Fred Eyre, lifelong Manchester City fan and future best-selling author of *Kicked Into Touch*, says: "Don had been at loggerheads with the manager all season but the Cup final went so well that supporters thought he was back in the fold. We presumed everything that had been said at the start of the season would be forgotten."

Revie did, indeed, start the 1956-57 campaign in his preferred centre-forward role, with the chance to again pull the strings from a deep position. However, a poor run of results – City lost six games in a row during September and October – brought about a change with Bobby Johnstone being restored to the number '9' shirt. Revie, shunted back to right-half, still managed one last England cap in a disappointing 1-1 draw with Northern Ireland in October but it was becoming increasingly clear to those close to him that their friend was becoming restless. And it was not long before the man whose 1955 autobiography had been titled *Soccer's Happy Wanderer* was on his way to a club whose place among the elite seemed as secure as the Bank of England.

Chapter 5

Bank of England Club

When Sir Alex Ferguson, after finally surrendering in the battle to keep Cristiano Ronaldo at Manchester United during the summer of 2009, chose to pour scorn on the lavish spending of Real Madrid, his analogy left many fans of the modern era scratching their heads in confusion. By comparing the Spanish giants' 'money no object' pursuit of Ronaldo and AC Milan's Kaka to how Sunderland built their side in the 1950s, the clearly furious Manchester United manager's intention was to prove that lavish spending does not necessarily guarantee success. In doing so, he stirred a thousand memories for anyone who watched football at a time when the Wearside club were causing a sensation by embarking on what, by the standards of the day, was a spending spree every bit as outrageous as that of Florentino Perez at the Bernabeu.

Having enjoyed immediate success with three league titles in just five years after being accepted into the Football League in 1890, Sunderland set a high standard from the very start. Two further championships followed before the outbreak of the First World War, while the 1930s brought another title success and a first FA Cup triumph. Attendances also flourished with a record 75,118 squeezing into Roker Park one Wednesday afternoon in March, 1933, to see the home side lose an FA Cup quarter-final replay to Derby County after extra-time.

Once English football had resumed following the end of the Second World War, though, the club's glory days had become little more than a fading, if pleasant, memory. Sunderland were still in the First Division and able to make the proud boast of never having been relegated. But, as the decade dragged on, the directors recognised drastic action was needed if Sunderland were to be jolted back to life as a football force. So, the Wearsiders embarked on a spending spree that saw Len Shackleton, the crowd-pleasing former Bradford Park Avenue inside-left, signed from Newcastle United for £20,500 a little over 12 months after Arthur Hudgell, a stylish left-back from Crystal Palace, had arrived for £10,000 – a record for a defender.

The spending did not pay immediate dividends, however, with even the presence of one of football's great characters not being able to prevent Sunderland suffering the great ignominy of becoming the first top-flight side to lose an FA Cup-tie to non-League opposition on Yeovil's notorious slope. Undeterred, the Roker Park board continued to release funds for manager Billy Murray as Shackleton was joined in the North East by Billy Bingham, George Aitken and Ray Daniel. Results improved markedly and the league title just eluded the club in 1950, Sunderland finishing just a point behind champions Portsmouth in third place. Further disappointment lay ahead in 1955 and 1956 with FA Cup exits in the semi-finals. By then, Sunderland had become known as the 'Bank of England Club' for the seemingly never-ending supply of money being spent on new players. It was a tag the newspaper headline writers of the day would make great hay with during the subsequent steep decline.

With 1955 bringing a fourth place finish, the feeling on Wearside was that further spending together with a little tweaking would bring the success the region craved. It was this desire to realise undoubted potential that persuaded manager Bill Murray to sign Don Revie from Manchester City for £24,000 in October, 1956. Goalkeeper Johnny Bollands had moved to Roker Park just a couple of months earlier and remembers the impact the signing made. "When the players discovered Don was signing, we were pleased," he says. "He was still a key player at Manchester City and had just won the FA Cup, so it was hoped he could make a massive difference to the team. We had been struggling quite a bit in the league that season and were in need of a lift."

Revie arrived with a big reputation after inspiring Manchester City to success at Wembley but it seems not everyone at Roker Park was over-enamoured with the new signing. Brian Leng, Sunderland's official historian and former editor of popular fanzine *The Wearside Roar*, says: "Len Shackleton once told me a great story about Don Revie. Seemingly, soon after arriving, he was chatting to a few of the Sunderland lads when he challenged them to try and copy a trick he had perfected of flicking a coin up with his foot and then catching it in his top pocket. Don made a small wager with them and, of course, they couldn't do it and had to pay up. Shack saw this and slipped away before Don, whom he regarded as something of a show-off, could challenge him. He then practiced for hours to perfect the trick, so much so that he eventually left Don open-mouthed by flicking the coin up and catching it on his head before landing it in his pocket. Shack loved the look on Don's face as he handed over his winnings."

Tricks with coins apart, the first thing that struck Revie on his return to the North East was how well Sunderland looked after their players. Nothing was too much trouble, particularly for those who had just signed and had not yet had time to find a new house in the area. Colin Grainger moved to Roker Park from Sheffield United in a £7,000 deal just four months after Revie's own arrival. He recalls: "It was a top-class club and only the very best would do. Don had not been there very long when I signed so the club put us both up at the Seaburn Hotel with our wives. The club insisted on redecorating our houses, something they did for all the new lads. It was typical of how Sunderland treated us that we should be put up in such a lovely place while the decorating was finished."

Sunderland's belief, and one Revie took with him to Leeds, was that players being happy off the field invariably contributed to better performances on it. Results over the 12 months or so leading up to Revie's arrival may not have added weight to the theory as Sunderland slipped into mid-table but the club, nevertheless, persisted. Unfortunately for the new signing from Manchester City, results were poor from the very start with five of his first six games being lost. Injury meant these appearances were stretched over the best part of five months and, with Sunderland struggling in his absence, relegation seemed a certainty by mid-March. That was, however, until a seven-game unbeaten run when Revie was an ever-present pulled Sunderland clear of the relegation zone and not even three defeats on the spin to end the season could prevent the club's unbroken run in the top division being extended by another year. Revie had scored twice in 16 appearances during that first season at Roker Park but his indifferent form was the least of Sunderland's worries as they were plunged into turmoil by an irregular payments scandal that shook English football to its very foundations.

The saga had begun in January, 1957, when a signed letter arrived at Football League headquarters in Lytham St Annes. The identity of the writer has been a fierce topic of debate ever since on Wearside with the finger being pointed at everyone from a disaffected director to a couple of former players. Whatever the source, the letter's contents were akin to placing a stick of dynamite underneath Roker Park and lighting the fuse with allegations of illegal payments to players leading to the launching of a joint inquiry by the League and Football Association. The eventual charges concerned the then law that made every footballer subject to a maximum wage of £15 per week, with an initial signing-on fee of £10 also allowed. It didn't matter whether a player was a seasoned international, a rookie or, like Len Shackleton, one of the game's great entertainers, clubs were forbidden to pay a player any more.

As the six-man commission quickly discovered, Sunderland paid little heed to the rule – as Colin Grainger, who moved to Roker Park a month after the initial allegations were made, confirms: "The payments were why so many players wanted to go to Sunderland. We would get a decent signing on fee, which was not allowed, and we would also get more money for winning than was allowed. The bonus should have been £4 but we got £10, quite a difference in those days. Footballers were paid more than the average wage, which was about £8, but still nothing like we should have been, bearing in mind all the money that came in through the turnstiles."

The joint inquiry meticulously examined Sunderland's accounts and one of the investigating team quickly found a huge receipt for a bulk order of straw, which was used to prevent the pitch being frozen. Attached to the receipt was a note reading, 'What shall I do with this?' Brian Leng, Sunderland's official historian and honorary member of the club's Ex-Players' Association, recalls: "The receipt for the straw made the Football League very suspicious so Alan Hardaker, the secretary at the time, rang up his brother, Ernest. He was the chairman of Hull FC rugby league club so Hardaker asked, 'If I gave you £3,000, would you be able to buy enough straw to cover the pitch for a season?' His brother replied, 'More like 20 seasons', and the Football League really got their teeth into it after that."

The commission eventually revealed that payments were being made and financed through orders placed with contractors. By charging more than was due for work done, contractors could then hand the club credit notes that were later cashed to pay the players illegally. In total, £5,450 was found to have been misappropriated this way over a period of five years. The punishment, when it came, was swingeing with the club fined a record £5,000, while chairman Bill Ditchburn was permanently suspended from football. Directors Stanley Ritson and LW Evans were also removed from the game indefinitely and manager Billy Murray fined £200. Murray subsequently resigned at the end of the 1956-57 season after having steered the club to 20th place and safety.

Several player registrations were also temporarily suspended by the commission, though in 1958 the players successfully sued on the grounds that the authorities had exceeded their powers. By then, however, the damage had been done and a shattered Sunderland were well on their way to a first relegation. In many ways, the Wearsiders could consider themselves unlucky to be caught out with several clubs left nervously watching events at Roker Park unfold. Perhaps the most unfortunate aspect for Sunderland, however, was that, just a few years after the scandal broke, the maximum wage for footballers was abolished. The club had been punished for defying a regulation system that was on its way out anyway, Professional Footballers' Association chairman Jimmy Hill winning his fight to abolish the maximum wage of £20 in January, 1961. Johnny Haynes of Fulham immediately became the first £100 per week footballer, a sum that dwarfed what the Sunderland players were pocketing.

Bill Murray's departure from Roker Park in the wake of the payments scandal meant a new manager was needed and the new board opted for Alan Brown. A former player with Huddersfield Town, Burnley and Notts County, he had returned to Turf Moor as manager for three years until 1957 and helped set up the youth scheme that would blossom in later years. Perhaps more importantly to a club so recently rocked by scandal was his almost puritanical outlook on life. Public confidence had to be restored so who better than someone who put so much store in honesty and integrity?

A host of new signings were made, including Charlie Hurley, destined to become Sunderland's most capped player with 38 appearances for the Republic of Ireland, but results were poor from the start as Brown's reign began with three straight defeats. Revie was also struggling for form and it took until the seventh game to register his first goal in a 3-1 defeat to Everton. Two further goals followed against Bolton Wanderers and Newcastle United but the players were not responding to the new manager. Colin Grainger made most of his 124 appearances for Sunderland under Brown but found it difficult to warm to him. "Brown's predecessor Bill Murray was a gentleman who wanted the best footballers in his team because he felt Sunderland should play the right way," says Grainger, who after football became a singer and appeared on the same bill as The Beatles. "He treated us all like adults and was very good on the man-management side, realising some players need an arm round their shoulder and some don't. Alan Brown was completely different. He was not my cup of tea at all, and a lot of the lads felt the same way. Don did not see eye to eye with him, mainly because Brown just wanted runners and kickers. He did not want footballers who could pass the ball like Don. He didn't want Len Shackleton and he didn't want Revie."

Despite the manager's apparent antipathy, Revie played in 39 of Sunderland's 42 games. Others, though, were not so lucky with Billy Bingham often being left in the stand despite the club's troubles near the foot of Division One. Brian Leng, a Sunderland supporter since 1955, recalls: "Alan was brought in to try and clean up the club. He was a very different character to what the players and fans had been used to and was determined to build the side around youth. He also wanted to get rid of those brought in during the 'Bank of England' days. In a way, he went a bit far with there even being one game when we were desperate for points to avoid relegation and yet Billy

Bingham was sitting in the stands because he didn't feature in the manager's plans. Just a few months later, Billy was playing in the 1958 World Cup. Alan went on to build a good young side around players like Charlie Hurley but in that relegation season it seemed the manager's desire to stick to his principles was to the detriment of the team."

By early March, a first relegation was looming for Sunderland only for the team, just as in the previous year, to rally. A draw with Sheffield Wednesday was followed by back-to-back wins over Tottenham Hotspur – Revie netting the only goal at White Hart Lane - and West Bromwich Albion before a point was secured from the trip to Chelsea. A Revie strike then helped Sunderland claim a draw at Manchester United to further raise hopes of avoiding relegation. Club historian Brian Leng says: "It really looked like we might escape for a second successive season after a good run. In the end, it all came down to the last day when we were at Portsmouth and Birmingham, our rivals for relegation, were at Leicester City. A win for us and Leicester getting at least a point would have been enough to save us. Anyway, we won 2-0 but so did Birmingham and that was that. It was a horrible feeling."

Sunderland's proud boast of never having been relegated was at an end. For Revie, fast approaching his 31st birthday, it meant a return to the Second Division and an uncertain future, with manager Brown even more determined to re-build with youth. It was a stance that saw Revie banished to the reserves as Sunderland lost 3-1 at Lincoln City on the opening day of the following season. Two defeats to Fulham, the second a 6-2 thrashing at Craven Cottage, then persuaded Brown to recall Revie by the first weekend in September but a parting of the ways still seemed inevitable. John Bollands, who remained at Roker Park until 1959 when the goalkeeper was sold to Bolton, recalls: "Sunderland is a huge football place so you can imagine what a blow it was for the club to go down. I blame Alan Brown entirely for the relegation, I didn't agree with his methods in training or in games. Don left a couple of months into the following season after becoming disillusioned. I was genuinely sorry to see him go as he could still play. But the manager wanted to go in a different direction."

Revie's priority was a return to the First Division but, unlike when leaving Hull or Manchester, there was no major clamour for his services this time around. Pace had never been his strength even as a youngster but it was still clear to many that time was catching up with Revie. Home-town club Middlesbrough, then in the Second Division, did show an interest but it was Leeds United, struggling in the top flight after winning just four of their opening 18 games, who eventually stepped forward and paid Sunderland £14,000.

The fee was a decent sum, Leeds being able to match the asking price thanks to the world record £63,000 banked when John Charles had moved to Juventus the previous year. Even so, it seemed a gamble for a club who had been forced to spend a decent proportion of the Charles transfer fee on rebuilding the West Stand following a devastating fire. Revie's better days, as even he admitted, were behind him and supporters rightly questioned whether the money could have been better spent elsewhere. History would show, however, that Don Revie's return to his native Yorkshire would change English football forever.

Chapter 6

A Fading Star

When Don Revie walked into Elland Road as a Leeds United player for the first time, the club's home had seen better days. A fire that had destroyed the club's main stand a couple of years earlier meant a brand new structure costing £180,000 could be found down one side of the pitch. With 4,000 seats and a large paddock capable of holding another 6,000 supporters, the West Stand was an impressive structure. Built courtesy of a public appeal that raised a third of the cost after it was revealed the old wooden stand had been under-insured, its modern façade and iconic entrance brought a sense of importance to Elland Road that only the likes of Villa Park and Highbury could better.

Elsewhere, however, a ground that had initially been home to Holbeck rugby league club before the founding of Leeds City in 1904 was showing its age. At the end backing on to Elland Road was the affectionately-known 'Scratching Shed', a shallow terrace with a wooden barrel-shaped roof that was identical in design to the 'Cowshed' at Huddersfield Town's old Leeds Road ground. Both had been built in the 1920s and were basic in the extreme. It was a similar story at the opposite end of Elland Road where a huge uncovered Spion Kop terrace could be found, while gazing enviously at the new West Stand was the rather primitive Lowfields Road Stand. John Reynolds joined the Leeds groundstaff in 1957 after the Welshman's promising playing career had been shattered by an injury sustained in an FA Youth Cup tie. He recalls: "I was out injured when the main stand burnt down one night in September, 1956. The owner of the fish and chip shop over the road raised the alarm but the fire had already taken hold and it ended up being so ferocious that the roof collapsed. The club lost everything – offices, kit, boots, you name it. The new West Stand that was built in its place was the bee's knees. It was very modern, not like now where it is Elland Road's worst stand by some distance. The only problem was that, in comparison, the rest of the ground now didn't look the best. The Kop was open and the whole place needed money spent on it. The problem was we didn't have any."

United were, of course, not alone in being unable to improve their ground due to lack of finance. Money had been tight at Leeds for several years, as illustrated by the decision after the Second World War only to buy the land immediately behind the old West Stand to convert into what became known as the Fullerton Park training pitches. The initial intention had been to snap up everything between the West Stand and the Leeds-London railway line, a move that would have given the club much more scope to expand.

On the pitch, Leeds' lack of wealth was also apparent as Revie prepared to make his debut at home to Newcastle United on November 29, 1958. Promotion – the club's fourth – had been secured under Revie's old mentor Raich Carter two years earlier but the sale of John Charles meant United were back in familiar territory at the wrong end of Division One. Carter had left in the summer of 1958 and been replaced on an initially temporary basis by Bill Lambton, the trainer who had been brought to Elland Road by the former Hull City manager the previous November. Lambton arrived with a reputation for unorthodox training methods with players at his previous club Scunthorpe United trying to improve their fitness with trampolining sessions.

Leeds won only one of the new manager's first nine games and fresh faces were brought in. Winger Billy Humphries boosted the club's Irish contingent and was joined by Burnley centre-forward Alan Shackleton. Lambton, mindful his side lacked creativity, then made the signing that would shape the future of Leeds United by bringing Don Revie from Sunderland.

Results immediately improved and Lambton was confirmed as manager shortly before Christmas. Leeds also had a new captain early in the New Year with Revie replacing Wilbur Cash but it was clear there were problems behind the scenes as, first, Jack Overfield and then Grenville Hair slapped in transfer requests. Matters came to a head in March when Lambton, the players and chairman Sam Bolton met to discuss the unrest and the manager decided to resign. Lambton's reign was the shortest-ever at Elland Road, though his signing of Revie means his place in history is assured. Despite that, the players did not mourn Lambton's departure. Jack Overfield, who made his Leeds debut three years before Revie's arrival as a player, recalls: "He was a Sergeant Major type who thought he could run a football club like you would the army. He didn't have a football brain and it was typical of the time that someone like that could manage Leeds United. He was sacked in the end but, even then, the directors tried to let it be known that it was the players who had got rid of him. Lambton had been Raich Carter's trainer and I never thought Raich should have been sacked. What did for Raich was not being afraid to give the directors a piece of his mind. John Charles was sold to Juventus but Raich didn't see much of the money for transfers and, in the end, he went in the newspapers and said he wouldn't trust the directors enough to send them out to buy a packet of Woodbines. He was sacked not long after that and the club went downhill."

With Lambton having followed Carter out of Elland Road, Leeds limped towards the end of the season and an eventual 15th place finish. Revie had missed only four games following his November arrival but a return of just two goals in 20 league games was disappointing. Jack Overfield again: "Don arrived at Leeds with a big reputation because of what had happened during his time at Manchester City. He was such a fine passer of the ball and he had also been the instigator of that plan of his. But it didn't really happen at Leeds. The plan when Don signed was for him to play inside-forward to me but I got injured. And by the time I was fit again, Leeds were ready to sell me to Sunderland so we never really got the chance to play together that much."

Lambton's resignation meant the Leeds board started the search for a new manager but it proved to be a frustrating affair. Arthur Turner, then manager of Southern League Headington United, was the first choice but he chose to stay at a club who would later join the Football League under the name of Oxford United. Similar rejections followed from Archie Macaulay of Norwich City, Hull City's Bob Brocklebank and Charlie Mitten of Newcastle United. In the end, Leeds settled for Queens Park Rangers' manager Jack Taylor, who was appointed in May, 1959, on a three-year contract worth £2,500 per annum. A well-established manager after seven years at Loftus Road, Taylor's first season was hugely disappointing and United were relegated in 21st place. Revie managed a healthy seven goals in 35 appearances from inside-right, the second highest tally in the team behind John McCole who found the net a commendable 22 times. What let Leeds down was a porous defence, a woeful 92 goals being conceded as Taylor's men were only kept off the bottom of the First Division table by Luton Town.

Revie's response was to surrender the captaincy to Freddie Goodwin, revealing his superstitious trait by insisting a change was needed as he had proved to be unlucky in the role. His mind was also turning to what lay in store once his playing days were over with a move into management becoming increasingly attractive. Such ambitions were put on hold, however, as Leeds kicked off their first season in Division Two for five years at Liverpool. Making his United debut in the 2-0 defeat at Anfield was Colin Grainger, Revie's former team-mate from Sunderland. He recalls: "Don was coming towards the end of his career and it showed. He had been no spring chicken when leaving Sunderland a couple of years earlier but now it was two years on. Don could still pass a ball as well as anyone, but he had slowed down and the formation Leeds played did him no favours."

Revie, a deep thinker on football even as a youngster, recognised his career as a player was drawing to a close. An offer to become player-coach at Chester City along with interest from Tranmere Rovers and Australia had already been rejected, when a vacancy came up at Bournemouth. Revie, tiring of the malaise that had descended on Elland Road following relegation the previous year, was keen and asked United director Harry Reynolds to write a reference in support of his application.

It has since become part of Leeds United folklore that Reynolds, while writing said letter of recommendation, suddenly tore it up after realising he was extolling the virtues of the very man needed at Elland Road following the resignation of Jack Taylor as manager. The Earl of Harewood, a Leeds United supporter since 1932 and president of the club, said: "Harry started to write the letter only to realise Don sounded like exactly the man Leeds needed. He thought, 'Don's our player so he should be our player-manager'. And with that, he screwed up the letter and threw it in the bin."

What is less widely known of Revie's aborted efforts to move to Dean Court is that Bournemouth also baulked at the £6,000 transfer fee Leeds were asking for Revie and opted to turn elsewhere. John Reynolds, who celebrated 50 years on the Leeds groundstaff in 2007, recalls: "It was Leeds' incredible good fortune that Bournemouth could not come up with the money. If they had, Don would have become their manager. It is amazing to think how different history could have been for Leeds United had that been the case."

The die was cast and Revie, then being paid the maximum £20 a week as a player, was named United's seventh post-war manager on March 16, 1961. Not everyone at Elland Road was delighted at the news, not least Jack Charlton who, at the time, was the most militant member of the squad. A tendency to question every decision and a refusal to conform for the benefit of the team often left Revie exasperated, as Charlton recalls: "Don was still a player when we had a training match one day. I was a bit hot-headed in those days and would go charging about all over. Eventually, Don had had enough and said, 'If I was manager, I wouldn't play you'. My response was to stick the finger up at him and say, 'Good job you're not then, isn't it?' Lo and behold, three weeks later and Don is being named manager. I did think my time at Leeds was up."

Charlton need not have worried. He and Leeds United were about to embark on a remarkable trip to the summit of English football.

Chapter 7

The Club That Don Built

When Don Revie embarked on the start of his managerial career in March, 1961, he did so in a city whose sporting affections were dominated not by football but rugby league and cricket. The sale of John Charles to Juventus four years earlier had robbed Leeds United of its one true sporting icon, the only man capable of competing with the crowd-pulling charisma of Lewis Jones at Headingley during the winter months or Fred Trueman in the summer. So disaffected had supporters become that the last two games at Elland Road of Jack Taylor's managerial reign attracted a combined attendance of just over 20,000. Six weeks after Revie had taken charge, the final home game of the season against Scunthorpe United was watched by a paltry 6,975.

It was not just the battle for the Leeds public's affection that was being lost at Elland Road, either, but also the fight for sporting supremacy in the city. A crowd of 52,177 had watched the Loiners be crowned the kings of rugby league in the 1961 Championship final at Bradford's Odsal Stadium. Eight months earlier, Yorkshire had clinched back-to-back County Championship successes. United, in contrast, were the very epitome of mediocrity. The malaise afflicting the club was best illustrated in that ten successive seasons had brought not even one solitary victory in the FA Cup. Even Hunslet and Bramley, Leeds' two other senior rugby league clubs, were considered superior to United in a city where football was still viewed by many to be an inferior sport.

Apathy ruled at Elland Road and there were some who questioned whether Revie would have been better served by accepting the Bournemouth job, after all. The new man, however, was quick to banish such thoughts from his mind as he set about the task. Helped by Harry Reynolds, who had by now retired from the family's steel firm, having an increasing say in the running of a club where he had become a director in 1955, Revie set about implementing the changes he felt were needed to revive Leeds. First, though, he made it a priority to seek the views of those he considered to be role models. Revie's son Duncan was seven years old when his Dad was appointed manager. He recalls: "Dad said one of the first things he did after taking over at Leeds was to ring Matt Busby at Manchester United and ask if he could spare an hour of his time one afternoon. Dad hugely admired Busby who had built the great team that had been so tragically cut down in Munich. Matt invited him across one day and was so helpful that Dad ended up spending the whole day there. Matt took Dad for lunch and dinner, and it was clear he just wanted to help someone who was starting out in management. Dad always said the advice he got that day was priceless and he never forgot what Matt Busby did for him. It meant in later days when young managers such as Alex Ferguson and Lawrie McMenemy rang up, he would always spare time for them just as Matt had done for him. He would invite them over to Leeds or to the England camp and spend the day with them."

Armed with advice from the likes of Busby and Bill Shankly at Liverpool, Revie set about implementing the changes he had felt were needed ever since arriving at Elland Road as a player in 1958. One of the first major decisions taken by Revie was to permanently change the team's shirts from the traditional Leeds city colours of blue and gold. United had played in white under Revie's predecessor, Jack Taylor, as long ago as September 1960 in a 4-4 draw at home to Middlesbrough. Revie was captain that day and Leeds continued to sport white shirts with blue and gold trimmings periodically for the rest of the season. It was, however, on Revie's insistence during the summer of 1961 that the club permanently adopted an all-white kit in the style of Real Madrid as a clear statement of intent. It was, depending on whose viewpoint was listened to at the time, a stroke of flamboyance, ambition or downright cheek on Revie's part. Imagine a club struggling in the Championship today suddenly adopting the colours of Barcelona in an attempt to emulate the Catalan giants and you get an idea as to the sheer audacity of the move. The laughter would reverberate all the way to the Nou Camp and back.

To Revie, however, it was a statement of intent designed as much for the rest of English football as those within his own club. And, just as importantly at a time when money was scarce, the switch in colours was relatively cheap. Colin Grainger, a former team-mate of Revie's at Sunderland, had joined Leeds 12 months before the permanent change of colours and was not impressed by the state of United. He recalls: "Sunderland was a top-class club to play for where the players were really well looked after so coming to Leeds was a big change. Don was just a player when Jack Taylor signed me but we talked about what a difference it was. Leeds were a club that seemed to lack pride and who felt inferior to the city's three rugby league teams. The stadium was not the best and the pitch was poor. Don knew things had to change."

A bold statement was required to change the defeatist mindset that seemed embedded at Elland Road after decades of struggle. Suggestions have been made since, most notably by Jack Charlton, that the switch was a purely practical one on Revie's part with the new Leeds manager feeling his players would be more able to pick each other out against the background of the crowd when dressed in white. But the Earl of Harewood, United's president since 1961 and a close confidant of Revie during his time as manager, insists: "Don was a huge admirer of Real Madrid and he did definitely change the team colours to show his desire to make Leeds United a success." Revie's son Duncan is equally sure of the real reasons behind the switch to all white. He says: "I am told the players looked at him at first as if to say, 'You must be mad'. But he just replied, 'We are going to be the best in the world, just like Real Madrid'. It was an amazing thing to say about a club near the bottom of Division Two, but it showed just how determined Dad was to be a success."

It was a bold move, and one whose significance was not lost on Revie's staff, with coach Syd Owen having been in the England side thrashed 7-1 seven years earlier by a Hungarian side inspired by Real Madrid striker Ferenc Puskas.

For the first 18 months, however, the change of colours looked little more than a gimmick that had gone badly awry as United struggled. Revie had inherited a mediocre squad that, for all the promise of a young Billy Bremner, was full of journeymen pros. Jack Charlton, who a little over five years after Revie's appointment would be a World Cup winner, was at the club but far from the player he would become and it was clear the new manager faced an uphill task.

One huge plus in Revie's favour was the presence of Les Cocker and Syd Owen on the staff. Cocker had made more than 300 league appearances for Accrington Stanley and Stockport County. But it was his move into coaching after retiring in 1958 that set him on the path towards the World Cup winners' medal, as a member of Alf Ramsey's backroom staff, that was awarded posthumously to his family in 2009. Cocker spent two years as a coach at Luton Town before moving to Leeds as one of the first generation to take the FA Coaching Certificate. Revie, then still a player, quickly realised the value of Cocker's fitness work – much of it having been developed during wartime service with the Reconnaissance Regiment - and he became an integral part of the revolution that would sweep Leeds to the top of the English game. Syd Owen had also joined Leeds from Luton at the same time after being lured to Yorkshire by United manager Jack Taylor but, unlike Cocker, he had enjoyed a more illustrious playing career. Named Footballer of the Year in 1959 after leading Luton to the FA Cup final, he had also played three times for England

– including that famous 7-1 defeat to Hungary in Budapest. Jimmy Greenhoff, who joined Leeds from school before going on to make more than 100 appearances, recalls: "I wanted to sign for Leeds because of Syd. He was a man who knew football inside out. He didn't smoke and didn't drink, he just lived and breathed the game. Leeds developed a real family atmosphere, which was what Don Revie wanted, and I always felt Syd played a big part in that." Eddie Gray agrees Revie was similarly blessed with his coaching staff. "Don had great staff around him," he says. "They all worked together really well but there was only one governor. Don also knew how to handle them. Syd was a great coach, but a bit of a perfectionist so Don would try and keep him away from the first team at times because nothing was good enough. Some of the boys would go home in tears after what Syd had said. When I became manager of Leeds in the 1980s, I noticed how much of a perfectionist Syd was. I would send him out to look at a player I was interested in signing but every time he would come back saying he wasn't good enough. We were in the Second Division at the time but he was looking at players as though they were joining the league champions."

Initially, Cocker and Owen, who would later turn down a coaching job at Tottenham to stay with Revie, had difficulty getting the Leeds players to accept their new ideas and methods with Jack Charlton, in particular, being most cynical. Revie, however, was an immediate convert and, once he had been appointed manager, the pair's influence increased markedly at Elland Road alongside that of Maurice Lindley. Again, it was Revie's good fortune that Lindley should already be on the staff as the club's chief scout when Revie took over. This backroom triumvirate would go on to play a major part in the club's success, not least in the development of promising youngsters and the compiling of the infamous dossiers that Revie would become synonymous with during his time with Leeds and England.

With money, as ever, tight at Elland Road, Revie, whose staff was completed by Bob English and Cyril Partridge, recognised that the only way to fulfil his ambitions of building a side in the mould of Real Madrid would be to develop the very best youngsters. Again, as with having a dependable backroom team already in place, the new Leeds manager was fortunate that predecessor Jack Taylor had put in place the foundations of a youth set-up, with Norman Hunter already on the groundstaff. It was, though, down to Revie that Hunter should stay with the club as Taylor had major doubts as to whether the 17-year-old from County Durham would make the grade and it was only after Revie took over that a defender who would go on to play for England was finally signed. Paul Reaney, who has played more games for Leeds than all but Jack Charlton and Billy Bremner, joined the club's juniors five months after the new manager's appointment and was followed by Gary Sprake. All three would go on to become stalwarts of United's success but Revie knew he had to spread the search as wide as possible if his plans for a truly great team were to come to fruition.

Harry Reynolds, whose growing influence at Elland Road was reflected in him being named Sam Bolton's successor as chairman in December 1961, agreed and the pair would regularly tour the country to speak to the parents of boys the club wanted to sign. There were times when such a direct approach failed, but more often than not they would return to Leeds with the requisite signature. One such capture was Eddie Gray, a schoolboy international who had been discovered in Glasgow by renowned Leeds scout John Barr. Gray recalls: "I was only 14 and had never even heard of Leeds, never mind Leeds United, when John Barr said they were interested. I had heard of the big clubs in England but Leeds had never won anything and were a very up and down team. I remember thinking at first, 'Why would I want to sign for them?'"

Revie was well aware of how unattractive a move to Leeds might seem compared to the pull of the bigger teams. He set to work on the parents, offering reassurances that their son would be much better looked after at a club where he mattered. It was a tactic that worked with the family of Eddie Gray, who recalls: "Don made sure everything was spot on. He looked after my Mum and Dad, getting them down to Leeds whenever they wanted and putting them up in a hotel. After I agreed to join Leeds, Don threw a big party for all my family back in Glasgow at the Central Hotel. My big pal Jimmy Lumsden was also joining Leeds and his family were invited as well. It sounds a little thing but it made every member of both families feel really special and that sort of approach definitely played a part in my parents being happy about me joining Leeds. No other club did anything like that and it was sensible on Don's part because he knew the only way to build up the club was by doing it the hard way as Leeds simply didn't have the money to spend on transfers."

The ace up Revie's sleeve was his personable manner and, having come from one himself, an ability to empathise with working-class families. He was the master at sitting in front rooms up and down the country, sipping tea and chatting with everyone from a boy's father through to his ageing grandmother as if he would like to do nothing more for the rest of the day. Above all, he made them feel special. The Lorimer family was another to receive the personal treatment from Revie. It had been clear from an early age that Peter had outstanding talent and a host of clubs had beaten a path to the family home in Dundee. A starring role for Scotland Schoolboys in a 4-2 win over England merely heightened the interest and eventually 30 clubs would be chasing his signature. Among them was Manchester United, as Peter recalls: "I had been down to Leeds for a trial at 14 and it looked like I was going to sign but then after playing really well when Scotland Schoolboys beat England, suddenly every club in the country wanted to sign me. Manchester United put the pressure on by leaving a suitcase full of money at my mother's house. Mum, who liked Don because of how he had treated the family, rang Leeds to explain what had happened and straight away Don said 'don't sign anything – I'll be there as quick as I can'. He jumped in his car and raced up to Scotland, being so keen to get there he picked up a speeding ticket on the way in Perth. He got me in the car and drove straight back to Leeds, before Manchester United could come back to the house in the morning. And that was that, I had joined Leeds. It looked a silly move at the time because Leeds had only just stayed in the Second Division that season. But Don was so convincing about how Leeds would become a successful team that he talked me and my family into it."

Revie's determination to go that extra mile – or almost 600 in terms of the return trip to pip Manchester United to the signature of Lorimer – served him well throughout his time at Elland Road. This desire to stay one step ahead did, however, rebound on him one day and almost cost Leeds a player who would become one of the most popular in their history. Eddie Gray recalls: "When I signed for Leeds, I actually did so before I should have done. Don got me to sign a blank form that he promised to date at the appropriate time. He was desperate for me to sign and was panicking a bit, basically because I could have signed for anyone. He put the contract in a drawer and said he would register it on the day I left school. Unfortunately, he jumped the gun and registered me a few days before I was due to play my last schoolboy game for Scotland against Ireland at Love Street in Paisley. Of course, the news leaked out so when I turned up for the game the selectors pulled me aside and said I could not play because I had signed for a professional club. My Mum was furious and said to Don, 'If he isn't allowed to play, he won't be coming to Leeds'. Don was mortified so quickly got to work and had a word with the selectors who relented and I played. He was a very persuasive man, as I found out a couple of days later. Don took me back to my house after the Ireland game and told my Mum he was taking me back to Leeds on the Monday. She said, 'What about his schooling?' So, on the Monday morning, he took me into school and marched straight into the headmaster's office without an appointment. I had to wait outside and, eventually, Don came out and said, 'We're off'. And that was that, I had left school. I never sat any exams or anything. I've no idea to this day what he said to change the headmaster's mind."

After working so hard to prevent Eddie Gray slipping from his grasp, Revie was soon faced with a new problem as rival clubs continued to circle the as-yet unsigned Scot. "Under Scottish football law, youngsters could not sign apprentice forms until their 17th birthday," says Gray. "It meant that for the first two years, I could have walked away for free. All the English lads like Norman Hunter and Mick Bates were signed to the club but the Scots had to stay as amateurs. Don got his fingers burned with this rule when Tommy Docherty, who knew all about it, lured Jimmy McCalliog away to Chelsea. Jimmy had been at Leeds for four months but Don could not do anything about it. There was a suggestion the same might happen to Peter Lorimer, but Don was by now wise to the loophole. After Jimmy had left, Don paid that extra bit of attention to the Scots. There was no way I was going to leave anyway, even though Celtic kept pestering my Dad by telling him, 'If Eddie is not happy at Leeds, we'd love to sign him'. Peter was the same, he was at Leeds because of the care and attention Don had shown his family. There was no way he was going anywhere else."

Revie's determination to build a side around youngsters was an admirable – and, ultimately, successful – policy but it also meant progress would be slow and patience vital. The priority in the early months of his reign, therefore, was to somehow cobble together as strong a team as possible to bridge the gap until his promising band of youngsters matured. The portents were, however, not good with the squad still clearly suffering a hangover from being relegated at the end of the previous season.

What Revie did do straight away, though, was change the ethos of a club for whom second best had become acceptable. He leant on experience gleaned when with Manchester City and Sunderland, two clubs who recognised the importance of their players preparing in the right manner. Jack Charlton, whose Leeds debut had come a little over eight years before Revie's appointment as manager, recalls: "Don changed the club overnight. Where before, we would get on the bus and travel to the game on the day, now we were suddenly staying overnight in nice hotels. Instead of things being done to suit the directors, things were being done for the players. It was a big change but one Don felt important."

Revie's son Duncan remembers his Dad being adamant that improvements had to be made. "The directors were skint but he just said, 'I don't care. I want to instil in these players' minds that they are the best. We can't do that if they are staying in third rate hotels or travelling on the same day'. So that is what happened. Tony Jacklin, who Dad played a lot of golf with at one time, once said he had learned a lot from what Dad said in that respect. When he became captain of the Ryder Cup team, he made sure everyone got new bags, new cashmere sweaters, new shoes etc. He also made sure they flew on Concorde, the thinking being that when they stepped on the first tee they would not feel inferior."

Former team-mates of Revie were not surprised to see the emphasis being suddenly placed on looking after the players at Elland Road. Colin Grainger had been with Revie at Sunderland before being reunited at Leeds in 1960. "Once he became a manager, Don was very big on looking after the welfare of his players and I think he picked that up from Sunderland where everything had been spot on. From travelling through to the hotels where we stayed, everything was the very best. And that was what Don quickly did at Leeds."

Those coming from other clubs to join Leeds noticed the difference straight away. Mick Jones, who became United's first £100,000 signing after moving from Sheffield United in 1967, says: "I soon learned that Leeds were a club who did everything right. If we had a long away trip that was not to London, Don would charter a plane for us. It meant we were a lot fresher when going to places like Southampton or Portsmouth. We also stayed in the very best hotels in London. Football is about results, Don knew that better than anyone. And that is why he wanted the best for us because he recognised that athletes perform best when happiest."

As much as improving standards off the field helped raise morale at Elland Road, there was one player whose own unhappiness troubled Revie during his early days in charge. Billy Bremner, after being rejected by Chelsea for being "too small", had signed for Leeds in December, 1959, and been quickly taken under the wing of Revie, then the club's senior pro. When, just a month or so after his 17th birthday, Bremner made his debut at Chelsea, Revie arranged for them to room together on the Friday night. Revie, almost twice Bremner's age, then made sure the teenager was up bright and early to enjoy a walk before the trip to Stamford Bridge. Bremner's debut was a success as United won 3-1 but the Scot soon became disillusioned with life in West Yorkshire and pined for a return to his native Stirling to be with his fiancée, Vicky. It was a problem Revie inherited from predecessor Jack Taylor and, before long, Bremner had submitted his first transfer request to the new manager. Hibernian immediately bid £25,000 but Revie, desperate to keep hold of a player whom he felt was integral to a brighter future for Leeds, held out for £30,000. The deal fell through, much to the disappointment of Bremner who continued to badger for a move. Bremner's fellow Scot Eddie Gray recalls: "Billy and Don became very close but in those early days Billy did cause him a few problems over wanting to go back home to Scotland. He was really homesick and missing Vicky. They had met at school, whereas most of the boys at the club had met girls in Leeds, and that made it hard for Billy because he missed her a lot."

This desire to be back in Scotland once led Bremner to go AWOL, opening the first team door for team-mate Peter Lorimer: "The reason I made my debut at 15 was because Billy had gone home," he says. "The gaffer called me in and said, 'You are playing tomorrow against Southampton because Billy won't come back from Scotland'. I didn't play again in the 1962-63 season but, thanks to Billy, I still hold the record as the club's youngest-ever player."

Revie, running out of patience but recognising how important the flame-haired midfielder was to his own ambitions, decided to sort the problem out once and for all by, unbeknown to Bremner, travelling to Scotland. Once there, he explained to Vicky that her future husband was integral to what he was trying to build at Leeds and that by leaving he would be doing himself a real dis-service. Revie's charm offensive worked and, when the couple were later married, they set up home in Leeds and all thoughts of returning to Scotland had been banished.

On the field, Revie's problems were much more acute than dealing with a bout of homesickness from one of his younger players. In the final nine games of the 1960-61 season that followed his appointment, Leeds won just once – a 7-0 thrashing of soon-to-be-relegated Lincoln City – to underline the size of the task ahead. Colin Grainger played in the first two games of Revie's reign at Leeds before suffering a cruciate injury that brought an abrupt end to his season. "I was disappointed to see Jack Taylor get sacked because I liked him and he had signed me," he says. "The club had been struggling financially for some time and it showed, so whoever took over was always going to face problems."

Despite an end to the season that would have left many demoralised, Revie set about trying to improve standards. Central to this was the introduction of the infamous dossiers on opposing teams that became such a staple part of Leeds' preparations for every game. Everything from strengths and weaknesses of both individual players and the opposing team as a whole were included for his own team to digest. Revie's son Duncan explains: "Dad was so meticulous in the crossing of t's and dotting of i's that he left nothing to chance, which is why the dossiers on opposing teams became such an important part of preparing for every game. A few years ago, I was going through some of Dad's belongings and came across some old books of handwritten notes on opposing teams. They were in Dad's handwriting and the detail was extraordinary. Basically, every opposition player's performance was broken down into 15-minute segments on things like dribbling skills, tackling and clearances. Clubs pay thousands of pounds a season today for something similar from Pro-Zone and yet Dad did it all by hand."

'Fail to prepare, prepare to fail' was a maxim that Revie could have dreamt up during his days as a manager with nothing being left to chance thanks to the exhaustive work put in by his backroom team. Eddie Gray recalls: "Syd Owen did some of the scouting and then reported back, as did Maurice Lindley. Don had total trust in both men. So much so that when he then delivered the findings of Syd and Maurice at a team meeting, it was as though he was passing on his own thoughts." The dossiers were individually tailored for each player's needs. "Everything was in there about the player you would be directly up against," says Gray. "If I was up against a particular full-back then I would know before running out for kick-off which his weaker foot was and whether I could beat him for speed. There was also information about the opposing team as a whole, such as details of how they lined up at corners or free-kicks. I know when Don went to manage England, some of their players didn't like the dossiers but I found them useful. I grew up with them because we even had them before youth team games when I was a kid. They were particularly useful in Europe because it was not like today where the opposition teams were on television all the time. Back then, it really was a step into the unknown."

With no point about the opposition considered too minor, the compiling of the dossiers was a laborious affair and one that involved long days and nights for those out doing the scouting on behalf of Revie. And woe betide any Leeds player who did not give the dossiers their full attention. Jack Charlton, who after Grenville Hair was United's second longest-serving player when Revie was appointed manager, recalls: "We would be handed these reports just before dinner the night before a game at our hotel and told to read them thoroughly. We would then talk about them. And if Don ever caught you looking away or not paying full attention, he would turn on you and say, 'I have people on the road bringing this information to you and you can't pay these lads the courtesy of listening'. Everyone listened after that. Thorough preparation was something we had never done before. By the end of that first season, I doubt there was a player in the league who we didn't know everything about, from what foot he preferred to whether he was aggressive or meek. In later years, we would be playing Manchester United and Paul Reaney would be handed a thick report on George Best to read. I always thought it was no coincidence that Paul, who was quicker and meaner than George, always had a good game against Manchester United. Paul would never leave his side and he could almost predict what George would do next – and that was mainly because of the information in those dossiers."

Revie did not confine his work to on-field matters, either, with one of his major aims being to foster a family spirit among every member of staff. Stories of office staff being given a few quid to put on a horse at the bookies are legendary, Revie's reasoning being that if the bet came in then the member of staff was happy. And if it didn't, they had not lost anything personally. Son Duncan recalls: "Every morning, I would be the first kid at Leeds Grammar School because Dad would take me on his way to Elland Road. He was always whistling, due to going to a place he truly loved to be – Elland Road. In the back, me and my sister Kim would be miserable as sin about going to school. It was the same for a banker who lived next door. Dad always gave him a lift to work on the way to Elland Road and this bloke would be miserable as well. Dad, in contrast, had a huge smile on his face. It was a big thing for him to be the first there at 8am. It was 90 minutes before the players were due in so Dad would spend the time going round everyone to say 'hello'. The tea ladies, the groundsman, the office staff – he knew all their names and made sure he went round them all in a morning. Dad was as keen to look after the tea ladies as much as Allan Clarke or Norman Hunter. He wanted everyone to feel part of the Leeds United family. Dad made sure there were no 'Big-time Charlies' at Leeds. If they tried anything like that, he would bring them down to earth with a bang." Revie's caring approach to club staff is confirmed by John Reynolds, then the assistant groundsman at Elland Road. "Don made sure he spoke to every one of us in a morning," he says. "As we looked after the pitch, we were in first so Don, after getting changed, would come to see us and have a chat. It could be about our family, football or anything. He was genuinely interested in our lives. He would go see the laundry staff next and then, once they arrived, the office staff. It was the same story for those of us on the groundstaff after a game. Don knew we would not be leaving until after midnight in winter due to having to put straw down to keep the frost out so he made a point of coming to thank us for our efforts before he left. And that happened after every match, without fail. I dare say we would have worked for free if he had asked, we loved him."

Revie wanted everyone at the club to feel equal, something he had picked up as a player at Manchester City. John McTavish, who was a little under five years younger than Revie when the pair became team-mates at Maine Road, recalls: "Don took me under his wing a bit at City as I was a young lad down from Scotland. He helped me settle and taught me a few valuable lessons, particularly about how everyone has to pull together. Don did not like how there was a divide between the first team and the reserves at Maine Road. When I first signed, there was a pool table for the first team to use – and even if a couple of the reserves were playing at the time, they had to vacate it if a first team player wanted to use it. Don felt that was daft as it was a divide between players of the same club. When he went to Leeds, I was told he made sure everyone mucked in together."

The summer of 1961, Revie's first as manager, brought the first minor tweak to the playing staff – an overhaul was impossible due to financial restraints – as Derek Mayers, a winger from Preston North End, arrived as the rest of the squad were told this was their chance to prove their worth. Some rose to the challenge, but others didn't and, by mid-November, United had won just four of their opening 17 games – two of which had come in the first week of the season against Charlton Athletic and Brighton & Hove Albion – and were slipping into relegation trouble.

By now, Revie had all but taken the decision that his playing days were over after two ineffective spells in the team. Having returned in the wake of an early season 5-0 thrashing by Liverpool and a demoralising home defeat to Rotherham United, the 34-year-old had been hoping to use his experience to inspire those around him. Playing in a role even more withdrawn than the one that had made his name at Manchester City, Revie soon realised that age and injuries had taken their toll. After back-to-back defeats against Norwich City and Sunderland, he returned to the dugout. A month later, however, United's poor form had persuaded Revie to once again pull his boots on, though this time in a more advanced role. He did manage one more goal – in a 3-2 defeat at Luton Town – to take his tally for United to 12 but after just four games the experiment had again been abandoned. Revie's brother-in-law David Duncan says: "Things were tough at Leeds so, against his better judgement, Don played a few games but he realised that it just wasn't possible to fulfil both roles. There was simply too much going on for him to do justice to both playing and managing. Maybe it would have been possible at a club lower down, but not at Leeds where he was trying to re-build everything. There was all the admin, the scouting and so on to do, which was far too much for someone who also needed to stay fit."

Revie made one last attempt to inspire his relegation-threatened team with his on-field deeds against Huddersfield Town in March, 1962, before finally admitting defeat. Mike O'Grady was in the Terriers side that beat United 2-1 at Leeds Road and is not surprised it proved to be Revie's final appearance. "I was only young but it was clear to me that Don's legs had gone," he says. "He was strolling around and a little frustrated at not being able to do what he had clearly done easily earlier in his career."

With results poor, it was clear drastic action was needed. It came in the form of boardroom changes that saw prominent Leeds businessmen Manny Cussins and Albert Morris become directors in return for an interest-free loan of £10,000 apiece. Harry Reynolds, on stepping up to replace Sam Bolton as chairman, also put up £50,000 to provide Revie with some much-needed spending power in the transfer market. Perhaps more importantly, what Reynolds, the man who had championed Revie's cause when United were looking for a new manager just a few months earlier, could also offer was time following his retirement after a hugely successful career in business. Reynolds being able to devote hour upon hour to the football club meant the bond and desire to make Leeds great between the new chairman and Revie was strengthened. The Earl of Harewood, who was invited to become United's first president just as Reynolds stepped up to the post of chairman in 1961, recalls: "Harry put the foundations down for the vastly improved fortunes of Leeds United. He was a wonderful man, very amusing and down-to-earth in his opinions. We got on very well. Unfortunately, Harry was not chairman for as long as he would have wanted due to ill health but I know Don valued very much the work he did."

Revie, with transfer funds finally at his disposal, signed former Manchester City team-mate Bill McAdams from Bolton Wanderers in an attempt to bolster a failing attack. Liverpool, who were destined to win the Second Division title under Bill Shankly five or so months later, were then beaten 1-0 at Elland Road on the final Saturday before Christmas but it proved to be a false dawn with just one win in the next nine games leaving Leeds in real danger of being relegated to the Third Division for the first time in history. A saviour was needed, not just for Leeds but also Revie. And he arrived in the form of a 31-year-old former Scotland international who was small in stature but huge in standing.

Chapter 8

Dirty Leeds

Dirty Leeds. Two words with such huge connotations that Leeds United are unlikely to be anything but damned forever more. A tag that, almost half a century on from it first being coined when Don Revie's young side came kicking and snarling out of the Second Division, is as much a part of the nation's lexicon as ever. Whether it be Sky's cult Saturday morning show *Soccer AM* or any one of the multitude of fan messageboards found on the worldwide web, any reference to the city of Leeds's football team is unlikely to be prefaced by anything but the word 'Dirty'. Even one of Revie's successors at Elland Road, Dennis Wise, used it as a motivational tool when trying to snap his players out of a rut by proclaiming at his first press conference as manager how he wanted them to be 'like the Dirty Leeds of old, who were horrible – I want that bit of nastiness'. It didn't work as the club was relegated to the third tier of English football for the first time in their history seven months later, but Wise's attempts to revive the ghosts of the past showed just how ingrained the reputation of Dirty Leeds had become in football.

How United became synonymous with all that is bad about the game, from being masters at time-wasting through to serial foulers and grand manipulators of referees, can be traced back to the arrival of Bobby Collins in March, 1962. Until then, Leeds had been the sort of club few outside its own city cared about with only John Charles being able to compete with the city's rugby league and cricket heroes. Signing Collins from Everton for the princely sum of £25,000 – or a little under £400,000 in today's money – seemed a huge gamble, especially as he had cost the Merseyside club the same price from Celtic four years earlier and the player was now 31. Revie, though, had been adamant that the money had to be found and on March 10, 1962, Collins made a goalscoring debut for Leeds in a 2-0 win at Swansea Town. Ian Lawson had also been signed from Burnley, along with Sheffield United left-back Cliff Mason, just before the transfer deadline. But there was little doubt Collins was the real signing of intent, as Johnny Giles – then of Manchester United – recalls: "It was a year or so before I signed for Leeds but I remember thinking that if Bobby had agreed to sign, the club must be really going places. Bobby was a great player and a real coup of a signing."

Collins, for his part, was not overly pleased to have found himself surplus to requirements at Goodison Park and vowed to prove a point to Harry Catterick, the manager who had let him go. Revie, recognising the desire that burned deep within the diminutive Scot, immediately made Collins captain. It was a masterstroke with the responsibility making the new skipper even more determined to succeed and prove Everton's folly. Collins made an instant impact and, along with fellow new signings Lawson and Mason, he helped Leeds build on that win at Swansea, their first in almost two months. United went on to lose just one of their final 11 games, the threat of relegation to the Third Division being finally lifted on the last day of the season when a team captained by Collins won 3-0 at Newcastle United thanks to a mesmerising display from Albert Johanneson. Years later, accusations would emerge that Revie had offered Newcastle captain Stan Anderson £10 per player providing they took it easy. Similar claims were also made in a *Daily Mirror* investigation into Revie following his decision to quit as England manager in 1977, namely how he had asked Bury manager Bob Stokoe to 'go easy' in return for £500 ahead of a key game between the two clubs. Both allegations were fiercely denied with Revie's supporters pointing out, with some justification, that as Newcastle had lost 17 games already that season and Bury 20, the subsequent 3-0 win and goalless draw hardly pointed towards the type of shock results that only the offering of sweeteners could produce.

In the summer of 1962, however, any allegations of match-fixing were some way in the future and the following season kicked off amid an air of optimism at Elland Road. The youngsters Revie had worked so hard to bring to the club were starting to blossom and were expected to make the step-up to the first team in the early months of the new campaign. The clear-out that would eventually see 27 unwanted players leave in his first two years was also well underway. Attendances were up even though relegation had only just been avoided, while Revie had headed off interest in Collins from Bill Shankly at Liverpool by offering the Scot a more lucrative contract. The return of John Charles from Juventus for £53,000, a staggering fee for a Second Division club, further fuelled the belief that this could be United's year. With Charles in the middle, much was expected of Albert Johanneson and Billy Bremner on each flank as both had the exuberance and skill to create the openings for the Gentle Giant to capitalise on. Unfortunately for Revie and Leeds, the Charles that returned to Elland Road was a very different attacking beast to the one that had left five years earlier and, by October, he was gone. The bonus for United, though, was a healthy profit due to Roma paying £70,000 to take

Charles back to Italy.

If the players left behind were unsettled by Charles' departure, they didn't show it. Collins continued to lead by example as Leeds stayed in the promotion hunt right until the final couple of weeks when a draining schedule of 14 games in 60 days – caused by the harsh winter of 1963 that saw the club unable to play between December 22 and March 6 – proved too much for a tired squad.

A fifth-place finish was, however, a pointer towards what lay ahead and the following year Leeds, with Collins firmly installed as the heartbeat of the side and Johnny Giles having been signed from Manchester United, won the Second Division title. Even their staunchest supporters would not claim the success had been earned the pretty way and there was fierce debate within the game as to just how ethical some of United's methods had been. And, in particular, the role of Collins in the mayhem that often surrounded Leeds. Eddie Gray says: "Bobby was the main man and I am certain that without Bobby signing, we would not have seen the Leeds United that we did. He taught the entire club how to win. Don realised he had to get someone in who could bring us younger lads on and that he had to get a born winner. A shrinking violet would have been no use. I will be perfectly honest, when I signed for Leeds in 1963 and watched Bobby in action, I was terrified. It was brutal stuff and, definitely, win-at-all-costs. Training was the same and the practice games where the English players would play the Scottish lads had, eventually, to be stopped by Don. They had turned into all-out war with Bobby right at the heart of it all. He was determined to win at all costs, even when turning out for the Ex-Players. In the end, we had to retire him at 65 because he was upsetting the opposition."

Whether Collins and his team-mates strayed beyond the laws of the game or not, there was little doubt that the promotion season had caused waves. The two games against Sunderland, who would eventually go up with Leeds, were particularly brutal, as the Wearside club's official historian Brian Leng remembers. "I used to go home and away then and the Leeds games were something else," he recalls. "They were no place for the faint-hearted and games where I used to shudder stood 50 yards away on the terrace. If you tell the supporters of today about what went on back then, they just don't believe you."

Such was the fearsome reputation developed by Leeds during the promotion campaign that it even started to work in the club's favour when it came to signing players. During the run-in, Revie felt his attack needed pepping up and saw Alan Peacock, Middlesbrough's England international striker, as the perfect choice. Peacock, 26 at the time, had developed a reputation as one of the best headers of the ball in English football and had formed a prolific partnership with Brian Clough at Ayresome Park. By the time Revie launched his attempt to bring the striker to Elland Road, Peacock had scored 126 goals in 218 league appearances. Such an impressive goal ratio meant, inevitably, that Leeds faced competition. Tottenham Hotspur, Liverpool and Everton all tried to sign Peacock, who admits an unusual reason was behind his decision to stay in Yorkshire. "A few people did ask me why I was joining Leeds when I could have gone elsewhere," says Peacock, who signed for a joint club record £53,000 from Boro. "I even turned down Jimmy Greaves, who made a personal appeal for me to go to Spurs. It goes without saying that Don was very persuasive. But I also fancied going there as I had played against Leeds a few times. They were bruising affairs and, if anything, my thinking was, 'If I'm on their side, then they won't be kicking me'. After some of the Middlesbrough v Leeds games, that was a big attraction."

Talk to any of Revie's players today and no-one will say their manager ever sent them out with an order to kick the opposition. But there can be little doubt that United possessed a ruthlessness – or 'professionalism' as it was referred to in Leeds – that many felt bordered on bullying. Referees giving much more leeway in the Sixties also helped with the first foul of the afternoon, no matter how bad by today's standards, being considered by many of the game's hard men as a 'freebie'. A booking would only follow if there was a repeat. This did, of course, work in their favour with many opposing teams, fearful of what lay ahead, being beaten before they even stepped out at Elland Road. A division where brawn often won out over brains was also, as Eddie Gray acknowledges "no place for shrinking violets", but Leeds insist they rarely went further than was legally permissible.

Despite that, the rumblings about Leeds' physical approach in winning promotion culminated in an article appearing in the Football Association's summer edition of FA News in which United were labelled a 'dirty team'. Revie was incensed; especially as he felt the article could influence referees the following season as Leeds ended a four-year absence from the First Division.

In the opening weeks of the season, Revie's fears proved unfounded as Leeds beat Aston Villa, Wolves and Liverpool in their opening three fixtures. A defeat in the return at Anfield against a Reds side who Leeds would meet in the FA Cup final the following May proved a rare setback and, by early November, Revie was happy with how his side had adapted to the step up in class. Alan Peacock, the striker whose eight goals after joining from Middlesbrough the previous February had helped clinch promotion, feels the belief Revie instilled in his players was a major factor in Leeds adapting so quickly to their new surroundings. He says: "Leeds had kicked their way out of Division Two but there were a lot of good players at the club. Young lads like Norman Hunter and Peter Lorimer had really come to the fore and I think Leeds took a lot by surprise in those early weeks. It was all down to Don who had this ability to send you out feeling ten feet tall. He was continually talking about Leeds becoming the new Real Madrid. It might be a team meeting or just in the dressing room, but he always seemed to manage to slip a mention of Real Madrid in to emphasise how far he thought Leeds could go. Don had changed the kit to all-white and he never let us forget the standards he wanted to reach. It rubbed off on the team."

Leeds' start had undoubtedly been a good one. Controversy lay just around the corner, however, with the trip to Goodison Park on November 7 set to become one of the most ferocious and ill-tempered games that the top flight had ever seen. It was Bobby Collins' first return to Everton since being transferred to Leeds two-and-a-half years earlier and the tone was set inside the opening five minutes, though not by the Scot. Instead, it was a foul by Everton full-back Sandy Brown on Johnny Giles that, literally, kick-started a battle that became so bad that referee Roger Stokes had seen enough after 35 minutes and ordered both teams off the field with the visitors ahead thanks to a Willie Bell goal. Missiles rained down from the terraces and one home fan tried to confront Billy Bremner as he left the field before order was eventually restored and play resumed. The kicking continued and Leeds were castigated in the national press the following day. What the reports omitted to mention, though, was that of the 32 fouls, Leeds committed just 12 and that only one – by Norman Hunter in the second-half – had warranted a booking from referee Stokes. The local newspaper, the *Yorkshire Evening Post*, also leapt to the defence of Revie's men, though the claim of reporter Phil Brown that 'the match was, in my view, nothing like as bad as United's two games against Sunderland last season' was hardly a ringing endorsement of the visitors' approach.

Nevertheless, Leeds were furious with the media coverage and put the blame squarely on the shoulders of the Football Association for branding the club 'the dirtiest in the Football League' the previous summer. In an open letter released following a board meeting two days after the win at Goodison Park, the board added: "We maintain that the 'Dirty Team' tag, which was blown up by the press, could prejudice not only the general public, but the officials controlling the game. It could have an effect on the subconscious approach of both referees and linesmen."

If this was the case, it was not reflected in the results that followed the trip to Everton with United winning eight of their next ten league games to go into the New Year firmly in contention for the title. The FA Cup third round draw then handed Leeds a straight-forward tie at home to Southport that was duly won 3-0 to set up a meeting with Everton at Elland Road. Fears that the game would descend into all-out war following the stormy league encounter failed to materialise as the visitors earned a replay. Goals from Jack Charlton and Don Weston secured a 2-1 win on Merseyside, which was followed by triumphs over Shrewsbury Town and Crystal Palace to earn Leeds a first semi-final appearance, their opponents being Manchester United. By now, Alan Peacock had returned to the side after injury and he recalls how Revie's tactical mind was causing all sorts of problems for the opposition. "Don was the first manager who ever sent me out with a tactical plan," he says. "At Middlesbrough, we had just been told to 'get out there and win'. It wasn't very scientific. Don could not have been more different and, often, it would be a little thing he had spotted that made all the difference."

Revie's influence could certainly be felt in the semi-final against Manchester United at Hillsborough as Leeds cancelled out the threat of their bitter rivals with a controlled display. It was a similar story in the replay at the City Ground where Revie's game plan worked perfectly as a header by Billy Bremner with just three minutes remaining was enough to book a first trip to Wembley. Even then, however, the club's physical approach meant their moment of triumph was shrouded in controversy courtesy of a foul count that revealed Leeds had committed 18 indiscretions to their opponents' five.

A first trip to Wembley was, despite the carping from elsewhere, a major achievement, though not one Revie could bask in for too long due to his side having eight fixtures to play in just 23 days before being able to turn their attention to the Cup final. Defeat to Manchester United at Elland Road on April 17 seemed to end any hopes of lifting the title. Back-to-back wins over the two Sheffield clubs then breathed new life into the club's title challenge, leaving Leeds one point ahead of their rivals from Old Trafford going into the final game of the season at bottom club Birmingham City. Matt Busby's side had the advantage of a game in hand but the league and cup double was still on. Nerves, however, got the better of Revie's men at St Andrews. By half-time they were 2-0 down despite the Blues having been reduced to ten men after a heavy challenge by Terry Cooper had left Alex Jackson unable to continue. Substitutions were not allowed and Birmingham stretched their lead further six minutes into the second-half through Geoff Vowden. Leeds, finally, woke up to set up a thrilling finale courtesy of a Johnny Giles penalty and a Paul Reaney goal on 73 minutes. United poured forward and Jack Charlton duly equalised two minutes from time but there was to be no fairytale ending as Birmingham held out for a draw. Manchester United, who 100 or so miles away had just beaten Arsenal, were able to celebrate clinching the Championship on goal average.

It was a heartbreaking way to lose the title but, not for the first time, Revie had to pick his troops up quickly with the FA Cup final just five days away. He was helped by Cup fever having taken a firm grip of the city with the level of interest in United's first trip to Wembley reflected in the black market price of a ticket that originally cost 7s 6d having soared to £25. One tout, who in the days long before selling on tickets for profit was made illegal had placed an advert in the *Yorkshire Evening Post*, told the local newspaper: 'I had 183 telephone calls in two hours last night. They are selling like hot cakes.'

Around 15,000 supporters made the trip to the capital from Yorkshire on May 1 as Leeds' football club finally followed in the footsteps of its rugby league cousins. Hunslet had already won at Wembley in the 1934 Challenge Cup final and were due back under the Twin Towers the following weekend to face Wigan, while Leeds had won twice in three visits to London for rugby league's showpiece final. Finally, in its 42nd year, Wembley would host Leeds United and hopes were high that the disappointment of missing out on the league by the narrowest of margins would be swept away with victory over Liverpool. Bill Shankly's team had enjoyed a much less strenuous passage through the rounds, even though in the third round Liverpool's captain Ron Yeats had given away perhaps the most bizarre penalty of the season when picking up the ball after hearing the whistle blown. Unfortunately for Yeats, it had been a rogue whistler in the crowd at West Bromwich Albion's Hawthorns ground and the referee had no option but to award a penalty that Bobby Cram missed as Liverpool progressed. Fourth Division Stockport County did cause Shankly a few anxious moments by holding his side to a draw at Anfield in the next round before being beaten in a replay but, otherwise, Liverpool made light work of beating Bolton, Leicester and Chelsea to reach their third Cup final.

On a spongy surface, the tackles were soon flying and it took just three minutes for Bobby Collins to clatter into Gerry Byrne. Trainer Bob Paisley rushed on to the field and initially seemed to treat Byrne's leg, only for the full-back, on getting to his feet, to realise there was numbness in his shoulder. Paisley immediately diagnosed a broken collarbone but, with substitutes not allowed, the player vowed to carry on. The Liverpool players realised it was crucial Leeds did not learn of their team-mate's problems and there was only one near miss when Ian St John threw the ball to Byrne and urged him to take a quick throw. St John realised immediately what he had done, but Leeds did not notice and Byrne's secret was intact. United also suffered their own injury blow during the first half when Jim Storrie pulled a thigh muscle. Liverpool adapted better to the conditions. Goalkeeper Gary Sprake turned out to be the Yorkshire club's hero by pulling off a string of saves to force the final into extra-time for the first time since Charlton Athletic had beaten Burnley 18 years earlier. The deadlock was finally broken three minutes into the extra half-hour when Byrne made light of his broken collarbone to centre for Roger Hunt to stoop and place a header into the net. Leeds, who until then had been distinctly second best, rallied and drew level when Billy Bremner thundered a 20-yard shot past the previously under-employed Tommy Lawrence, only for justice to be done in the 111th minute when Ian St John netted the winner. It was a shattering blow to Leeds but, even in his hour of disappointment, Revie still found time to console his then five-year-old daughter, Kim. She recalls: "I remember going to the FA Cup final in 1965 but not really understanding it. I still enjoyed the day, though, and asked Dad afterwards, 'Can we come back next year, please?' He smiled that big smile of his and replied, 'I can't guarantee it, but I will do my very, very best'."

Once the dust had settled on the Wembley defeat, there were plenty of positives to glean from United's first season back in Division One – not least that runners-up spot was enough to secure European qualification for the first time. And it was here, on the often unforgiving football fields of the continent, where the finer arts of gamesmanship that Revie's Leeds are still renowned for were fine-tuned.

The Inter-Cities Fairs Cup had started life as a competition to promote international trade fairs whereby only cities that hosted them could enter. There was also a 'one city, one team' rule that led to the first two-legged final in 1958 being between Barcelona and London, the latter featuring players from no less than five clubs based in the English capital. The Catalan XI, which triumphed 8-2 on aggregate, was effectively Barcelona's first team plus one player from Espanyol. By 1965-66, the Inter-Cities Fairs Cup had evolved into a respected competition and Revie was determined his team would shine on the international stage. His squad was unchanged from the previous May as United prepared for their first expedition into Europe against Torino, though Huddersfield Town's Mike O'Grady would be added a month or so into the campaign. The Italians arrived at Elland Road with a fearsome reputation as a physical team who thought little of bending the laws of the game for their own means. Revie, displaying a penchant for trying to unsettle the opposition that would later be seen during his time in charge of England, sent out his players wearing unfamiliar shirt numbers in the hope it would confuse the Italians and their rigid man-marking system. Leeds triumphed 2-1 so a goalless draw in the return leg meant safe passage to the next round. It came, though, at a terrible price with Bobby Collins, voted Footballer of the Year during United's remarkable double runners-up season, breaking his thigh bone. The injury, caused by a tackle from Fabrizio Poletti that had left Revie incensed, underlined to the maturing Leeds youngsters the need to look after themselves in European battle. The injury led to Revie partnering Johnny Giles with Billy Bremner in central midfield to create a vacancy on the flank that was filled by Mike O'Grady, the Huddersfield Town winger signing a week after Collins had suffered such an unfortunate break. O'Grady recalls: "What happened in those early European games had a big impact on how Revie wanted us to play. He knew we had to look after ourselves. Some of the things that went on in European games were beyond belief. Someone spat in my face and I also had one opponent who tried to poke me in the eye. There was another game against Napoli when, after passing the ball, I felt a tap on my shoulder. Naively, I turned round and was head-butted in the face. Straight away, he threw himself to the floor and the referee booked me - even though I had blood dripping down my face. Afterwards, Don called us all together in the dressing room and said, 'This is what we are up against, lads'."

Losing Collins was a massive blow with the second leg in Turin so finely-balanced, but Leeds displayed great maturity to hold out for the remaining 40 minutes and progress to the second round. They had also started well in the league, losing just two of their opening 14 games. But there was no denying what a huge loss Collins would be following his injury in Turin. Eddie Gray, then 17 years old but whose first team debut was only a couple of months away, says: "Losing Bobby was huge. Bobby was the governor of the team at the time and everyone looked up to him. Bobby used to scare the life out of Albert Johannesen, but he got him to play by saying things like, 'If I get the ball, make sure you're there' and would point at the wing. Don knew just how vital Bobby was to the team and he never criticised him for anything he did. That is not to say they didn't have words at times. I remember one night when Bobby had an accident when messing about with Big Jack. He cut his arm. Don went ballistic as it was a nasty cut but Bobby just turned round and said, 'I'll be playing tomorrow and I'll be the best player on the park'. And he was. Nothing fazed Bobby and it was his determination to win that was passed down to Billy Bremner and Norman Hunter."

Revie knew what impact the absence of Collins could have on his fledgling team. But, displaying the tactical know-how that had helped turn Manchester City into FA Cup winners almost a decade earlier, he decided to shuffle his pack and bring Johnny Giles into the centre from outside right to partner Billy Bremner in midfield. To fill the vacancy on the wing, O'Grady was brought in from Huddersfield for £30,000. He recalls: "Bill Shankly signed me for Huddersfield but, once he left, the training went pear-shaped and the club was just treading water so I wanted to leave." O'Grady, who had scored twice on his England debut against Northern Ireland only to be overlooked for the rest of his time at Leeds Road, was desperate to sign for his home town club, but Revie, typically, was still determined not to leave anything to chance. "I had played against Revie for Huddersfield at Leeds a couple of years earlier but never spoken to him," recalls O'Grady. "So, the first I knew he rated me as a player was when there was a knock at the door one day. It was the Bishop of Leeds' secretary. He was a little Irish fella, who said, 'Don Revie is very interested in you and he wants me to pass on my best wishes'. Revie had somehow found out that we were a Catholic family and this was his way of getting my Dad on side. It worked as well. After that, we also had a visit from two Leeds City councillors who said Revie wanted me, as did a reporter friend of his called Tom Holley who had been a Leeds player. Don had sent him round as well. It was an illegal approach but it did the trick as I trained so hard that summer that when I signed for £30,000 early the following season I was as fit as I had ever been. It was very clever of Revie, who I only met for the first time after I had signed."

Any hopes the opposition harboured that the loss of Collins from the United engine room for several months - he eventually returned on the final day as Leeds drew 1-1 with Manchester United at Old Trafford - would mean a less physically demanding afternoon were soon dispelled as the Bremner-Giles axis prospered. Before long, they had become one of the most feared partnerships English football had ever seen with the pair's ability to mix it with the opposition only being matched by their ability to out-play them. Alan Hudson, who joined Chelsea in the late 1960s before going on become a key figure in the 1970 FA Cup final success against Revie's men, recalls: "People complain about the game being physical these days but it is nothing compared to what Leeds were like. I knew every time I walked out on to the pitch to face Leeds that I would be kicked all over. Bremner and Giles were the worst. They were a couple of pocket-sized assassins. You could never turn your back on them for one second or they would have you. If I ever got whacked or done from behind by either of them, I always used to blame myself for turning my back. The great thing about Bremner and Giles was that they were also great players. Truly great players, but who would always mix it. That is how Revie loved it."

United's two-legged victory over Torino on their European debut earned a second round tie against SC Leipzig, a genuine step into the unknown behind the Iron Curtain. The journey to East Germany would be arduous, Leeds having to fly to West Berlin before passing through Checkpoint Charlie and completing the rest of the journey by coach. It would be a tough enough assignment for seasoned travellers such as Manchester United who were embarking on their fifth campaign in Europe. But for a side playing only their third competitive game against foreign opposition it was a huge ask. Peter Lorimer recalls: "The travelling was unbelievable compared to now. I went on a few of the European trips when David O'Leary was Leeds manager and a trip to somewhere like Moscow in the UEFA Cup would see the players landing back at Leeds-Bradford Airport at midnight after the game. For us, going to Leipzig involved getting a rustbucket of a bus to and from the border with the west before flying home. We would get back to Leeds sometime on the Thursday and then often have to travel to London or some other long journey on the Friday for a big game. It was tiring."

If Leeds were just learning the ropes in terms of the logistics involved in European competition, on the field they were maturing fast – as Leipzig soon discovered to their cost. Lorimer recalls: "Gamesmanship was rife in Europe and English sides would get little help away from home. We had to adapt fast. Leipzig stands out in that respect because a foot of snow had fallen overnight. There was no question of calling the game off. Instead, the snow was compacted with a roller, some blue lines painted on it and an orange ball provided for us to play with. We knew it was going to be treacherous so Don shaved off the bottom of our studs so that the nails came through. This way we would be able to get some sort of grip on the ice. Of course, we knew the referee would inspect our studs before we went out so cardboard was fixed over the top and the referee was happy. Once we were on the field, the cardboard was kicked off and soon the Leipzig players had blood pouring down their shins. They kept complaining, but the referee just insisted everything was fine as he had checked our boots before kick-off."

Goals from Lorimer and Billy Bremner earned Leeds a precious lead to bring back to Elland Road where a goalless draw in the second leg again saw Revie's men progress to the next stage. United's next sortie into Europe would be in the New Year, by which time Liverpool were starting to pull away in the title race despite both sides claiming a win apiece from the Christmas double-header. Leeds would go on to once again finish runners-up, six points behind Bill Shankly's champions. Chelsea knocking Leeds out of the FA Cup at the fourth round stage meant the focus turned to Europe and a two-legged third round meeting with Valencia that would once again see the 'Dirty Leeds' headlines dusted down and given another airing.

The tactic of Jack Charlton being positioned just in front of the opposition goalkeeper at corners, something he had developed after realising how it upset brother Bobby during England training sessions, was the catalyst for a bust-up that would see Dutch referee Leo Horn forced to take the players off the field for 11 minutes to allow tempers to subside. The score was 1-1 and 15 minutes remained on the clock when the Spanish goalkeeper's frustration at Charlton's presence in the six-yard box boiled over and he kicked the Leeds man. Defender Francisco Vidagny then lashed out at Charlton whose retribution sparked a mass brawl that took a dozen police officers and officials coming on to the pitch to break-up. Valencia's goalkeeper also decided jumping into the West Stand paddock would be preferable to facing Charlton as the Leeds defender tore after him during the melee. Referee Horn sent Charlton and Vidagny off before taking the players off the field in an attempt to take the sting out of a fiery game that would later see Jose Maria Sanchez-Lage also dismissed. The game eventually resumed and was played out with no further addition to the score, leaving Leeds with a potentially difficult away trip to southern Spain to negotiate a fortnight later. United's preparations were nearly harmed when Maurice Lindley, travelling alone on a scouting trip to Las Palmas in the Canary Islands, was refused entry to Valencia's next game. Several telegrams had been sent but Lindley's pleas to speak to someone in authority were ignored and, eventually, he had to buy a ticket on the black market. After the stormy first leg in Leeds, it did not need a scouting report to predict further trouble but the anticipated bloodbath never materialised as a controlled display by United brought a 1-0 victory courtesy of a Mike O'Grady goal. He recalls: "Some of the Valencia players tried to provoke us with one asking me to help pull him up after a fair tackle and then trying to head-butt me as he got off the ground. But we didn't let it faze us and went through. Don was really pleased with the control we had shown."

This increased maturity was evident in the next round of the Fairs Cup as Ujpesti Dozsa, a Hungarian team Revie had rated very highly in the pre-match dossiers handed out to his players, were comprehensively beaten 4-1 in the first leg at Elland Road. A 1-1 draw in the return then set up a semi-final against Real Zaragoza that remained locked at 2-2 after two legs. With the Fairs Cup not yet under the auspices of UEFA and no away goals rule in place, a coin was tossed to decide where the play-off would be held. Leeds called right and the replay was set for May 11, only to be brought forward eight days when it was discovered the tie clashed with England's trip to Yugoslavia – Norman Hunter and Jack Charlton having been selected by Alf Ramsey. Zaragoza objected and a telegram arrived from Spain at Elland Road, outlining that flights had already been booked and they would, therefore, not be coming to the rearranged game. Eventually, the Fairs Cup organising committee stepped in and found in Leeds' favour. The game was to go ahead on May 3. Unfortunately, United's luck then ran out and their first European adventure ended in disappointment despite Revie using one last trick to try and unsettle a Zaragoza side featuring several Brazilians. Having noticed the silky skills of the visiting players when training on the bone dry Fullerton Park training pitch that used to stand behind the West Stand at Elland Road, Revie ordered the fire brigade to flood the pitch with gallons of water. The move failed dismally as Zaragoza triumphed 3-1 en route to lifting the trophy courtesy of a 1-0 win over Barcelona in the final.

A defeat to Newcastle United and a draw with Manchester United then rounded off what had, despite not having yielded a trophy again, undoubtedly been another season of progress by Leeds. Success seemed to be just around the corner for a group of players who were maturing fast. Revie, after back-to-back runners-up spots, was determined to leave nothing to chance and made a move for Alan Ball that would, more than a decade later, land him in hot water with the FA. Ball revealed in his autobiography how Revie had tried to lure him to Elland Road with three illegal £100 payments, something that led to both men being charged with bringing the game into disrepute. The meeting had taken place on Saddleworth Moor but Ball opted instead to join Everton, adding to Revie's frustration by pocketing the cash knowing the Leeds manager would be able to do little about it.

Missing out on Ball as a player was a blow for Revie, whose side won just three of their opening 11 games once the 1966-67 season got underway. Already, a sustained title challenge looked beyond Leeds and they eventually finished fourth. Instead, it was Europe – a second consecutive runners-up spot having again secured a place in the Inter-Cities Fairs Cup – and the FA Cup where United hoped to finally end the search for silverware. Once again, however, the stigma of gamesmanship and foul play would continue to dog Leeds – accusations that are given short shrift by those involved who instead point to the culture of a sport that, back then, had Ron 'Chopper' Harris and Tommy Smith among its household names. Johnny Giles, often referred to by United's critics as one of the more uncompromising members of Revie's team, says: "When people talk about Leeds being dirty, they forget that was the culture back then. You had to look after yourself. There were so many players around who would now be suspended all season long. We just made sure no-one ever managed to bully us."

Leeds-born Mike O'Grady had played against Revie's side for Huddersfield and also come up against a combative right winger by the name of Billy Bremner during his youth team days. He said: "What happened in Europe in those early games after I joined Leeds in 1965 did have an effect on how we played abroad. But what I always say is that while Leeds tackled hard and were competitive, we never resorted to some of the things that went on in Europe like spitting. It was not as bad in the First Division, but there were still a lot of players who thought nothing of straying outside the rules. Eddie McCreadie and Ron Harris were dreadful to play against at Chelsea. There was one game at Stamford Bridge when the game had stopped and Terry Cooper had the ball. McCreadie came up and kicked him so hard on the back of the calf that it cracked his shin. Nothing was done about it by the referee or the FA and yet we were known as 'Dirty Leeds'."

Others, and particularly those who had admired Revie as a player, found United's physical approach a major surprise. Brian Glanville, chief football writer of the *Sunday Times*, had followed Revie's career since his days as a Leicester City reserve and thought him to be a wonderfully talented footballer. But he was less of a fan of the Leeds side that came up from the Second Division under Revie's stewardship. Glanville recalls: "In many ways, it was similar to what became known in later years as the 'George Graham Syndrome' whereby someone renowned for their elegance as a player would turn into the exact opposite as a manager. Watching that Leeds team of his, it became clear to me that Revie now despised flair – despite him having been such a skilful player himself. The team he built at Leeds was one many had a great antipathy towards due to their cynical and abrasive approach. They were not liked at all. Pat Crerand was a very good friend of mine and I recall bumping into Pat outside the ground before Manchester United were due to face Leeds one year. We were discussing the game and Pat was not looking forward to the game at all, saying what a horrible experience it was playing Leeds due to their rough approach. He was, by no means, alone in thinking that, either." Former team-mates also found the transformation from cultured player to manager of a team with an, at best, questionable approach difficult to fathom. Andy Davidson had been at Hull City with Revie and admits: "I always thought Don would be a manager because he thought a lot about football, but what I didn't expect was he would end up in charge of a team like Leeds. Don was not a vicious player at all, if anything he needed people alongside him who could handle themselves to provide protection. But Leeds seemed to thrive on confrontation."

Leeds put aside the mounting criticism of their approach to progress in the FA Cup with comfortable victories over Crystal Palace (3-0) and West Bromwich Albion (5-0) to set up a fifth round tussle with Sunderland. Such was the interest in the meeting of two clubs who had slugged it out so memorably to win promotion just three seasons earlier that 55,763 packed into Roker Park to see a Jack Charlton goal earn United a replay. Staged just four days later, the tie was not all-ticket due to the time factor and such was the demand that the gates were shut 23 minutes before kick-off with a record 57,892 fans inside. Some fans were so desperate to see the game that they watched the entire 120 minutes perched on the roof of the Scratching Shed. Disaster almost struck 10 minutes into the game when a 10ft crush barrier collapsed under the weight of the crowd and dozens of fans were left injured. Referee Ray Tinkler, who would later earn infamy among Leeds fans following a controversial defeat at home to West Brom in 1971, halted the match and a fleet of ambulances took 18 people to hospital as United chairman Harry Reynolds made appeals for calm over the public address system. The game eventually resumed with the pitch ringed by fans sitting on the touchline and the club's record crowd saw a John O'Hare goal for Sunderland cancelled out by Billy Bremner. Extra time could not split the two teams so a second replay was ordered for Boothferry Park, Hull, where Leeds, thanks to a controversial late penalty by Johnny Giles, won a stormy encounter that saw George Herd and George Mulhall sent off for Sunderland.

Manchester City were beaten 1-0 in the quarter-finals to set up a meeting with Chelsea that again ended in controversy, though this time with Leeds the side left seething by a referee's decision after Ken Burns disallowed a last-minute 'equaliser' by Peter Lorimer because the Chelsea defensive wall had not retreated the requisite 10 yards. United's subsequent appeals fell on deaf ears, leaving Revie with the task of again having to galvanise his players in the hunt for what was turning out to be an elusive first trophy. With Leeds having suffered a spectacular 7-0 defeat at West Ham United in the League Cup, the Inter-Cities Fairs Cup was their last hope with wins over DWS Amsterdam, Valencia and Bologna – the latter coming courtesy of Billy Bremner calling correctly the toss of a coin after the sides could not be separated over two legs – earning a semi-final meeting with Kilmarnock. A Rod Belfitt hat-trick in the home leg effectively booked United's first appearance in a European final but, as with Chelsea in the FA Cup, only disappointment lay ahead in a two-legged affair against Dinamo Zagreb that was held over until the start of the following season due to fixture congestion.

Leeds were hampered by Syd Owen, the compiler of the dossiers that Revie made such an integral part of his preparations, being unable to watch the Yugoslavs in action before the first leg due to a flight cancellation. The die was cast as a 2-0 first leg defeat in Zagreb was followed by a goalless draw at home in the return when Revie adopted an initially cautious approach despite the need for goals. Mike O'Grady played in both legs of the final defeat to Dinamo. "I was surprised we didn't go for it more," he says, "especially at home. I felt we were too cautious and too much attention was paid to the opposition's strengths rather than our own." More than four decades on, it is a sentiment Peter Lorimer shares. The club's all-time record goalscorer said: "I don't think Don ever really believed until the last couple of years what a great team he had. He could be quite negative, probably because he hated losing so much. Everything was geared towards making sure we didn't lose in the early years and that probably didn't change until the early Seventies. Underneath it all, I just don't think he was the most secure person. He was always worried what might go wrong."

This fear of events conspiring against his team manifested itself in all manner of personal traits, from the painstaking preparation that went into the legendary dossiers handed out to players before every game through to the superstitions that he increasingly became a slave to. By the autumn of 1967 – and with Leeds having finished runners-up twice in the league while also having suffered further heartache in the FA Cup and Inter-Cities Fairs Cup – Revie was starting to wonder if that first trophy would ever arrive. He would soon have his answer.

Chapter 9

A Trophy At Last

When it comes to superstitions, footballers are in a class of their own. Actors may refuse ever to utter the word 'Macbeth', instead referring to Shakespeare's work as 'the Scottish play'. They may also insist on wishing each other good luck before a performance with the words 'break a leg'. But the peculiarities of the stage pale into insignificance when compared to those who make a living in what Pele once called 'the beautiful game'. It could be wearing the same boots, visiting the same toilet immediately before running on to the field or even kissing the bald head of a team-mate ahead of kick-off, but one thing is for sure – footballers will do anything if it makes them believe the result will be a better performance. Even the very best have succumbed, Bobby Moore always made sure he was the last player in the dressing room to put on his shorts. Team-mate Martin Peters is said to have found the ritual so amusing that he would mischievously wait until Moore had put his shorts on before taking off his own, causing England's World Cup winning captain to do the same.

Moore's behaviour may have been anything but rational, but compared to Don Revie's own eccentricities it was nothing. Revie's superstitious leanings had been apparent very early during his reign as Leeds United manager. When still in the Second Division, for instance, Revie believed the spirits were conspiring against his team and vowed to take action, as Jack Charlton vividly recalls: "There was this one time Don brought someone over from Blackpool because he thought the ground was haunted. Don wanted this person to get rid of whatever spirits were there so we were all blessed, as was Elland Road itself. We weren't convinced but, funnily enough, from that moment on results improved and we won promotion the following season. And, a year later, we finished runners-up in the First Division."

The blessings were just the start. Any incident that happened before a game that Leeds went on to win, such as the afternoon Norman Hunter absent-mindedly threw the ball to captain Bobby Collins in the dressing room, would have to be repeated every week. The club's nickname of the 'Peacocks', so named because of the two pubs – imaginatively named 'New' and 'Old' - that stood near Elland Road, was soon banished due to Revie's fear of feathered creatures, as was the owl that used to adorn the front of the club's shirts. One local reporter was even sent home to change after he turned up to a match wearing a green suit, a colour the United manager considered unlucky.

In later years, Revie's list of superstitions grew. He would wear the same 'lucky' blue suit to every game each season, while also following the same ritual of a short walk to a particular set of traffic lights, which he would touch before retracing his steps.

Revie's slavery to such quirky rituals was so ingrained in those around him at the time that it even became a stick with which to beat the makers of the 2009 film *The Damned United*, the account of Brian Clough's dramatic 44 days as Leeds manager. The Earl of Harewood, who often travelled with the team to away games when Revie was in charge, says: "The film was a travesty of the truth, apart from Brian Clough saying those rude things to the players about throwing their medals away. That bit was fact. The film claimed Don and the players had walked to a match against Derby after their coach stopped nearby. But, as Jack Charlton said to me after also watching the film, if it had happened and Leeds had won then Don would have got the players to do it every week'."

Revie's players were not immune to superstitious behaviour, either. Jack Charlton ran out of the tunnel last before kick-off and Eddie Gray pushed a photo of his wife down one of his socks before every game. Even those who felt they were beyond such nonsensical claptrap found themselves drawn in eventually, as Peter Lorimer explains: "Don went over the top with his superstitions, but that was the kind of man he was. Like everything, if we had lost and he had not stuck to his usual routine then he would blame himself. Whether that was the thick dossiers being as detailed as usual or not sticking to his routine of walking round a lamppost 55 times, Don felt he wasn't doing his job unless he stuck to it. But, it's funny, because quite a few of the lads picked up their own superstitions over the years. I didn't go in the dressing room a lot before a game, I would rather sit in the lounge and watch the racing on television. I would just sit there with my kit on and my boots next to the chair on the floor. Then, someone would come and get me when it was time to go. Maybe, subconsciously, it was something I had picked up from watching the others."

Unsurprisingly, superstitious behaviour had been a common trait in the Revie family, as Don's son Duncan admits: "The family has always been superstitious about things like not putting new shoes on the table and touching wood for good luck. We all developed our own matchday routine as well. There were a lot of games when all the relatives from Scotland came down and that was when it went into real overdrive with everyone having to do exactly what they had done before the last game. Mum was the same with pictures of birds, which she deemed to be unlucky. So she made sure we had none of them in the house." Another ritual Revie closely adhered to was never returning to his house if he had forgotten something. John Wray, who was the Leeds United writer for the *Bradford Telegraph & Argus* for 20 years, recalls: "Don was so superstitious that if he forgot his briefcase when leaving for work, he refused to go back indoors because he considered it to be unlucky. Instead, Elsie or some other family member would have to find the left-behind article and pass it to Don through a window or door."

To many, Revie's superstitions were a form of neurosis that did his players few favours. He was seen as sowing doubts in the minds of a team who had enough talent to beat the opposition without relying on such nonsense. Those within the Leeds camp, however, beg to differ and insist Revie's superstitious bent made no difference to the players once out on the field. "He had to wear the same lucky blue suit of his to every game," says Mick Jones. "And if he couldn't find it on matchday there was a major panic on. It had so many holes in the backside, by the end you could have combed your hair in it but he would not change that suit. He was a one-off, though having said that there are a lot of footballers who have their own little quirks. Don was no different and I can honestly say it made no difference to us players at all."

To a man so locked into superstitious forebodings as Revie, losing a major cup final in the opening three weeks of a new season as Leeds had done against Dinamo Zagreb in the Inter-Cities Fairs Cup was the worst possible start. Having brought a medium to Elland Road in his early days as manager, Revie had gone one step further during the summer of 1967 by inviting a gypsy to Leeds. He believed a curse had been put on the site that became United's home when travellers had been forced off the land several decades earlier so the subsequent defeat to the Yugoslavs came as a real kick in the teeth.

Revie, however, was not a man to dwell on failure for too long as he stuck to the mantra that had been drilled into his players after previous major disappointments. Forget it and move on.

Determined not to dwell on the defeat, he moved to raise spirits by breaking the club's transfer record as Mick Jones was signed from Sheffield United in a £100,000 deal. Revie and his staff had searched tirelessly for a striker for much of the previous season. A lack of goals had hindered the push for honours during a campaign that saw Leeds challenge on three fronts but only Johnny Giles, a midfielder, reached double figures in the league with 12 goals. Revie had bought Alan Peacock for a joint club record £53,000 from Middlesbrough in February, 1964, with not only securing promotion in mind, but also prospering at the top level. Unfortunately, injury would restrict the 6ft 1in forward to just 40 appearances in the First Division before he was sold to Plymouth Argyle, though he did manage two more England appearances while at Elland Road to take his tally of caps to six. Peacock's fitness problems meant Revie needed a reliable replacement and he eventually settled on Jones, an aggressive hard-working forward who had shot to prominence at Bramall Lane and already had a couple of England caps to his name.

Jones signed a couple of weeks after United's Fairs Cup final defeat and his debut came in a 3-2 home victory over Leicester City, the third time in four games that Revie's side had claimed maximum points. Two weeks later, a Chelsea team in disarray following the resignation of manager Tommy Docherty were thrashed 7-0. Strangely, Jones failed to score but his unselfish and energetic display underlined just why Revie had been so willing to break the club's transfer record. Third Division Bury, with Bobby Collins in midfield making his first return to the club he served with such distinction since being sold the previous February, were the next visitors to Elland Road in a third round League Cup tie. The Shakers duly lost 3-0 as United, who had already knocked Luton Town out, embarked on a run towards Wembley that included victories over Sunderland and Stoke City before culminating in a 4-2 aggregate win over Brian Clough's Derby County in the semi-finals. United, ironically without their Cup-tied record signing Jones, were through to their third major final and this time Revie was determined there would be no repeat of the disappointments against Liverpool and Dinamo Zagreb.

The League Cup had been the brainchild of Football League secretary, Alan Hardaker, and Sir Stanley Rous, the secretary of the Football Association. The League wanted a rival to the FA Cup – Hardaker would later claim 'the FA Cup final is football's Ascot, the League Cup its equivalent of Derby Day at Epsom – and the new competition made its debut in the 1960-61 season. It was, however, far from an immediate success with Arsenal, Sheffield Wednesday, Tottenham Hotspur, Wolverhampton Wanderers and West Bromwich Albion refusing to take part over fears of fixture congestion. By 1968, however, the League Cup had gained much more credence thanks to a combination of the winners qualifying for Europe and the ditching of a two-legged final format in favour of a one-off game at Wembley. United reaching the final was, therefore, big news back in West Yorkshire as thousands of fans started planning their trip to north London for the March 2 encounter with Arsenal. Captain Billy Bremner spoke for his team-mates when telling the

Yorkshire Evening Post on the eve of the game: "The boys are all very confident of winning this one. We only hope we don't suffer from over-confidence."

The Football League's lack of marketing nous saw the final take place on a Saturday, a practice that continued until the 1980s, and that meant the rest of the country was engaged in a full programme of games. The final was also, unlike in the FA Cup, not shown on television thanks to League secretary Alan Hardaker's strong belief that live broadcasts would drive down attendances.

In the end, the nation's football fans missed little with the 97,887 fans inside Wembley enduring a dour affair punctuated by a series of ugly flare-ups between two teams who clearly couldn't stand the sight of each other. Whether nerves had played a part or not is open to question, though Revie and assistant Les Cocker were so concerned about how tense the players looked in the dressing room half-an-hour before kick-off that they held an impromptu sports quiz. Eddie Gray says: "They did things like hold sports quizzes all the time, just to defuse a bit of tension."

United settled first and took the lead after 18 minutes when the Arsenal defence could only clear an Eddie Gray corner as far as Terry Cooper, who thundered a volley past Jim Furnell. United's left-back later claimed to have visualised scoring the winner while asleep on the three nights leading up to the final and the goal did, indeed, boast dream-like qualities. It was, however, the only thing of beauty in the entire 90 minutes, as United winger Jimmy Greenhoff readily admits. "As a spectacle, the final was a complete non-event," he says. "Us scoring so early was probably the worst thing that could have happened for the neutrals because we just shut up shop. Don Revie was a very cautious man and, once 1-0 ahead, he always wanted us to protect what we had. It happened every week and Wembley was no different. I was on one wing and Eddie Gray the other, but all we did once ahead was sit in front of the full-backs. I helped Paul Reaney out, while Eddie did the same for Terry Cooper. It was effective, but I doubt anyone outside Leeds enjoyed the 1968 final very much."

The final whistle was the signal for captain Billy Bremner to enjoy a celebratory forward roll in the centre-circle before rushing to join his overjoyed team-mates and manager. Only England's Jack Charlton, in the World Cup final two years earlier, and Johnny Giles, with Manchester United in the 1963 FA Cup final, had tasted victory at Wembley. The Leeds party left the national stadium with a mixture of joy, pride and relief at winning a first trophy. A huge burden had been lifted from their shoulders and Giles, who along with Bremner had fought for every challenge in the heart of the United midfield as though his life depended on it, insists lifting the League Cup was a major step forward for the club. He says: "A lot had been made about us not having won a trophy despite finishing as runners-up a couple of times in the league and being the losing finalists on a couple of other occasions. But what people often forget is just how young that side was at the time. We stayed together for a lot of years after 1968 without too many changes and that shows how young we still were. What the League Cup win proved to be was something of a breakthrough as it gave us increased confidence as a team going forward."

Disappointingly, the players' triumphant home-coming in Leeds the following day saw just 15,000 fans line the streets after organisers failed to take into account that highlights of the Wembley final were due to be shown on television at the same time as the team arrived home. In an age before video recorders, many opted to stay home and relive the game in the comfort of their own armchairs. Revie, unhappy his players had been denied the homecoming parade they deserved, made it clear no such clash must be allowed to happen again. The significance of the United manager, notoriously such a cautious character, feeling able to suggest publicly that further successful homecomings lay ahead for his team was not lost on anyone.

Revie's ambition before the 1967-68 season had been to win 'any two' from the four available trophies. With the League Cup already in the Elland Road trophy cabinet, attention turned to the league where the team's Wembley success was followed by a run of five wins and three draws from the next nine games. United's tendency to choke at the vital moment returned with a vengeance, however, as four consecutive defeats to finish the season saw Revie's men slip from top spot to fourth. It was a similar story in the FA Cup. Everton benefited from a Gary Sprake mistake that led to Jack Charlton having to handle a goalbound shot from Jimmy Husband on the line, the resulting penalty turning out to be the only goal of the Old Trafford semi-final. Attention turned quickly to Europe and the Inter-Cities Fairs Cup where Spora Luxembourg, Partizan Belgrade, Hibernian and Glasgow Rangers had all been knocked out by Leeds to book a semi-final meeting with Dundee. A Paul Madeley header earned a 1-1 draw in the first leg at Dens Park before the return became enveloped in a row after Leeds duo Norman Hunter and Jack Charlton had been called up by England for their European Championships quarter-final against Spain, a game that clashed with the Fairs Cup tie's scheduled date of May 7. Dundee wanted to stick to the original date but Leeds protested and, eventually, the matter was referred to the Fairs Cup Management Committee. Keen to sort out the mess, but also desperate to avoid a repeat of the previous year when the final between Leeds and Dinamo Zagreb had been put back to the start of the following season, the Committee tried to strike a compromise before accepting there was no alternative to a delay. When Leeds won the return leg against the Scots on May 15 their prize was again being forced to wait three months to play in the final. The decision back-fired on United in financial terms with just 25,268 fans watching the home leg against Ferencvaros on August 7 as it fell in the middle of the traditional Leeds holidays. Nevertheless, Revie's men earned a precious 1-0 lead to take to Budapest for the return five weeks later, thanks to Mick Jones being on hand to prod a Jack Charlton knockdown over the line from a yard out just before half-time. It proved to be a decisive advantage to take to Hungary for the return leg. Ferencvaros threw everything at Leeds but, thanks to an outstanding display by Gary Sprake, United claimed a goalless draw to become the first British team to lift the Fairs Cup. The unusually long gap between the two legs of the final meant Jimmy Greenhoff, who had come off the bench to replace Johnny Giles in the 1-0 win at Elland Road, had the unwanted distinction of becoming the first player to be transferred halfway through a Cup final. He recalls: "I was sold to Birmingham not long after the first leg to become the subject of a question that I am told has been asked in countless pub quizzes ever since. I did find Don's decision to let me go a bit strange and, to be honest, I can't remember now whether I ever got a winners' medal or not. But at least I played my part."

Revie's joy at lifting the League Cup at Wembley and then the Fairs Cup in Budapest six months later was tempered slightly by his good friend Harry Reynolds, the chairman who had been so supportive in his early years as manager, being unable to share in the club's success. Reynolds had stepped down as chairman in August, 1967, at the age of 67 through ill health after overseeing a dramatic change in the club's fortunes both on and off the field. A debt that had stood at £250,000 when he succeeded Sam Bolton shortly after Revie's appointment had been turned into a £138,000 profit by the time he quit. Despite being crippled by arthritis, Reynolds had insisted on travelling to London in March for the League Cup final against Arsenal by train but was unable to take his seat due to his condition. The absence of his good friend upset Revie; Reynolds had accompanied him on many of the trips to far-flung parts of the country that had brought to Yorkshire the very same players who had just ended the club's hunt for silverware. Revie had made sure one of the first things his players did on their return from Wembley was to go and visit Reynolds with the League Cup. There were similar feelings of regret for the

United manager in Budapest as his team battled gamely for a goalless draw. John Reynolds, a member of the Leeds groundstaff for more than half a century from 1957 and close to both men, is in no doubt as to the debt Revie felt he owed his chairman. "Harry helped Don a lot in the early days and Don never forgot that," he says. "Not just in terms of making sure Don got the job in the first place but by also matching his ambitions for Leeds United and providing the funds. They got on well because Harry, who had been a scrap merchant, preferred a sandwich and a game of dominoes to the boardroom. Don was the same and they worked well together. It was sad that ill health forced Harry to stand down before we had won a trophy. He actually died at an Elland Road game several years later in 1974. The reserves were playing at home and Harry, ever the fan, had come to watch. I was with him at the time along with Tom Holley, a reporter for the *Yorkshire Evening Post* and *The People*. It was very, very sad."

Harry Reynolds had been succeeded as chairman by Albert Morris, a director since 1961, but again tragedy struck with the new man passing away just four weeks after the League Cup triumph. Into the breach stepped vice-chairman Percy Woodward, a member of the board for more than 20 years. Relations between manager and new chairman remained cordial. But there was little doubt to those inside Elland Road that Reynolds' decision to step back from the day-to-day running of the club, coupled with success on the field, meant Revie was well on his way to becoming the all-powerful figure that would dominate Leeds United in the coming years.

Chapter 10

Champions, Champions, Champions...

Long before the days of 24-hour rolling news channels and the influx of billions of pounds from television that turned football into a mix of big business and showbusiness, the life of a chairman was a simple affair. Some, such as Bob Lord at Burnley, were familiar figures to supporters but, in the main, the Turf Moor chairman's peers were rarely seen and even less likely to be heard. These largely silent heads of the board were either self-made men from humble origins or members of a family dynasty who had been in charge of the club for decades. Some were dictatorial, while some just enjoyed the social standing that came with the position, plus the seemingly endless supply of G&Ts that came their way in oak-panelled boardrooms up and down the country. Most were anonymous, being more than happy to make the big decisions behind closed doors while offering little by way of an explanation to those who handed over their hard-earned money at the turnstiles.

Now, of course, the picture has changed dramatically. Some chairmen are every bit as high profile as the players and managers. Few of the hourly sports bulletins churned out by Sky Sports and their ilk are broadcast without a soundbite or two from a media-savvy chairman, while local newspapers will wipe out entire pages to chronicle the thoughts of the man in charge of even a League Two club. Peter Ridsdale, known by some within Yorkshire football during his spell as Leeds United chairman as 'Publicity Pete', is by no means alone in courting the media, though it is doubtful many of his contemporaries have had a DVD entitled *My Leeds United* released by their own club's media department. Likewise, few but Ridsdale could have been the subject of a joke from Sky Sports presenter Richard Keys at the Leeds Player of the Year awards night one year that suggested the then Elland Road chief was so used to being in front of the cameras that, on opening the fridge door at home, he 'immediately did five minutes to camera when the light came on'. But in being high-profile and an easily recognisable face, Ridsdale is one of many in the brotherhood of football chairmen.

Even those who choose not to speak to the media, such as Malcolm Glazer at Manchester United or Chelsea's Roman Abramovich, are as familiar to the man in the street as the players who bring the trophies to their respective clubs.

The position football now has in the nation's conscience is such that the days when the chairman of the local basement division club could wander around his own town unnoticed have long gone. One area that has changed little, however, is where the ultimate power lies within a football club. If, for instance, Abramovich wants a successful manager such as Jose Mourinho to go, he is gone and not even two Premier League titles in three seasons will save him. Little has changed in that respect with even Brian Clough at Derby County having, eventually, to admit defeat in his 1973 battle of wills with chairman Sam Longson despite having the majority of the Baseball Ground on his side.

There have, of course, been exceptions and one of these came at Leeds United when Don Revie ruled the roost. By 1968, he had overcome initial difficulties to build a formidable team whose considerable talents had finally been rewarded with the League Cup and Inter-Cities Fairs Cup. Revie had achieved his success working in tandem with chairman Harry Reynolds, the pair proving such an irresistible combination of ambition and gritty determination that success had followed both on and off the field. Not only had Leeds got their hands on two major trophies, the club's bank balance had swelled through increased attendances and the funds had allowed Revie to shatter the club record transfer fee when signing Mick Jones. The money coming through the turnstiles had also allowed for a much-needed improvement in facilities at Elland Road. John Reynolds had been appointed assistant groundsman 12 months before the arrival of Revie as a player in 1958 and four years before Harry Reynolds would succeed Sam Bolton as chairman. He recalls: "The club had no money when I started to look after the pitch, not even to buy some straw to try and prevent it becoming frozen. I became friends with Don, who knew I had been a footballer before injury ruined any chances of making a career in the game, when he was a player and he thought it ridiculous that the club could not spare some money for something as important as the pitch. But that was how it was then. Things changed when Don became manager and Harry chairman, and particularly once Leeds had started to become successful. All of a sudden, we could replace a bit of machinery here and do something else there to try and improve the surface."

It was in the surrounds at Elland Road, however, where the success of Revie's team was becoming most apparent by 1968. With cash in the bank, the board vowed to turn United's home into a venue worthy of the great side Revie was building. Not long after Leeds had ended the search for a first trophy by lifting the League Cup, work began on clearing the huge open terrace that filled the north end of Elland Road to allow the building of a new covered Spion

Kop. To create space for future building plans at the opposite end, the new terrace was built behind the old terrace and right up to the extremity of United's land. It created the unusual sight for several months of a vast, gaping area of emptiness behind one goal – a problem the club moved to solve once turf had been laid by moving the pitch 30 yards to the north, meaning the new Kop and old Scratching Shed both stood 30 yards from the nearest goalline. The work cost £250,000 and fitted in with the grandiose plan of Revie and Harry Reynolds to turn Leeds United into a first-class football club, both on and off the field.

Reynolds' retirement through arthritis, followed by the death of his successor Albert Morris just four months later, meant there had been a rapid turnover at the helm of the club as Percy Woodward took charge. It had little impact on the team but Revie had started to miss working alongside his good friend Reynolds. His relationship with Woodward remained cordial but the new chairman, a former Lord Mayor, was more old school than his predecessor and never had the same affinity with Revie. The relationship between manager and board would never be as close again and Revie soon felt his worth was not appreciated by the powers-that-be at Elland Road, something that would later be a factor in him seriously listening to offers of employment elsewhere. Certainly, during Reynolds' tenure as chairman, he had firmly rejected the advances of former club Sunderland in 1964 and interest from Sheffield Wednesday. Italian clubs Torino and Juventus received the same response in the wake of Leeds' first league title success despite lucrative contracts being dangled in front of Revie.

Later, however, Revie became more open to approaches from outside, with Everton in 1973 being one of a couple that went the distance before a lucrative offer was rebuffed at the last minute amid talk of a new, improved contract at Elland Road. Whatever the truth about manager and board, from 1968 onwards there was only one man in charge of Leeds United. And it wasn't anyone on the board. Club president, the Earl of Harewood, recalls: "Once Harry Reynolds had left, I very much had the impression that Don wanted to run things on his own. Before too long, he was doing that very thing. He had the final say on everything and he was very much Leeds United. Whether some of the directors resented this, I don't know. But I did feel that there perhaps wasn't a true appreciation of just what Don was doing for Leeds United, even when we were the league champions."

The growing influence Revie, a powerfully-built man, had at Elland Road meant that few, if any, major decisions were taken without the board seeking

Steely
determination.
From a young
age, Don Revie
had an inner
belief he would
make it as a
footballer.
(Yorkshire Post)

The family
home. 20 Bell
Street,
Middlesbrough,
was a typical
two-bedroom
terrace,
complete with
outside toilet.
(YP)

Playground fun. Revie would arrive 45 minutes before class at Archibald Elementary School, to hone his footballing skills. (YP)

Swift action. Signing for Middlesbrough Swifts meant playing for Bill Sanderson, a coach whose methods would hugely influence Revie's own thinking later in life. (YP)

A professional at last. Revie takes his first tentative steps as an apprentice with Leicester City. (YP)

A close family. Revie's dad, Donald senior, and stepmother Emily are flanked on the extreme left and right by his sisters, Joyce and Jean. Donald senior died in 1962. (YP)

Away from home. Revie relaxes at his first lodgings in Thirlmere Road, Leicester. (YP)

On the road. Revie prepares to set off to an away game on the Leicester City team coach. (YP)

Hooked. Revie proves that football is not the only pastime where he can land the big prize. (YP)

Hole-in-one. Golf became an enduring passion for Revie after first discovering the game in his teens. (YP)

Cup winner. Revie hoists captain Roy Paul on his shoulders in celebration after Manchester City's 3-1 win over Birmingham City in the 1956 FA Cup final. (Press Association)

Head-to-head. Revie, then captain of Sunderland, shakes hands with Leeds United counterpart, John Charles, ahead of the two sides meeting in the First Division. (YP)

Sign here. Watched by (L-R) director Harold Marjason, secretary Cyril Williamson and manager Bill Lambton, Revie joins Leeds on November 28, 1958. (YP)

The new boy. Revie sports Leeds United colours for the first time. (YP)

First class. Harry Reynolds realised Revie was the man for Leeds when writing a reference for the Bournemouth job. (YP)

The return of the Giant. John Charles joins Leeds from Juventus in August, 1962. (YP)

Leeds United, 1965. Back (L–R): Norman Hunter, Jack Charlton, Gary Sprake, Paul Reaney, Willie Bell. Front (L–R): Johnny Giles, Jim Storrie, Alan Peacock, Don Revie, Bobby Collins, Albert Johanneson, Billy Bremner. (YP)

First trophy. Revie proudly shows off the League Cup in front of the uncovered Gelderd End at Elland Road. (YP)

One of the lads. Revie joins in a sprinting session on the old Fullerton Park training pitch. The greyhound stadium that used to stand on Elland Road is in the background. (YP)

Club president,
the Earl of
Harewood, helps
Billy Bremner
show off the
Charity Shield
after a 2-1 win
over Manchester
City at Elland
Road in August,
1969.

Royal appointment. Revie greets Princess Anne ahead of the 1970 FA Cup final
against Chelsea at Wembley. (YP)

Leading out his lads. Revie and his players stride out of the tunnel at Wembley before the 1970 FA Cup final. (YP)

Back in front. Mick Jones puts Leeds 2-1 up in the 1970 Cup final with a low shot past Peter Bonetti as Allan Clarke waits to pounce on any rebound. (YP)

Running repairs. Les Cocker, Revie's invaluable right hand man, tends to Mick Jones on the Wembley turf. (YP)

Rallying the troops. Revie issues orders to his exhausted players ahead of extra-time at Old Trafford in the 1970 Cup final replay. (YP)

Building blocks. Revie joins his team for training as building work continues on Elland Road during the summer of 1970. (YP)

Capello clash. Mick Jones challenges future England manager Fabio Capello during the second leg of the 1971 Fairs Cup final against Juventus. (YP)

Cup clincher. Allan Clarke nets against Juventus in the second leg of the 1971 Fairs Cup final to prompt joyous celebrations around Elland Road. (both YP)

his approval. The players, many of whom had been brought to the club by Revie as youngsters, were in awe of their manager and hung on his every word. To them, he was not only the 'Boss' on the field but also off it – a point reinforced on one particular trip to London when two of United's directors pushed Revie's patience to the limit. Mick Jones recalls: "The players always came first in Don's eyes with everything else coming second. I always remember one game at Crystal Palace where Don had said before we got off the coach that we had to be back on board by 5.30pm to make it to King's Cross to catch the 7pm train back to Leeds. As a result, all the lads were back on the bus on time but a couple of directors weren't. They were still in the boardroom enjoying a drink with the Palace directors. The lads were wondering how long we would have to wait when, suddenly, Don turned to the coach driver and said, 'Right, come on – we're off'. And with that, the coach drove off. The directors had to make their own way home. We were astounded and wondered what would happen on the Monday but, as far as the lads were aware, nothing was ever said about it again. Don had made the decision and the directors just had to accept it." The directors could not claim they had not been warned, as Revie had done exactly the same a couple of years earlier after a game at Newcastle United. John Wray, of the *Bradford Telegraph & Argus*, recalls: "Phil Brown covered Leeds for the *Yorkshire Evening Post* in those days and had been delayed filing his match report for the Green Saturday night sports paper. I had finished my own for our Pink but decided to wait for him. Unfortunately, by the time we got back to the coach, it had gone. Don had told the driver to set off, leaving Phil and I to catch the train back to Leeds. Phil wasn't best pleased but he was never late again after that."

Revie's standing at the club had increased through the winning of two trophies but he was determined not to rest on his laurels. By the time Leeds had triumphed in the delayed Inter-Cities Fairs Cup final against Ferencvaros, the 1968-69 league season was already seven games old and Revie's team had dropped just one point. He had welcomed the players back to pre-season in July with a challenge to chase the big one, the League Championship. Usually, the aim was to win every competition United entered but Revie's thinking had changed. He knew only the league title could promote Leeds to the list of English football greats. He also shrewdly recognised that the likes of Manchester United and Liverpool were on the wane, just as other rivals such as Arsenal and Everton were undergoing a re-building process that would not yield success until a couple of years later. The stage was set for an all-out assault on the league title, and the feeling that this could be Leeds United's year only grew after the Fairs Cup triumph over Ferencvaros. Revie's single-minded focus on being crowned league champions had already been evident during the trip to Nottingham Forest on August 24 – and it almost proved fatal for his players. Mike O'Grady, who would miss just four league games that season, recalls: "We were drawing 1-1 at the City Ground when, just before the break, smoke started appearing in the main stand. The referee blew the whistle for half-time and we trooped off, not thinking much more about it. We just presumed whatever was causing it would be dealt with quickly. We got to the dressing room and Don started his team-talk. Gary Sprake, who thought he could hear the fire crackling, then tried to speak, but Billy Bremner just said, 'Shut up, the boss is talking'. Don continued and it was only when one of the lads opened the door to go to the toilet that all this black smoke poured in. Don said, 'We need to find somewhere a bit quieter, lads'. He only wanted to carry on the team-talk, even though it was clear the stand was ablaze! Talk about being focused. Eventually, it was suggested we should get the hell out of there and that's what we did – though not before Norman Hunter had turned the wrong way out of the dressing room and almost been burnt alive." The United party retired to the nearby Bridgford Hotel where Revie hired a room and provided the players with lemonade to help ease the effects of smoke inhalation. Thankfully, no-one was injured even though the £100,000 stand was destroyed and Revie, with tongue firmly placed in cheek, told the following Monday's *Yorkshire Evening Post*: "We just don't seem to be able to stay out of the news, do we? But at least no-one is blaming us for the disaster, like they blame us for most things."

Blazing stands apart, the start to the season was proving something of a breeze for Leeds who leap-frogged over Arsenal into top spot with a 2-1 win over the Gunners at Elland Road in late September. A 3-1 defeat to Manchester City at Maine Road a week later was a setback, as was a 5-1 hammering at Burnley on October 19. But it would prove to be the team's last defeat of the season as Revie's men powered through the next 26 games to leave the trip to Anfield on April 28 as the potential championship-winning fixture. Leeds had two games left and led Liverpool by five points, Bill Shankly's men being the only side able to prevent the title coming to Elland Road due to still having three games to play. The stage was set for an almighty tussle. John Helm, now a respected football commentator but then a budding journalist, had just moved from the now defunct *Shipley Times* to the *Yorkshire Evening Post* and was sent to cover the title decider from the famous Anfield Kop. He recalls: "It was a huge game, made all the more special by night games always having that extra atmosphere. You could feel the tension before kick-off. The Kop was packed full of Liverpool fans and they were all desperate for the victory that would keep their chances of winning the title alive." Nerves were evident in the United dressing room with Billy Bremner admitting to being unable to sleep the previous night. Once on the field, however, it was a different story with Leeds producing an ice-cool display as Paul Madeley dropped deep to provide extra protection for the back four. Liverpool became more and more desperate as the night wore on but United refused to buckle and when referee Arthur Dimond blew the final whistle, the joy was etched across the faces of every player. Revie was similarly overjoyed but insisted on grabbing a quiet word with his inspirational captain. The United manager had told Billy Bremner before kick-off that, if they got the point they required, he must take the team to the Kop end. Bremner thought his manager was mad but Revie reinforced the point after the title had been clinched. The diminutive Scot still had his doubts but, as with everyone at Elland Road, he did what he was told by his boss and duly started to lead the Leeds team towards the famous terrace housing almost 27,000 Liverpool fans. Plus John Helm, who recalls: "I remember seeing the Leeds lads come towards us. Billy looked reluctant, to say the least. You could hear a pin drop as they got as far as the penalty area and I did wonder how it was going to end. Eventually, this chant of 'Champions, Champions, Champions...' began and, within seconds, it seemed everyone around me was joining in. The Kop could see the Liverpool players had given it everything but had lost out to the best team in the country. The reception was amazing and totally genuine. It was a magical moment, and one I will never forget. And all thanks to Don Revie, wisely as it turned out, sending Billy and his team-mates to the Kop end."

Once back in the dressing room, the champagne started flowing as the players celebrated. Two nights later, Leeds would round off their season with a 1-0 win over Nottingham Forest to ensure the setting of a host of new records. United had earned more points than anyone in history with 67, won the most games (27), suffered the fewest defeats (2) and conceded just nine goals at Elland Road. As gratifying as those deeds were for Revie, it was instead what happened in the away dressing room at Anfield that gave him the most satisfaction. Revie's son Duncan says: "Bill Shankly had been a big friend of my dad's for many years so to win the championship at Liverpool was very special. What Dad appreciated most, though, was Shanks asking if he could speak to the lads after the game. Dad asked for quiet and, suddenly, the dressing room was silent. Shanks stepped forward and said, 'We have not lost the title, you have won it and you're the best team in the country'. That little speech meant the world to my Dad because he was not only good friends with Shanks but he also respected him hugely. They were so close that every Sunday morning would see Dad having breakfast in bed before spending an hour on the phone to Shanks talking about their respective games the previous day and football in general. Leeds and Liverpool were huge rivals at the time but you would never have guessed it from those chats. Put it this way, I can't imagine Sir Alex Ferguson spending his Sunday mornings on the phone to Arsene Wenger or any of his other big rivals."

With the league championship residing at Elland Road for the first time, Revie's control of the club was now total. Nothing happened without his approval and his influence extended right across the city of Leeds. Little went on without the manager finding out, something his players had long ago come to appreciate. Jack Charlton recalls: "He had a host of people out in the city reporting back. For instance, me and Billy Bremner would go to our local pub, The Woodman Inn, every Thursday for a game of dominoes. The pub was only 200 yards from where we lived and it helped us relax and we wouldn't drink – well, apart from maybe the odd half a shandy. Anyway, word got back to Don that we were drunk as Lords in there every week so he called us into his office. It was all lies, which we explained to him. Don listened and then said, 'If it relaxes you two boys, then that's fine by me'. It was an adult way to treat us and we both appreciated it." John Helm admits to being impressed with Revie's common sense approach when dealing with his players: "In Don's last couple of years at Leeds, I used to go round his house and we would chat off-the-record. He would always talk about the relationship between Jack and Billy. They were not the bad boys of the team or anything like that but they would share a quiet bottle the night before a game. Because Don knew the pair would still perform the following day, nothing was said. If it had been Paul Reaney or anyone else, I think Don would have made an issue of it. To me, it was great man management – treating everyone different to ensure he got the best out of them. It was a big strength of Don's."

Peter Lorimer was another of Revie's squad who would be called into the manager's office from time-to-time. He recalls: "Don was a very strict man and had a host of spies across Leeds reporting back whenever any of the lads were out. Sometimes, he would call me into his office and read the riot act. With the younger lads, he even went so far as to check out any girls they were seeing. And if he didn't like what he heard, he would say, 'She's not the right girl for you – get rid'. He wanted to know every aspect of your life, in case it impacted on how you played on a Saturday."

As keen as he was to know what was going on in the lives of his players, Revie felt, at least off the pitch, able to trust them to make the right choices. Mike O'Grady, whose final full season at Elland Road ended with the league title triumph, recalls: "He did trust the lads to behave. If we went to London a couple of days before playing Chelsea or Arsenal, he would let us do what we wanted as long as it did not impact on the game. He would say, 'If you've been drinking, I'll be able to tell in your performance'. It meant that if I wanted to go to the theatre or the cinema, I could. Even if it was just me going on my own. The only stipulation under Revie was that everyone had to be together at 10.30pm for coffee and biscuits back at the hotel, usually the Royal Garden in Kensington. No-one abused that trust, as far as I am aware. I noticed the difference straight away when I signed for Wolves from Leeds. The manager Bill McGarry would even say what food we could and couldn't have. He didn't like that I had beans on toast, something I had started at Leeds as I found out it was good for energy."

Revie's determination to keep his players' minds focused on football was legendary. As well as ensuring they were not getting up to anything untoward, he would also instruct his staff to keep an eye out for anyone being unusually quiet in the dressing room or looking troubled. Mike O'Grady recalls: "My Dad was ill with leukaemia in my first year at Leeds and died that season at the age of 62. Don found out he was ill - even to this day, I've no idea how - and tried to help. He got it into his head that the worry and stress of it all was making me tense up. And that this was aggravating a back problem I'd had since being at Huddersfield. Don sent me to a couple of specialists to try to help me relax, while also trying to find out if there was anything he could do for my Dad. I had discovered soon after joining how keen he was to try and prevent players bringing their troubles to work. He sat us all down and said, 'If you have financial problems, gambling problems, family problems or problems with your wife...come to see me as I don't want you worrying'. It was not the same at other clubs. I remember once going to see Bill McGarry after I had signed for Wolves and his response was, 'If you've done something wrong, it's your fucking problem'."

O'Grady was, however, to see what he still considers to be the flipside of Revie's character during his time at Elland Road. The Leeds-born wideman had suffered a serious back injury at Huddersfield that had kept him out for six months. It was an injury that had never really gone away, with O'Grady suffering problems for much of his stay at Leeds. He puts a lot of those down to Revie's refusal to trust a player's own judgement on football matters ahead of his own. "I could manage the back problem providing I did a warm-up routine that I had developed at Huddersfield. I also had to rest when I could feel the pain coming on. Unfortunately, at Leeds, I was told to stop doing the routine because it was felt the back problems were all in my head. I knew that wasn't true but I stopped the routine. Sure enough, the injury problems came back and it was only when Paul Madeley and Johnny Giles suffered a similar injury that Don finally accepted my point. I knew my body better than anyone and felt I should have been trusted more. Once the pre-match routines had started again, I played 38 games as we won the league title."

Just a few months after Leeds had clinched the championship at Anfield, O'Grady was sold to Wolves. The former wide man today describes his time at Elland Road as the happiest of his career but admits the actions of Revie in the aftermath of the fire that destroyed Nottingham Forest's main stand during the abandoned game against United 12 months earlier did leave a nasty taste in the mouth. He recalls: "The fire destroyed the entire stand at Forest so all our belongings went up with it. At first, the club said, 'Don't worry, you're all covered and will not lose anything'. Unfortunately, it turned out that Forest didn't have the correct insurance. All the other lads were married and had house insurance, which they could claim on. But I didn't. I had been wearing a new suit for the Forest game and had £200 cash in my pockets. It was over this that I felt Don let me down as at that earlier meeting he said we would all be covered. I went to see Don when it emerged Forest's insurance did not cover us but he continued to fob me off and refused to help. I don't know if it was because I was not married or what, but I was annoyed. I felt I deserved a lot better, not just from Don but also Leeds. It left a sour taste in my mouth."

Despite being left out of pocket and then subsequently sold to Wolves against his wishes the following September, O'Grady admits Revie was a great manager. "You only have to look at the team he built at Leeds to realise how good he was. He had played in the 1950s when, basically, players were treated like slaves so was adamant that only the best would do for his own team. Training was never boring and he would always try to keep us on our toes by changing sessions. Sometimes, we would just do a quick loosener before travelling to the Craiglands Hotel in Ilkley for lunch and a nap in the afternoon. It was my misfortune to be sold before Don really let his team go out and play in the early 1970s. I stayed in touch with Billy Bremner after leaving and he would say, 'You'd love it now – he has let us off the leash'. I used to grit my teeth as I always felt during my time at Leeds that Don was too cautious and too reliant on getting the first goal and then concentrating on protecting the lead."

In the summer of 1969 and with a first crack at the European Cup on the horizon, Revie was still a few years away from taking the shackles completely off his side. But he was certainly moving towards a more free-flowing style, a point illustrated by Leeds smashing the British transfer record to sign Allan Clarke from Leicester City for £165,000. Hailed as the most lethal finisher since Jimmy Greaves had burst into the First Division goalscoring charts, Clarke's arrival to play with Mick Jones meant United now had arguably the most devastating strike partnership in the country. Don Revie, who had just been named Manager of the Year, also hoped the signing would prove to be the final piece in the jigsaw as Leeds prepared to take on Europe's elite.

Chapter 11

Chasing The Dream

Success, as many of those who reached true sporting greatness have insisted over the years, is a drug where the high of winning an Olympic Gold or an Ashes Test series can be enjoyed only fleetingly before an overwhelming desire to repeat the triumph kicks in. Football is no different, except opportunities for further success usually come round every 12 months as opposed to the longer wait required in many other sports. For the newly-crowned champions of England and their manager, however, the summer of 1969 brought the exciting prospect of one prize in particular for the first time. The European Cup was, unlike the Champions League misnomer of today, the preserve of champions from across the continent. Only the winners of Europe's domestic leagues could enter and, for Don Revie, it was the culmination of eight years' hard work. Ever since changing Leeds United's colours from blue and gold to all white in honour of Real Madrid, he had craved the chance to take on the cream of Europe. Here, at last, was the fulfilment of that dream. Real, having won their 15th La Liga title in the same season Leeds had been crowned champions, were just one of several previous winners taking part alongside AC Milan, Celtic and Benfica. With beaten finalists Fiorentina plus established European names such as Bayern Munich also in the seeded first round draw, it was clear Leeds faced an uphill challenge in the quest to become only the third British club after Celtic and Manchester United to lift the trophy. Not that this seemed to unduly bother Don Revie, who told the *Yorkshire Post*: "Of all the competitions open to us this season, this is the one we would like to win more than anything." Anyone in the United squad, however, taking this public declaration as a signal that the European Cup was being prioritised ahead of the league and two domestic cup competitions soon had the notion dispelled. On returning to pre-season training, Revie called his players together to reveal they were, in fact, chasing the treble. Never mind that only one club had managed the league and cup double since the turn of the century, Revie believed his players were capable of creating history by retaining the title as well as bringing the FA Cup and European Cup to Elland Road. Such was the sway Revie held over the Leeds squad, the players immediately bought into the plan. Eddie Gray recalls: "The lads believed in Don totally. They would have run through brick walls if asked and they trusted him implicitly."

Because the World Cup finals were to be staged in Mexico the following summer, the start of the Football League season had been brought forward to August 9th to provide extra preparation time for Alf Ramsey's squad. Initially, the change had no effect on Leeds as wins over Tottenham Hotspur and Nottingham Forest sandwiched a draw against Arsenal in the opening eight days. Both victories featured goals from new signing Allan Clarke, while the 4-1 triumph at the City Ground also saw United set a new top flight record dating back to 1920-21 by eclipsing Burnley's 30-game unbeaten run. Three draws followed before Everton inflicted Leeds' first defeat of this truncated season on the final Saturday in August. Mike O'Grady departed to Wolves soon after in an £80,000 deal, a transfer that had been made possible by a re-jig in tactics following Allan Clarke's arrival in the summer. With Clarke installed alongside Mick Jones up front, Revie tinkered with the formation as Peter Lorimer, never a conventional winger despite playing on the right, was handed more licence to get forward in support of the front two. As a result, the attacking instincts of Billy Bremner and Johnny Giles were curtailed slightly. Lorimer, who is unlikely ever to be overtaken as Leeds' record goalscorer with 238, adapted quickly to the new role and was just as responsible as new signing Clarke for the dynamism that began to characterise Revie's previously defensive-minded side.

Spotting previously untapped potential in a player had been a feature of Revie's previous eight-and-half years in the job. "Don had a real eye for where a player's best position was," recalls Eddie Gray. "It started in the early days with Norman Hunter being moved from inside-forward to central defence and Terry Cooper converted from outside-left to left-back. Johnny Giles had been an outside right at Manchester United but Don wanted him as a central midfielder, while Billy was also moved inside. All of those players went on to be great players in the positions Don felt suited their ability best. I was also fortunate to play for Don, who moved me from wing-half to outside-left. People forget that when I scored the two goals against Burnley in 1970, it was from midfield because that was where I played. It was only later when Don wanted to improve his attacking options that he came to me in training and said he wanted to try something different with me at outside-left."

Revie's more attack-minded approach was illustrated in his side keeping just eight clean sheets in 1969-70, compared to the 24 that had played such a major part in the previous season's league title triumph. It was also reflected in a European Cup debut that saw Lyn Oslo thrashed 10-0 at Elland Road in the first leg with a further six goals without reply landing in the net of the Norwegian part-timers in the return. Ferencvaros, the Hungarian side beaten by Leeds in the 1968 Inter-Cities Fairs Cup final, were dispatched 6-0 on aggregate in the next round to set up a two-legged meeting with Standard Liege – a pairing made particularly memorable by a Leeds director announcing on radio, 'We have been drawn against Standard Liege and the first leg will be in Standard'. Thankfully, the member of staff in charge of United's travel plans knew exactly where Liege was and the players duly turned up at the Sclessin Stadium only to be refused entry by an over-zealous Belgian gateman. After 10 uncomfortable minutes, Revie's patience finally snapped and he leapt off the team coach before pulling the gate open himself to allow his team to enter. The plan had clearly been to unsettle the visitors but it didn't work as Peter Lorimer ensured Leeds returned with a precious 1-0 advantage. A mischievous suggestion by his players that the Belgians be made to walk the final 100 yards to Elland Road ahead of the return was not acted upon by Revie but his team, nevertheless, progressed to the semi-finals with another one-goal victory.

By then, Revie's dream of an unprecedented treble was well and truly on. Just three days after confirming a place in the last four of the European Cup, United won 2-1 at Wolves to move to within three points of Everton at the top of Division One with six games still to play. The FA Cup had also been a fruitful competition with Swansea Town, Sutton United, Mansfield Town and Swindon Town being beaten en route to a semi-final meeting with Manchester United. Due to the looming World Cup finals in Mexico and the insistence that Alf Ramsey's side be given as long as possible to acclimatise, the semi-final date had been set unusually early for March 14. With the fixtures backing up as Leeds chased glory on three fronts, Revie's men badly needed the maxim of being '90 minutes from Wembley' to come true. What they got instead was a tie that would only be settled after two draining replays, Billy Bremner scoring the goal at Burnden Park that eventually booked United's place in the final at Wembley after the first two games had finished goalless. Bremner had discovered ahead of kick-off that he had won the Footballer of the Year award.

Fatigue had, however, now well and truly set in and something had to give. It came two days after the semi-final replay triumph in the form of a 3-1 home defeat to Southampton in the league that, coupled with Everton beating Chelsea at Goodison Park on the same day, all but ended any hopes of wrestling top spot away from the Merseysiders. Leeds, jaded and with Revie claiming six of his players had been diagnosed with mental and physical exhaustion, were becoming the victims of their own success. Peter Lorimer, for one, believes

Revie had asked too much of his players by chasing an unprecedented treble. "The problem was that while Don would say he had 16 internationals in the squad," he says, "the reality was he wanted to play the same XI every week. I think it was his biggest failing. Lads like Rod Belfitt and Mick Bates should have played a lot more than they did in the lesser competitions."

As if to prove Lorimer's point, a glance at the appearance chart for the 1969-70 season shows eight players featuring in 50 or more of the 62 games with another four's tally being in the mid-40s. "Don should also have taken into account another couple of factors when picking his team for some games," insists Lorimer. "The pitches were very heavy and nothing like the pitches today where they are so smooth you could play snooker on them. We would go to Derby's Baseball Ground in winter and there would hardly be a blade of grass on it. Playing on such heavy pitches made it even more tiring to play 50 or 60 games each season, as did all the travelling. When we were competing in Europe, it could take the best part of 24 hours to get home and then we would have to prepare for the weekend's game. It eventually took its toll."

Two days after the shock home defeat to Southampton, Leeds travelled to Derby County on Easter Monday with what was effectively a reserve team. Revie's reasoning was simple, with a European Cup semi-final first leg against Celtic just 48 hours away his players needed to rest. It sounds a reasonable argument but Football League secretary Alan Hardaker, a long-time Revie adversary, showed little sympathy. Over the previous two years, Hardaker had tired of pleas to postpone fixtures for what he saw as Revie's own ends and Leeds were fined £5,000 for the weakened team that lost 4-1 at the Baseball Ground.

Just one win from the final six games, secured against Burnley by two goals from Eddie Gray in midfield that included the mazy dribble that 25 years later would be voted the club's best of all time, meant United finished second. The focus had now switched to the 'Battle of Britain' double-header against Celtic. The first leg at Elland Road was United's 57th game of an arduous season and it showed as Celtic won much more comfortably than the 1-0 final score suggested. Gray did hit the crossbar but, in truth, Leeds were lucky to still be in the tie ahead of the return in Glasgow a fortnight later.

Unbelievably by the standards of the modern game when even two games a week can be enough to incur the wrath of top managers, United were back in action the following night against West Ham United and again two days later at home to Burnley. Still bridling at being fined for playing a weakened team at Derby, Revie did select a handful of first team players – a decision that backfired spectacularly as Paul Reaney suffered a broken leg in the 2-2 draw at Upton Park. Not only was the lightning quick full-back out of the crucial European Cup semi-final second leg against Celtic, he would also miss the FA Cup final against Chelsea and the World Cup. He did not return until the following December.

It was a shattering blow for both player and club but Leeds re-grouped and headed back to London just over a week later for the Cup final. With the two previous visits by United to Wembley hardly setting the football world alight, the neutrals could have been forgiven for thinking another dour affair lay ahead against Chelsea. In fact, the match turned out to be a classic. On a pitch covered in 100 tonnes of sand after the Horse of the Year show had ripped up the surface, Leeds rediscovered the attacking verve of earlier in the season. An unusually weak Jack Charlton header gave United a fortuitous lead that was cancelled out just before half-time by an equally daft goal, Gary Sprake allowing a tame shot from Peter Houseman to squirm under his body. Leeds, with Eddie Gray tormenting David Webb at full-back, regained control after half-time and duly went ahead for the second time through Mick Jones. Just seven minutes remained but any hopes of the Cup coming to Leeds for the first time were dashed when Ian Hutchinson equalised. Thirty more minutes could not separate the two clubs to make the 1970 final the first since Wembley had been built to require a replay, the last thing United needed. Forty eight hours later, this most unrelenting and punishing of seasons continued with a trip to Glasgow and a European Cup semi-final second leg tie against Celtic that had been switched from Parkhead to Hampden Park to satisfy the demand for tickets.

A crowd of 136,505 poured through the turnstiles to set a new record for a European Cup tie. Among the Glaswegian throng was Frank Gray, the then 15-year-old brother of Eddie and future Leeds United player. The Scot recalls: "All the family were mad Celtic fans so even though I had been visiting Leeds since the age of eight or nine to see Eddie and was in the process of signing for the club, I still wanted Celtic to win. I was in what is known as the 'Celtic End' at Hampden and the noise was unbelievable as the players came out of the tunnel. There must have been 50,000 in that end alone. The Celtic fans were all confident after winning the first leg 1-0 that we would be going to the final."

Predictably, Celtic tore into the visiting Sassenachs but it was Leeds who took the lead on 14 minutes through a 25-yard rocket from Billy Bremner that flew past Evan Williams in the home goal. Hampden Park fell silent, save for a few hundred Englishmen brave enough to make the trip north of the border. Revie's son Duncan recalls: "Billy's goal put us right back in the tie but I'll admit to never having felt as lonely as when jumping up to celebrate that goal – even though there were 136,000 people there."

Leeds, already missing the dependable Reaney, suffered a further blow six minutes into the second-half when goalkeeper Sprake had to be stretchered off following a collision with John Hughes. By then, Celtic's lead had been restored by a Hughes strike and Sprake's replacement, David Harvey, was unable to do anything about the host team's second goal of the night when Bobby Murdoch finished from close range. The noise levels as the Glaswegians celebrated a second European Cup final appearance in four seasons were such that none of the players could hear each other on the pitch in the closing stages.

Going out in the last four was a huge disappointment to Revie, as son Duncan remembers: "Dad always felt his team should have won more trophies and the one that really rankled was the European Cup. He won the rest but the European Cup was his Holy Grail and he came so close. Dad loved winning the league title twice and the FA Cup, but without the European Cup it was as if something was missing. That team certainly deserved to win it but the fixture pile-up in the spring of 1970 just proved too much."

The 3-1 aggregate defeat to Celtic also shattered Revie's dream of competing in the inaugural World Club Championship, FIFA having floated a few months earlier the idea of six teams doing battle to be crowned the best team on the planet. Revie was not alone in hugely fancying the chance of representing Europe in such a prestigious tournament, chairman Percy Woodward's response in the *Yorkshire Evening Post* to the suggestion being: "What a terrific idea, and one which I'm sure my board will look favourably on – if we win the European Cup." Defeat at Hampden Park ended any such hopes, though any regret at missing out on the new World Club Championship was soon banished when the plan was dropped by FIFA as the status quo of the champions of Europe and South America going head-to-head for the Intercontinental Cup continued. It would be almost 30 years before the World Club Championship became reality, the first tournament becoming infamous in England as the reason for Manchester United failing to defend the FA Cup in favour of flying out to Brazil to compete.

Defeated by Celtic but determined to rescue reward from the wreckage of an audacious assault on three trophies, Leeds returned to England and began preparations for the FA Cup final replay against Chelsea at Old Trafford on April 29. The league game with Manchester City scheduled for the same night was pulled forward 11 days, while all nine Leeds players selected for international duty on the weekend before the Cup final replay were released from their respective squads.

Even so, it was still a tired United party that travelled across the Pennines for their 62nd – and now most important – game of the season. Eighteen days on from escaping with a draw at Wembley, Chelsea made a tactical switch that saw Eddie Gray, man of the match in the first game, marked by Ron 'Chopper' Harris as opposed to David Webb. Since the drawn final, the feeling within the Blues' dressing room had grown that Leeds had missed their chance. Alan Hudson had been an integral part of Chelsea's Cup run only to miss the final through injury. He recalls: "You have to remember that everyone hated Leeds back then. We certainly did at Chelsea and I realised after signing for Stoke a couple of years after the 1970 Cup final that they felt the same, too. It gave the Chelsea lads that extra incentive to win the Cup final to go with the confidence that had grown since the first game at Wembley."

The thinking behind Harris' switch to full-back was made clear in the opening stages when he deliberately scythed down Eddie Gray, restricting the Scot's movement for the rest of the game. Despite that, Leeds went in front through Mick Jones only for Chelsea, just as at Wembley, to show tremendous resilience by equalising 12 minutes from the end of normal time courtesy of a Peter Osgood header. Then, as the tackles became even more ferocious and players from both sides squared up to each other, David Webb gained retribution for his tormenting at the feet of Eddie Gray under the Twin Towers by heading in the extra-time winner.

The Leeds dressing room was devastated. Nine months on from Revie setting his side the target of an unprecedented treble, they had ended the season with nothing. Unlike future years when refereeing controversy or just downright bad luck could be blamed, this time it seemed the damage had been self-inflicted. Certainly, Revie's insistence on chasing every available honour at Leeds is held up by former members of his team as a major reason why the team never got its just rewards. Jack Charlton says: "We should have won a lot more than we did, no question. I think even our critics would agree with that. But Don going for every tournament we entered meant our resources were spread too thinly at the vital stage of a season."

Revie's son Duncan admits failing to prioritise during the season when Leeds went so close to achieving greatness was a factor in the club ending the season empty-handed. But he also makes a valid point on behalf of his Dad. "With hindsight, he would have done things differently – he admitted as much later in life. But, in the case of 1970, which competition do you leave out? Is it the league? Or do you say, 'Let's forget the FA Cup?' Or do you sacrifice the European Cup? It would have been a tough decision, no matter which way you look at it."

Chapter 12

The Boss

After the heartache of missing out on three trophies in the space of a month, Leeds United's dejected players and management could have been forgiven for wanting to get as far away as possible from football once the 1970 close season was underway. For five members of Don Revie's Leeds, however, this proved an impossibility as the World Cup finals in Mexico were looming large. Allan Clarke, Terry Cooper, Jack Charlton and Norman Hunter had all been named in Alf Ramsey's 23-man squad and joined up with the rest of the England party once the FA Cup final replay against Chelsea was out of the way. Paul Madeley was also offered a late berth by Ramsey but, realising his chances of featuring were slim at best, he declined. Completing the Leeds contingent heading to Mexico, therefore, was Les Cocker, Revie's loyal lieutenant who for the past nine years had been on the England coaching staff. Typically, in terms of the finale to the season they had just endured, all five of the Leeds representatives would suffer further heartache in South America as West Germany came from two goals behind to knock Ramsey's men out at the quarter-final stage.

For the rest of the United squad, the summer brought unwelcome time to reflect on where it had all gone wrong and it was a subdued squad that returned to pre-season training for the traditional running sessions around Roundhay Park.

Don Revie's own spirits and enthusiasm had been partly restored by a stint as an expert summariser for BBC Television at the World Cup. Watching an exuberant Brazil lift the Jules Rimet trophy in style may not have exactly been a life-changing 'Road to Damascus' moment for the Leeds manager, but it did start to colour his own thinking. Revie, named Manager of the Year for a second consecutive season despite his side failing to win anything, realised the implications such an attack-minded team's success on the greatest stage of all would have for English football and his Leeds team in particular. The 1969-70 season had already seen Revie's side lose some of their renowned conservatism but it would be another year or so before he finally allowed his players the freedom they craved. Nevertheless, he could see the direction the game was heading and knew Leeds could not afford to be left behind.

A far more pressing concern, however, in July, 1970, was how to lift the spirits of a squad still bearing the mental scars of those devastating final few weeks of the previous season. It would be a huge challenge and a real test of the leadership qualities honed during Revie's career as both a player and a manager. One supporter who felt Leeds had the ideal manager to pull the players out of their gloom and depression was the club president. The Earl of Harewood says: "When I first met Don, I realised immediately that here was a man who was a leader. Everyone at Leeds United looked up to him. We became good friends and the way everyone from the tea-ladies to the captain of the team had faith in Don reminded me of a particular commanding officer I was fortunate to serve under in the War." The mention of the Second World War by the seventh Earl of Harewood, a first cousin to Queen Elizabeth II, is a telling one. Born George Henry Hubert Lascelles, the Old Etonian had become a captain in the Grenadier Guards after leaving King's College, Cambridge. He was wounded and captured in battle. Due to his Royal links, he was sent to Colditz on the direct orders of Adolf Hitler. "This commanding officer that Don's leadership skills reminded me of was a man who, funnily enough, I didn't like very much at all," recalls the Earl. "But he was a great leader, no question. We all believed in him and had total faith in what he said. You must have that to make things happen. I saw the same leadership qualities in Don at Leeds and the way his players listened to his every word reminded me very much of how I was with my commanding officer. Don could persuade those players to try anything that he thought possible – and even if the players initially thought it beyond them, they would still definitely attempt it. Don once said to me, 'Norman Hunter would run through a brick wall for me – but only once'. They were devoted to him because they trusted him."

The English football season may have been a long way from the battlefields of the Second World War but Revie appreciated he would need all his powers of persuasion to prepare his troops for the fast-approaching campaign. As if to illustrate his own stomach for the fight, Revie swatted away Birmingham City's attempts to lure him to St Andrews with a £100,000 four-year contract and quickly got down to work.

Revie displayed his faith in the players who had gone so close the previous season by refusing to enter the transfer market, the only movement during the summer being out of Elland Road as Albert Johanneson joined York City on a free. A key player in the side promoted to the top flight six years earlier, the South African had made just five appearances in the previous two seasons due to a combination of injury and Eddie Gray's blossoming talent.

Revie felt the biggest threats to his side in 1970-71 would come from Tottenham Hotspur and Everton. The manager's vote of confidence in not having felt the need to make a summer signing meant Leeds were able to shake off the disappointment of the previous April by winning their first five league games. A 3-2 victory over reigning champions Everton at Elland Road proved particularly satisfying for Revie. United dropped their first point at Arsenal in a goalless draw – a result that would take on huge significance come the season's end - before an Allan Clarke goal after just 21 seconds of the home game against Chelsea exacted more revenge for the previous season as the Cup holders were beaten 1-0.

Such was the consistency shown by Leeds in the league that they would lose just once, a 3-0 aberration at Stoke City in September, before the turn of the year. Only Bertie Mee's Arsenal, fresh from having beaten Anderlecht in the 1970 Inter-Cities Fairs Cup final, seemed capable of lasting the pace with Leeds. Defeats to Spurs and Liverpool in the first two league games of 1971 at Elland Road then handed the initiative to the Gunners only for Revie to display his tremendous motivational skills again as Leeds hit back to win five of their next six games. By the first weekend of April, United were six points clear of an Arsenal side proving to be surprisingly resilient thanks to a happy knack of scoring decisive late goals. Two weeks later and the Gunners had cut the leaders' advantage to two points when West Bromwich Albion arrived at Elland Road. The *Match of the Day* cameras had also made the trip north, hoping to capture more drama in what was turning out to be a thrilling title race. The producers would not be disappointed.

Revie's Leeds went into the game as overwhelming favourites, West Brom not having won away from home in 16 attempts. A United win seemed a formality to everyone but those in the away dressing room. John Kaye was Albion's captain for one of the most extraordinary matches ever shown by *Match of the Day*. He recalls: "The thing that really fired us up that day was Don Revie on the television before the game. He was being interviewed on either *Football Focus* or *On the Ball* at lunchtime and we were watching at our hotel. I can't recall his exact words but he was, basically, suggesting Leeds should win easily. He said something like, 'We could get five today'. Well, we weren't having that. In a way, Revie did us a favour as we didn't need a team-talk that afternoon. We were determined to prove him wrong."

Angered by Revie's pre-match confidence, West Brom had raced into a shock lead and were still in front when referee Ray Tinkler blew for half-time. Revie got to work on his players during the interval, stressing the need for patience and his belief that by full-time their title challenge would be back on course. What Revie did not know, however, was that Tinkler was about to write himself into the history books with one of the most controversial decisions of all time. A misplaced pass by Norman Hunter was the catalyst as the ball rebounded into the Leeds half off Tony Brown. With Colin Suggett sauntering back towards halfway and standing a full 10 yards offside, linesman Bill Troupe immediately flagged. The home defence stopped, as did Brown as he raced into the Leeds half to collect the ball. Under today's laws, play would be waved on, Suggett being deemed not to be interfering with play. But, in 1971, it was a clear case of offside. Imagine the horror, therefore, on the faces of the home players as referee Tinkler suddenly waved play on and Brown, his initial embarrassment soon giving way to a sense of glee, burst into a sprint before squaring the ball for Jeff Astle to tap into an empty net. Elland Road was outraged as the players surrounded Tinkler. Several fans came on to the field, as did Revie to plead his team's case but the referee was adamant. The goal stood. Viewers watching at home later that night on *Match of the Day* were treated to a breathless commentary from Barry Davies. 'Leeds will go mad,' said the BBC man. 'And they have every justification for going mad!'

John Kaye admits to being relieved when the police came on the pitch to arrest the interlopers from the terraces. "It was a frightening situation," he says, "though it would probably have been worse today as more of them would have come on. The Leeds players were all protesting as well but, thankfully for us, the referee would not be swayed." As for the Baggies' second goal, Kaye is adamant there was nothing wrong with it. "I know Leeds still insist to this day that the goal was offside but I don't necessarily agree with that. Colin Suggett had closed Gary Sprake down when he rolled the ball out to Norman Hunter. When Norman's pass was then blocked by Tony Brown, Colin was still standing offside but, in my opinion, not interfering with play. Under today's rules, he definitely wouldn't be. Browny then ran through as the Leeds players stopped and squared it for Jeff Astle to score."

An indignant Leeds pulled a goal back through Allan Clarke but it did nothing to prevent the initiative in the title race swinging the way of Arsenal, who had taken over at the top on goal difference. The recriminations went on for months, or, in some cases, even years with just the mention of Ray Tinkler's name today being enough to get a Leeds fan of a certain vintage frothing at the mouth. The referee, for his part, was adamant in the immediate aftermath of the game that the correct decision had been made. Tinkler told Monday's *Yorkshire Evening Post*: 'He was in an offside position and the linesman flagged, but he was not interfering with play. So, no offence was committed and I could let play go on. I was perfectly correct in doing so.' Tinkler adopted an identical stance on Sunday's *Big Match* programme when interviewed by Brian Moore.

Nevertheless, the official from Boston, Lincolnshire, was withdrawn from the following Tuesday's Fourth Division game between York City and Oldham Athletic in an attempt to let the furore die down. Any hopes the football authorities had of the saga slipping out of the headlines were soon dashed, though, as Leeds united in its condemnation of Tinkler. Revie made an impassioned plea for the advent of professional referees, pointing out that paying part-time officials a match fee of £10.50 was an outdated practice in an era when one decision could cost a club tens of thousands of pounds.

The behaviour of the Leeds fans was also in the spotlight following the West Brom defeat with linesman Colin Cartlich having been felled by a missile. Cars and shops outside Elland Road were also damaged as the 36,812 crowd left, while police had to disperse around 100 fans waiting for Tinkler in the car park after the game. The instances of hooliganism would have serious repercussions for the club once the following season got underway.

Once the initial furore over Tinkler's decision had eased, Revie had the task of getting his aggrieved players' minds back on the title race. The championship was, undoubtedly, now Arsenal's to lose but with Bertie Mee's side still to visit Elland Road all hope was not yet lost. A controversial Jack Charlton goal that, ironically considering the circumstances of the West Brom defeat, came with the big defender standing offside was enough to beat their only rival for the title 1-0 in the penultimate game of the season. And with Southampton dispatched 3-0 and Nottingham Forest 2-0 either side of the win over the Gunners, it meant the League Championship race would go down to the final game. Leeds, their 42 games now over, could only cross their fingers while taking part in a testimonial for Hull City's Chris Chilton at Boothferry Park and hope Tottenham Hotspur would do them a huge favour by winning the north London derby. Nearly 52,000 crammed into White Hart Lane as Arsenal chased the goalless draw or victory that would be enough to clinch the title, Leeds needing either a score draw or a Spurs win to snatch top spot. As it turned out, a goal from Ray Kennedy in the closing stages was enough to seal the first half of what would, five days later, become a famous league and cup double for the Gunners as Liverpool were beaten 2-1 at Wembley.

Leeds United's own Cup campaign had ended in rather more ignominious fashion when Colchester United of the Fourth Division performed one of the most famous giant-killings of all-time. Revie's side had travelled to Layer Road three points clear at the top of the Football League and not even the Essex club's supporters held out much hope of an upset. For a start, six of the home team's starting XI were over 30. Seventy-four places also separated the two clubs in the Football League. Such pessimism did not, though, deter the airmen at RAF Wattisham from welcoming the Leeds party after their charter flight had touched down with a blackboard reading 'Colchester 2 Leeds 0'. One man who did genuinely believe Revie's Leeds were beatable was Colchester manager Dick Graham. Not averse to a few psychological tricks of his own such as surrounding the pitch with chairs to make it look smaller, Graham also had a shrewd eye when it came to tactics. Throughout the week leading up to the fifth round tie, the U's manager had his wide men practicing their crossing due to a belief Gary Sprake would struggle in the air if put under sufficient pressure. Practice did, indeed, make perfect for Colchester come the day of the game as Ray Crawford, who before the game had told sceptical reporters, 'I always play well against Jack Charlton', netted twice inside the opening 28 minutes. David Simmons adding a third shortly after half-time finally jolted Leeds into life, Norman Hunter and Johnny Giles quickly reducing Colchester's advantage to a solitary goal. However, no matter what Revie's men threw at the mid-table Fourth Division side in the final 17 minutes, they stood firm to claim a famous Cup scalp. United's critics rejoiced and it was a chastened Revie who flew back to Leeds from Essex with his players. Chairman Percy Woodward took defeat so badly that, on the return flight from Essex, he suggested to *Telegraph & Argus* football writer John Wray that teams from the lower divisions should not be allowed to take part in the Cup.

With Sheffield United having knocked Leeds out of the League Cup in the second round, the prospect of another season without a trophy was looming large. Thankfully for Revie, Europe had once again proved to be a profitable hunting ground for his team.

Back in the Inter-Cities Fairs Cup following their failure to land either the European Cup or league title in 1970, Leeds had swept aside Norwegian amateurs Sarpsborg and Dynamo Dresden in the opening two rounds. Less pleasing for Revie were the attendances for the two home legs with just 19,283 witnessing the 5-0 hammering of Sarpsborg and 21,292 a narrow 1-0 win over the East Germans. Crowd levels at Elland Road had frustrated Revie for some time, his desire to be the biggest and best club in the country extending to numbers coming through the turnstiles. The ground would be packed for certain games, most notably the titanic tussles with great rivals such as Manchester

United and Liverpool. But there were also plenty of other occasions when Leeds were watched by a crowd that paled into insignificance compared to their rivals. In the 1971-72 season, for instance, Leeds came within a whisker of winning a league and cup double but the average crowd of 35,636 was lower than those boasted by Arsenal, Chelsea, Everton, Liverpool, Manchester City, Manchester United and Tottenham Hotspur. Even in the club's second league title winning success of 1973-74, almost 86,000 fewer fans watched the 21 league games at Elland Road than at Old Trafford as Manchester United were relegated. The feeling that Leeds was a rugby league city, a notion that was never truly dispelled until David O'Leary's ill-fated reign as manager when Elland Road was sold out every week, continued to gnaw away at Revie.

The crowd of 25,843 that turned out for the visit of Sparta Prague in the Fairs Cup third round shortly before Christmas, 1971, did little to appease the manager. On the pitch, however, he could have few complaints as the Czechoslovakians were comprehensively thrashed 6-0 en route to a 9-2 aggregate passage to the quarter-finals. The competition resumed in March with a home tie against Portuguese side Vitoria Setubal. Just 90 seconds had elapsed when the visitors went in front and it required a Peter Lorimer special from 25 yards to get Leeds back on level terms. The home side began to exert more and more control after half-time but it took a hugely controversial penalty award by East German referee Gunter Manning for handball against Carlos Cardoso for United to earn a 2-1 victory. The Setubal players were incensed and jostled the referee, an action that prompted the visitors bench to be pelted with missiles before police moved in to restore order. Once the furore had died down, Johnny Giles kept his cool to score from the spot.

Ahead of the return, Revie decided his Leeds players should be based in the fishing resort of Sesimbra. It was here where news filtered through that the club had announced a profit of £172,000. Further good news followed as Peter Lorimer extended his scoring run to seven consecutive matches as the second leg finished 1-1. The United squad were flying back to Yorkshire when the semi-final draw threw up a mouth-watering tie – Leeds v Liverpool. Revie took a major gamble in the first leg at Anfield by selecting a fit-again Billy Bremner for his first game in three months. The manager was so worried over whether his captain was up to the task that he organised a behind-closed doors friendly against Bradford on the morning of the game. It was only after Bremner had come through that Revie selected him for the Fairs Cup tie on Merseyside just a few hours later. The gamble paid off when United's talisman netted the only goal of the game midway through the second-half. It was the club's 100th of the campaign but, more importantly, enough to earn a place in the final when the return at Elland Road – happily for Revie, played in front of 40,462 fans – ended goalless.

The Fairs Cup may have lacked the prestige of the European Cup but a second final appearance provided, with memories of the league title being snatched from their grasp by Arsenal still fresh, one last chance to avoid finishing a second successive season empty-handed. Juventus, who had once lured away Leeds' then greatest footballer John Charles, were the opponents with the first leg scheduled for May 26 in Turin. This being Leeds, once again little ran smoothly as a six-hour thunderstorm over the Italian city left the Stadio Comunale pitch under water. Peter Lorimer recalls: "The pitch looked more like a lake and the game should never have started. The ball wouldn't run properly and a lot of the time would just stop dead. It became dangerous." Referee Laurens Van Raven eventually admitted defeat six minutes into the second-half and abandoned the tie, which was rearranged for 48 hours later. Juventus, whose Serie A season was still going on, generously offered to play both legs in Leeds if the rain failed to stop but, in the end, the weather improved and the game went ahead.

The Italians adapted quicker to the still heavy pitch and went ahead in the 27th minute through Roberto Bettega. Paul Madeley equalised shortly after half-time only for future England manager Fabio Capello to restore Juventus' lead with a ferocious shot past Gary Sprake from 20 yards. Once again, however, Leeds dug deep and substitute Mick Bates netted a precious equaliser 13 minutes from time. The game had been preceded by a rare row between Revie and his players, which was triggered by the initial postponement on the Wednesday. Peter Lorimer recalls: "The first leg was rearranged for the Friday night and Don wanted us to return to our hotel in the hills above Turin rather than meet up with the wives and girlfriends in the city on the Wednesday night as planned. Don's thinking was that because the game had been postponed, we should also postpone getting together with the wives by two days. Paul Madeley was the first to say he was not happy. Paul was speaking common sense. We went away before every game, which meant our families were hardly seeing us at all. It was no fun for our wives as they were left sitting at home with the kids on their own five nights a week. All we wanted was for Don to allow us some time together, as had been planned before the game was postponed. But Don was having none of it. In the end, he won and we drove back to the hills. But Don sulked about the lads standing up to him and it created an atmosphere. I think it was the first time Don started to think, 'These lads are growing away from me and are losing faith'. We weren't losing faith at all, though we did think it stupid that we weren't allowed to see our families."

Domestic arrangements aside, the Leeds party flew back to Yorkshire in fine heart ahead of the return six days later. By now, June had arrived and Elland Road was bathed in sunshine as the two teams entered the field. Allan Clarke then settled home nerves with a 12th minute strike only for the Italians to equalise through Pietro Anastasi. Play raged from end to end as tempers boiled over in a second-half clash that saw Fabio Capello and several of his team-mates square up to their Leeds counterparts in front of the Scratching Shed. Eventually, the 42,483 crowd's pleadings to referee Rudi Glockner were answered as the East German blew the final whistle and Leeds celebrated winning the Fairs Cup for a second time. Even in the euphoria, however, there was a feeling that United were under-achieving considering the undoubted talent in their ranks. Eddie Gray, injured in the postponed first leg, said: "I am convinced that, had we been in the European Cup that season as opposed to the Fairs Cup, we would have had a very good chance of winning it. The team was maturing and seemed better equipped for success. We were a good team, as was shown by going to Liverpool and inflicting their first defeat at Anfield in a year and then beating a very good Juventus side over two legs."

Chapter 13

The Great Entertainers

If ever a football club needed a public image makeover it was Leeds United in the early 1970s. Despite having challenged at the top of English football since the middle of the previous decade, Leeds were an unpopular side, to put it mildly. Where neutrals would cheer Manchester United or Liverpool on against European opposition, the only public rejoicing surrounding Don Revie's side would come with a shock defeat. Their standing as the club everyone loved to hate had been evident in February, 1971, when the country's response to Leeds United being knocked out of the FA Cup fifth round by Fourth Division Colchester United had been to poke fun at the humbled giants.

The 'Dirty Leeds' tag that had followed the side out of the Second Division and into the top flight was proving difficult to shake off. It meant few were ambivalent towards Leeds, the hatred many rival supporters felt towards Bremner, Giles, Hunter et al continuing long after Revie and his team had left Elland Road. In 1990, and almost 12 months on from Revie's death, Howard Wilkinson's Leeds side won promotion from the Second Division at Bournemouth amid shameful scenes of rioting outside Dean Court. Leeds' by now notorious supporters, who seemed to take literally the 'Keep Fighting' sign Revie had once hung in the Elland Road dressing room, had turned up in their thousands without tickets for the Bank Holiday weekend game and fought running battles with the police. The back page of one Sunday tabloid newspaper simply read 'Leeds Scum Are Back'. To some, it was an intentionally ambiguous headline with the 'Scum' alluded to quite possibly referring to the return to Division One of the club itself rather than the hooligans who had wreaked havoc across the Dorset town. The condemnation in other newspapers was equally fierce with one double page spread being titled 'Say the Leeds and you're snarling', a clever play on the slogan 'Say the Leeds and you're smiling' made famous by George 'Arthur Daley' Cole in a series of adverts for the Leeds Permanent Building Society in the 1980s.

Don Revie, by the summer of 1971, deeply resented the negative publicity surrounding his team. OK, he could understand, at a push, how some may have found Leeds a functional side in those early seasons that followed promotion. But, as Revie would bemoan to anyone willing to listen, his United team had moved with the times. Leeds had finished runners-up in 1969-70 and 1970-71 playing a much more expansive style of football. Revie could not understand why the critics refused to acknowledge the shift of emphasis. Personal recognition had come his way in the form of two Manager of the Year awards and an OBE from Buckingham Palace. But still his players' considerable talents were not being acknowledged by the wider public, something he was determined to change.

Unfortunately for Revie, his hopes of engineering more positive publicity during the close season were scuppered as the fall-out from the Ray Tinkler debacle against West Bromwich Albion continued. After the pitch invasion that had led to the police having to deal with a number of interlopers determined to confront Tinkler, the Football Association launched an immediate investigation. Revie and United chairman Percy Woodward gave evidence to the Disciplinary Commission, both apologising for their reported post-match comments that Tinkler's performance had played a major part in the disturbances that followed. Revie then went away on holiday with his wife Elsie, confident the FA would take the mitigating circumstances into account before making their judgement. Unfortunately for both Leeds and the Revies' holiday plans, the punishment, when it arrived, was swingeing. Revie's son Duncan recalls: "Mum and Dad had gone away to Spain for their annual two-week holiday and were relaxing on the beach one morning. Suddenly, there was a shout from the hotel bar of, 'Telephone call for Mr Revie'. It was a long time before mobile phones would be invented so Dad trudged off to answer the call, while Mum stayed on the beach. Mum said a few minutes went by before Dad marched back down the beach and she could see from his face that all was not well. He got to her, started packing up his towel and said, 'Elsie, they've closed the ground, we've got to go back and sort it all out'. And that was the end of their holiday. They had only been there three days."

The FA had come down hard on Leeds, ordering Elland Road to be closed for the opening four games of the season. The club was also fined £500 and ordered to compensate visiting clubs for the loss of gate money from playing at a neutral venue. Unlike today, when the home side keeps the lion's share of the receipts, in 1971 the cash was shared between the two teams. The United manager and chairman were also censured for their post-match comments and warned about their future conduct.

Revie, now back in situ at Elland Road after his abandoned holiday, was faced with having to find alternative venues for the 'home' games against Wolverhampton Wanderers, Tottenham Hotspur, Newcastle United and Crystal

Palace. In the end, he at least managed to keep United in Yorkshire with Huddersfield's Leeds Road ground staging the visits of Wolves and Palace. Hull also hosted its first top-flight match when Boothferry Park was used for the Spurs game, while Sheffield Wednesday's Hillsborough was the venue for the Newcastle encounter. With the fixture compilers having also handed United two away games against Manchester City and Sheffield United in the opening weeks of the 1971-72 season, it added up to a difficult start for a team harbouring hopes of another assault on the league title. The one characteristic that Revie's side were renowned for, however, was an ability to respond positively to adversity. They did just that by winning four and drawing two of those opening seven matches. Only the trip to Bramall Lane three days into the new campaign resulted in defeat, the Blades running out surprisingly comfortable winners.

United's exile from Elland Road ended in mid-September when Peter Lorimer clinched a 1-0 victory over Liverpool to start an incredible run that would see just two further points dropped on home soil for the rest of the season. It was, however, a different story on the road as United followed the early 3-0 defeat at Sheffield United by losing to Huddersfield Town, Coventry City, Arsenal and Southampton before the turn of the year. By then, Leeds' involvement in the Inter-Cities Fairs Cup and the League Cup had also come to an end with the exit in Europe coming in unusual circumstances. The holders had been drawn against SK Lierse in the first round, the first leg in Belgium ending with a 2-0 victory for Revie's men. United's passage to the next round seemed assured only for a rare display of complacency to allow the Belgians to pull off a major shock. Out went several first choice players for the home leg as teenagers, goalkeeper John Shaw and forward Jimmy Mann, were handed their debuts in Europe. Even so, Leeds were still expected to make light work of an opposition featuring just seven full-time players. Three goals in six first half minutes changed all that, however, and Revie's response was to bring Gary Sprake on for Shaw and replace Mann with Norman Hunter during the half-time interval. Leeds needed to score at least twice to rescue the tie but it was the Belgians who went on to grab a fourth goal 10 minutes from the end through Peter Ressel.

Typically, United's humiliation was a source of amusement to the rest of English football - making Revie keener than ever to try and change the public perception of his team. His chance came in the unusual form of a 38-year-old illustrator and budding inventor. Paul Trevillion had made his name in the 1960s as the illustrator behind the *Roy of the Rovers* comic strip but had since branched out into sports marketing. He had been invited out to America by legendary American sports agent Mark McCormack in 1971 and the trip made a huge impression. Now back in England, Trevillion, who would later illustrate the popular 'You are the Ref' column in *The Observer*, had vowed to bring some of the US-style razzmatazz he had experienced at a Cleveland Indians baseball game to the Football League. His first choice was Tottenham Hotspur, the team he had supported since childhood, but Bill Nicholson was not keen. The Spurs manager did, however, recommend he contact Don Revie at Leeds. Trevillion recalls: "Bill listened to my ideas before saying 'it is not for me, but try Leeds because they need to entertain the public more – Don is a good manager and they can play a bit, but their image is poor'. I thought Bill was winding me up at first. Why would someone like Don Revie be interested? But Bill had praised Don and Leeds, which he didn't do much with anyone, so I thought I'd give it a go."

Paul Trevillion wrote to Revie at Elland Road, outlining his ideas and how they could help improve Leeds United's wretchedly poor public image. On the face of it, persuading a notoriously cautious and introverted manager to adopt gimmicks more commonly found at American sporting occasions seemed an impossible job. But Trevillion's timing was perfect and Revie, by now desperate for his team to be appreciated beyond the boundaries of West Yorkshire, replied with an invite to Elland Road. Trevillion recalls: "I had done a bit of work with Terry Cooper for an illustrated article in the *Sunday Times* so got him to have a word but, as it turned out, Don was receptive anyway. He really badly wanted his boys to get the recognition he felt they deserved, so much so that Don once said to me in a reflective moment, 'Why can't my boys get the praise Manchester United get?' He then added, 'Why is the country behind Liverpool and Manchester United in Europe but wants Leeds to lose? Just because my boys are competitive and win every second ball, they come in for criticism'."

Sitting in Revie's office at Elland Road, Trevillion began running through his innovative ideas. Leeds, he suggested, should develop a pre-match salute to all four sides of the ground. They should also start wearing sock-tags that could then be autographed and handed to kids after every game, while plastic footballs should be kicked into the crowd and the players' names emblazoned across the back of tracksuits that should be worn before every game. The list went on and on, Revie listening patiently to what his guest had to say. Trevillion says: "Don never interrupted as I rattled through my ideas and, at one stage, I thought I had lost him. I paused but he just said 'And...?' So, I carried on. We had initially broken the ice because of Don's love of golf. I knew Lee Trevino and Don was fascinated how I had once helped Trevino bring a bit of his character to golf. Basically, I gave Trevino a list of golf gags ahead of a major tournament and then a rundown of what holes the television cameras would be positioned at. Once he went out to play, Trevino would then make a point of stopping at the holes with cameras and reeling off a joke to the fans. The cameras loved it, so did the people sitting at home and Trevino's reputation as a character was made."

Revie continued to listen as Trevillion outlined how he would turn his players into superstars, something the Leeds manager was desperate to achieve. He paid special notice during the outlining of some psychological tricks Trevillion had dreamed up, such as getting the players to wear long sleeved shirts that could be rolled up if they went a goal behind to send a clear message of intent out to the opposition. Revie was, finally, convinced, though the rider attached to possibly adopting Trevillion's ideas was that Jack Charlton, a hugely influential figure in the dressing room, had to agree or the deal was off. Big Jack duly raised no objections, so the upcoming FA Cup quarter-final against Tottenham Hotspur was pencilled in as a suitable launch date. United had already knocked out Bristol Rovers, Liverpool (after a replay) and Cardiff City but Spurs, even at Elland Road, were expected to be a tough prospect. The Londoners had Pat Jennings, considered one of the best goalkeepers in the world, along with an outstanding forward line of Martin Peters, Alan Gilzean and Martin Chivers.

Revie almost lost his nerve during the last couple of days, arguing to Trevillion such an important game was not the right place for such a bold experiment. Eventually, though, he gave the go-ahead and the United players duly embarked on an elaborate pre-match training routine on the field half an hour or so before kick-off. They then returned to the dressing room for final instructions from their manager before, a couple of minutes ahead of the opposition, running back out on to the pitch. "The idea was to go out early, run to the centre circle and assemble in a line before waving to all four sides of Elland Road," explains Trevillion. "Then, after milking the applause, the players would go into one half of the field and allow the fans to boo the opposition as they emerged from the tunnel."

Leeds beat Spurs 2-1 but got almost as much press for the presentation as a stylish and impressive display. Some mocked and some accused United of arrogance, pointing out the wave to the crowd could incite trouble away from Elland Road. But others raved about the new practice and it quickly became an established part of pre-match preparations under Revie, much to the delight of their creator. Trevillion recalls: "People did start to appreciate Leeds United more and the players began to get more credit. Whether that was down to what happened on the field or what happened before a game, I don't know. Though a big part of me hopes it was a mixture of the two. Leeds had been constantly criticised for being mean and Don Revie painted as some sort of dour dictator, but the reality could not have been more different. Don was a very warm man and I have never known a laugh like his, nor the big bearhug he would give friends and family. He was completely different to my other hero manager of that era, Bill Nicholson at Spurs. Bill was hard and unapproachable, and he never gave any praise. Don would always talk up his boys and do anything for them. People on the outside criticised Leeds. But, to me, Don Revie's Leeds United were not a football club – more like a sporting version of the Waltons."

Billy Bremner or Jack Charlton living an existence similar to the wholesome and warm-hearted American family made famous by a fictional television series may be a difficult one for anyone who saw them play to visualise. But there was no doubting the close-knit atmosphere that existed at Elland Road as team-mates pushed each other forward on behalf of their manager. After all the heartache and disappointment of the past couple of years, here was an opportunity to make amends. Through to the FA Cup semi-finals and drawn against Second Division Birmingham City as Arsenal were paired with Stoke in the other tie, United's league challenge was also building nicely. Some of the football seen at Elland Road that season had been truly breathtaking with Manchester United being thrashed 5-1 on February 19. A fortnight later came the performance Revie rated among the very best during his time at Leeds, the 7-0 demolition of Southampton. Peter Lorimer's hat-trick together with two goals from Allan Clarke and a strike apiece by Mick Jones and Jack Charlton were responsible for the third seven-goal league victory under Revie, following identical scorelines against Lincoln City in 1961 and Chelsea six years later. But it was the manner in which Leeds played keep-ball during the closing stages that elevated the Southampton game to legendary status. For over a minute and more than 30 passes, United toyed and teased the Saints with a succession of back-heels, outrageous flicks and spell-binding feints that eventually moved *Match of the Day* commentator Barry Davies to proclaim, 'It's almost cruel'. Only Jack Charlton of the outfield players was not involved in the move, though not for the want of trying as he waved frantically for the ball only for his team-mates to claim not to have seen him. Johnny Giles would later wind up his team-mate by answering Big Jack's query of 'Why didn't you pass to me?' with the response, 'Because we wanted to keep it!'

Three-and-a-half weeks later and it was Nottingham Forest's turn to be put to the sword, losing 6-1 as Leeds made it five wins and a draw from six games. The plaudits Revie craved were now pouring in as even United's fiercest critics grudgingly praised the high standard of football on show. One match report pleased him in particular as it included a comparison between Leeds and the club Revie had been so in awe of almost 11 years earlier that he copied their all-white team colours. Alan Hoby of the *Sunday Express* wrote: 'I used to think in their golden heyday that Real Madrid, Manchester United, Celtic and Spurs represented poetic perfection in soccer. I used to think they were the best club sides I have ever seen, but I am beginning to wonder if Leeds, with their advanced tactics, their exciting elegance and flair, may outstrip them all.'

Supporters and players alike have, in the subsequent years, often debated what would have happened if Revie had given his side more freedom earlier. Johnny Giles, however, insists the manager's approach was spot on. "People praise the football we played once Don had allowed us to play with more freedom, while suggesting he should have done it a lot earlier," he says. "But what they forget is that the team needed patience to mature. We had been a young team in the mid to late 1960s, particularly after Bobby Collins left, and needed guidance. Gradually, the team matured and I think too much is read into this 'the shackles came off' line. It was more that Don could see we were now mature enough to make our own decisions – and that those decisions would be the right ones."

Having netted 17 goals in four straight home wins, March had been a profitable month with the visits to Leicester City and West Ham United also having yielded a point apiece. A 2-0 defeat at title rivals Derby County just 24 hours after the draw at Upton Park was a setback but Leeds responded in typical style by beating Huddersfield Town and Stoke City. Birmingham City's attempts to unsettle Leeds ahead of the FA Cup semi-final at Hillsborough by aping their new Trevillion-inspired pre-match warm-up routine back-fired as two goals from Mick Jones and a strike by Peter Lorimer sealed a comfortable passage to Wembley. The prospect of a league-cup double had again moved tantalisingly close.

Leeds were, however, brought down to earth just four days after the semi-final victory during a rearranged trip to Newcastle United. Revie was again unhappy with the now familiar fixture pile-up as his side chased honours but, according to Football League secretary Alan Hardaker, this latest instance had been entirely of the Leeds manager's own making. Newcastle had offered to play the game the previous month, the day after the lifting of a ban on midweek floodlit games. No night games had been allowed during the three-day week sanctions imposed by the Government in the wake of the miners going on strike. Hardaker passed on Newcastle's offer to Elland Road but Revie turned it down, saying Leeds did not play on Thursdays. It meant the game at St James' Park would eventually take place less than two-and-a-half weeks before the end of the season. Compared to the chaos of the 1969-70 season when Leeds were chasing the treble, the run-in did not seem too arduous – apart from the final game of the league campaign at Wolves being scheduled for just two days after the FA Cup final. Injuries were, though, beginning to mount with Terry Cooper having broken his leg in the victory over Stoke to join Gary Sprake on the sidelines. Fatigue was also becoming an increasing problem among the rest of the squad. The swagger that had seen Manchester United and Southampton humbled so emphatically just a few weeks earlier had disappeared.

Revie had attempted to strengthen his squad earlier in the season by signing Asa Hartford from West Bromwich Albion. An attacking midfielder, Hartford was hugely admired by Revie, who agreed a £177,000 fee with the Baggies. The transfer seemed to have been done only for Leeds to pull out at the eleventh hour after the player's medical revealed a heart defect. The club's caution would turn out to be misplaced with Hartford going on to enjoy a successful career and make 50 appearances for Scotland. Had the deal not been abandoned in haste, Hartford could have become an important weapon for Revie to fall back on during those crucial final weeks of the season. As it was, the Leeds manager travelled north to St James' Park with depleted resources and his side lost 1-0. The damage was not as serious as first feared, though, thanks to leaders Derby County losing to Manchester City on the same night. United remained three points behind the Rams in fourth place but had two games in hand. By the following Saturday, the picture at the top of the First Division had become a little clearer. Leeds' 1-0 win at West Brom meant they had two games remaining to overhaul a two-point advantage enjoyed by new leaders Manchester City, who had just completed their season. Derby and Liverpool, meanwhile, were both a point in front of Leeds, with one and two games outstanding respectively.

With the FA Cup final looming, Leeds again approached the Football League for assistance in rescheduling one of their remaining fixtures – namely the trip to Molineux that was due to take place just two days after the Wembley showpiece with Arsenal. Leeds wanted the game delayed by either 24 or 48 hours but, again, League secretary Alan Hardaker vetoed the suggestion on the grounds that it would impact on England's preparations for the following weekend's European Championships game against West Germany. Revie and Hardaker had clashed several times in the past, so the official's reluctance to help came as no surprise to those involved at Elland Road. Club president, the Earl of Harewood, recalls: "Hardaker was perfectly pleasant to me whenever we met but he and Don never got on. It continued for many, many years. It got so bad that anything Don asked for, whether it be a postponement or co-operation when he had become England manager, would be turned down straight away. He just didn't like Don. I never found out why." Others within the Leeds camp had their own views on why the Football League secretary was so unwilling to help their manager. Peter Lorimer says: "Don was the sort of man who could make enemies and, unfortunately for us, he made an enemy out of Hardaker. He would often try and use the rules to our advantage, such as when appealing against a red card for one of the lads, and Hardaker took exception."

Whatever the reason for the enmity between Revie and Hardaker, the League secretary was unmoved. Leeds would play Chelsea at home on the Monday, travel to Wembley for the Cup final against Arsenal on the Saturday and finish 48 hours later with a trip to Wolves. Three games in eight days would decide whether the name of Leeds United was to be added to those of Arsenal and Spurs in the exclusive list of clubs to have won the prestigious league and cup double since the turn of the century.

Goals from Billy Bremner and Mick Jones ensured the week that would decide United's destiny got off to a fine start with a 2-0 win over Chelsea in front of Elland Road's biggest crowd of the season, 46,565. Derby had beaten Liverpool to go top but, with their own 42-game season having now been completed, Brian Clough and his players could only wait anxiously to learn their fate. For Leeds, the situation was simple – win or draw at Wolves and the title would be theirs. Only a win for the home side at Molineux would open the door for Liverpool, sitting a point adrift of United but with a weaker goal average and one game to play.

The League would, though, have to wait as Leeds prepared for their third FA Cup final appearance. Niggling injuries sustained in the league victory over Chelsea had left Revie sweating over the fitness of Johnny Giles, Paul Reaney and Allan 'Sniffer' Clarke but, come Cup final day, all had recovered and were fit to start. The players had managed to find time to enjoy the traditional recording of a Cup final song, the B-side *Leeds, Leeds, Leeds* being more commonly known today as the club anthem, *Marching On Together*. The recording session proved an opportunity for the players to relax but, come the day of the game, the mood was deadly serious. United were staying at Hendon Hall where, after a relaxing morning walk, Revie called his squad together to go through the dossiers his coaching staff had compiled on the Arsenal squad. Opinion was split among the players as to how useful the dossiers were any more, Leeds having all but completed their eighth season in the top flight and knowing the vast majority of the opposing sides inside out. Peter Lorimer, for one, felt they had past their sell-by date. "The dossiers were quite useful and informative, particularly early on after we had just won promotion," he says. "But Don went on too long with them. It was good to know about free-kick routines and things like that, but what started as a 15-minute look at the opposition had become more and more detailed over the years. We had already shown with the big victories over Manchester United and Southampton what a good side we were and I felt we should have been concentrating on our own game rather than dwelling too much on the opposition and their supposed strengths. It got so daft at one stage that we were playing a Third Division team in the FA Cup, a game that was a formality. Don had compiled this usual long dossier and he made them sound like a great team. I remember coming out of the meeting and discussing the dossier with Allan Clarke. 'Sniffer' said, 'Fucking hell, this lot sound like Real Madrid! What are they doing in the Third Division?' But that was how Don was. His motto was, 'If I don't tell them and it happens, I have failed'. He was so thorough but, personally, those dossiers had become a ballache by the end."

Despite some players having reservations, the squad duly paid attention as Revie outlined what they could expect from Arsenal. Bertie Mee's side had won the double the previous season but had slipped to fifth place this time around. But Revie, though, was still wary. He knew this was a golden chance to make up for the disappointment of the final defeat to Chelsea two years earlier but, still, his doubts remained.

Once at Wembley, any negative thoughts had been put to the back of the manager's mind as the team bus edged its way through the crowds. He had been reassured by seeing a bride on her way to church as the Leeds party made the journey from their hotel. John Wray, the Leeds correspondent for the *Telegraph & Argus*, recalls: "Leeds United had so often been the bridesmaid as opposed to the bride in major finals that Don took it as an omen that his team would lift the Cup." Wembley Way was already full of supporters sporting the red and white of Arsenal or the all white of Leeds. The Football Association, to mark the Centenary Cup final, had added to the sense of anticipation by inviting the Queen and Duke of Edinburgh to present the famous old trophy to the winners. A parade of past winners was also organised and the hope of all neutrals was that there would not be a repeat of the last meeting between the two teams when Leeds had edged a truly turgid League Cup final four years earlier. The pessimists need not have worried as, while the game was far from a classic, it did prove to be an entertaining and dramatic affair.

Revie, a very different manager to the one that had claimed that first trophy against the Gunners in 1968, had sent his side out to attack. With Arsenal also hoping to take the game to the opposition, albeit on the counter-attack, the stage was set for a game worthy of the occasion. The kicking match that had been the League Cup final meant a few robust challenges were always likely and Bob McNab became the first of four players to be booked for a late challenge on Peter Lorimer inside two minutes. Arsenal were the first to settle and David Harvey, preferred to the fit-again Gary Sprake, had to save smartly from Frank McLintock before Alan Ball's volley from 20 yards was kicked off the line by Paul Reaney. Ironically, it was a planned free-kick routine going awry that presented Leeds with their first serious chance of the afternoon when Johnny Giles' poor pass rebounded to Peter Lorimer who drilled a low shot that Geoff Barnett bundled round the post. Allan Clarke then hit the crossbar with a header after being picked out by Lorimer before the most famous goal in Leeds United's history arrived eight minutes into the second-half.

Jack Charlton started the move by cutting out an attempted pass by Alan Ball and finding Paul Madeley. The man once dubbed 'a Rolls Royce of a footballer' by Don Revie for the smooth manner he glided around the pitch then passed to Peter Lorimer who, in turn, rolled the ball out to Mick Jones on the right. Clarke, showing the awareness that had persuaded Revie to break the British transfer record three years earlier to sign the Leicester City forward, raced into the penalty area in the hope his strike partner could get to the by-line. Jones duly obliged so, when the inch-perfect cross arrived near the penalty spot, Clarke was on hand to throw himself at the ball and power a diving header beyond the reach of Geoff Barnett.

The Leeds players were overjoyed but Revie, mindful of how fate had conspired against his team so often in the past, calmly rose from the bench to remind them of the need to stay focused. The United manager needn't have worried, with Arsenal going close just once in the remaining 37 minutes when Charlie George's stinging shot crashed against the crossbar. The rebound was then stabbed well wide by Peter Simpson and Leeds had won the Cup. Once again, however, misfortune had struck Revie's team due to Mick Jones having dislocated an elbow after colliding with Arsenal goalkeeper Barnett in the final minute. With the last league game of the season at Wolves just 48 hours away, Revie realised the ramifications immediately as Jones lay flat out on his back in the six-yard box at the Tunnel End with Les Cocker tending to the striker. The injury meant Jones was unable to join the rest of the Leeds players as they climbed the steps to the Royal Box to collect the Cup, though he did make it up several minutes later. Heavily strapped and needing Norman Hunter for assistance, the sight of Jones collecting his medal from the Queen is one of the enduring images of the 1972 final. Unfortunately, the drama of Jones' injury and excitement of winning the Cup meant one of Revie's ideas to try and improve his team's battered image was forgotten. Paul Trevillion, the football illustrator who had brought US-style razzmatazz to Elland Road earlier in the season, recalls: "The saddest thing about the 1972 FA Cup final for me was the missed opportunity that came after the game. Don, always looking for ways to make the public view his team more positively, had come up with the idea of presenting the Queen with a bunch of roses if Leeds won the Cup. Don loved roses and Terry Cooper, who had broken his leg and was not playing, was put in charge of getting the roses to the dressing room. He delivered them before kick-off. But then, in all the excitement, the roses were forgotten about and left in the dressing room. It was a real shame as the gesture would have shown Don in a completely different light and just what sort of a club Leeds were away from their public image."

Once back in the dressing room, the players were rationed to one plastic glass of champagne and a sip from the Cup as attention quickly turned to Wolverhampton. Leaving their wives and the Cup behind - club secretary Keith Archer had the task of ensuring the trophy's safe arrival back in Leeds - the squad, minus the injured Jones, were on the road to the Midlands within an hour of the final whistle at Wembley. Eight draining matches inside a month had taken their toll and several players needed patching up to take the field at Molineux. It meant a busy couple of days for the United medical staff as Eddie Gray was troubled by a thigh injury and pain-killing injections were administered to Allan Clarke and Johnny Giles. Revie later claimed all three would not have played under normal circumstances.

The game against Wolves was, of course, anything but normal with Leeds needing just a point to clinch the league and cup double. If United lost, Liverpool would be crowned champions with a win at Arsenal. Leaders Derby

County, whose season had ended nine days earlier, could only sit and wait for news in Majorca where assistant manager Peter Taylor had taken the players for their traditional end-of-season break.

Wolves were midway through a two-legged UEFA Cup final against Spurs and were expected to have their minds elsewhere. Revie, sensing attack was the best form of defence even when a draw would be enough, vowed to take the game to the home side. Leeds dominated but, not for the first time, were left raging at the officials after having three strong penalty appeals turned down. Referee Bill Gow may be nowhere near as familiar a name to modern day Leeds fans as that of Ray Tinkler, but those from Yorkshire who were in the sell-out crowd at Molineux on May 8, 1972, are unlikely to have forgotten – or forgiven - the Welshman.

Wolves went ahead through Frank Munro just before half-time so when Derek Dougan added a second on 65 minutes, United's title hopes lay in tatters. Billy Bremner, now playing up front as a hobbling Allan Clarke finally admitted defeat and was replaced by Terry Yorath, did pull a goal back shortly after by converting a Paul Madeley cross. But, try as they might, the equaliser would not come with Bremner going the closest with a back header that Wolves full back Gerry Taylor cleared off the line. Once again, Leeds were left cursing their luck as referee Gow blew the final whistle. The memory of how United came so close still rankles with Jack Charlton, whose 37th birthday coincided with that fateful game in the Black Country. "Fixture congestion cost us a few times, but particularly in 1972," says the England World Cup winner. "People in the Football Association and Football League were out to get us. Can you imagine a team now having to play their final league game on a Monday night, just two days after winning the FA Cup? Why they could not have delayed the game to the Wednesday or Thursday was something we never had explained. In the end, it was too much and we lost the game. But it should never have taken place so close to the Cup final."

Leeds were not the only team left cursing their luck that night with Liverpool having what would have been a League Championship-winning goal chalked off two minutes from time at Arsenal when John Toshack was adjudged to be offside when bundling the ball into the net. Bill Shankly raged at referee Roger Kirkpatrick after the final whistle, insisting: 'He cost us the title.' Liverpool's failure to win combined with Leeds' defeat at Molineux meant the title went to Derby County, Revie's frustration only being added to by the knowledge that Leeds' arch-critic Brian Clough and not his friend Shankly was the beneficiary of his own side's slip-up.

The ramifications for Revie of that defeat to Wolves would, however, extend way beyond annoyance that Clough had been handed the title. Allegations would surface a few months later in the *The People* of attempts by Leeds to bribe three Wolves players to 'take it easy' in return for £1,000 apiece. The FA and the police both investigated but no charges followed. Several years later, however, the scandal was revived in an investigation into Revie by the *Daily Mirror*. The *Mirror* attempted to fill in some of the gaps in their sister newspaper's original story and named Mike O'Grady, the former Leeds player who had been sold to Wolves, as the intermediary. O'Grady had been on loan at Birmingham City by the time of the title-deciding fixture at Molineux but the *Mirror*, whose investigation also included an extensive interview with Gary Sprake, quoted the one-time Leeds winger as saying he had made an offer to the Wolves players on behalf of Revie. O'Grady admits today he did speak to the *Mirror* but is keen to distance himself from the subsequent allegations that appeared in the newspaper. "I don't know where it (the initial *People* story) came from," he says. "There were rumours but where they came from I don't know. When it all got dug up again (in 1977), I knew people would automatically say I had something to do with it. But I didn't. The *Daily Mirror* came to me and said, 'we will print it whatever'."

The People followed up the allegations in their sister paper and were rash enough to name Billy Bremner, who sued successfully for libel damages and won £100,000. Mike O'Grady adds: "It hurt Billy and he sued over all sorts of things." On the game itself and Leeds again falling short, O'Grady adds: "I was at Birmingham on loan from Wolves but I came back to watch the game when Leeds were trying to win the league. I was gutted for the lads, I really was. Wolves raised their game. Had they played like that all season, they would have won the title themselves. Leeds should not have been made to play that game 48 hours after the Cup final. There was a lot of nonsense said about that game but most of it was just spiteful."

Revie, unlike his captain Billy Bremner, never sued over the allegations – something that those close to the United manager felt even then was a big mistake on his part. The Earl of Harewood, club president for all but the first few months of Revie's 13-year reign, insists: "I was very keen for him to sue, like Billy had done. I said to Don I wished he would do the same and donate the money to charity when he won damages. And he would have won, I am certain of that. Why he didn't, I never found out. It would have helped his reputation. Billy winning his case was good, but it was not the same as if Don had done the same."

Eddie Gray, who played hundreds of games under Revie after being signed as a 15-year-old, adds: "I would hate to think I played in any game that wasn't right. As a professional, you like to think you would be able to tell. I certainly never had the impression it was going on. The allegations were made but, even if it was true, how would they prove it? What I will say is it never occurred to me in the slightest that something was going on."

Whatever the rights and wrongs of the case – and there are plenty in football who insist to this day that Revie was corrupt, just as those who worked alongside him are adamant nothing untoward went on – the defeat to Wolves ensured a season where Leeds had played their best football to date under Revie had ended in yet more disappointment. After five runners-up finishes in eight years and three in a row - the United manager knew time was running out if the title win of 1968-69 was not to prove to be an isolated success.

Chapter 14

A Great Football Manager But An Even Better Dad

More than two decades after his death, Don Revie remains a deeply divisive figure in English football. On one side of the argument are largely those whose loyalty remains to Leeds United, a defiant group of ex-players, supporters and club officials who will not hear a bad word said about the man who built from scratch one of the finest teams Europe has ever seen. They will speak of a warm, caring man who found time and a kind word for everyone. And of a manager so far ahead of his time that his rivals took years to catch up and who was only denied the trophies his work deserved by a combination of refereeing injustices and rank bad luck. On the other side of the divide are those from outside Leeds who talk with disdain about the nastiness of his team. They point to the nickname 'Don Readies' and his defection from the England job to take up a lucrative contract in the Middle East. And of the corruption and venality for which Revie has since become renowned.

What both his supporters and critics do agree on, however, is that what he built at Elland Road was a band of brothers so committed to each other that if you kicked one, you incurred the wrath of them all. They were family and the fostering of such a strong bond between his players had been no accident, as club president, the Earl of Harewood, explains: "The atmosphere changed at Leeds United almost the moment Don was appointed manager in 1961. He wanted the club to feel like a family and he set about that task straight away. He wanted everyone from the ladies who served the tea to the captain of the team to feel part of the club."

Central to Revie's plan to create a family atmosphere was to sign players who he felt would fit in with his ethos. Careful vetting was done of every potential signing, combing through backgrounds and making sure their character was such that new ideas would be taken on board. And they must not be troublemakers – at least not off the pitch, as Revie's critics would wryly note in later years. These youngsters, once signed, were then taught important lessons such as the need for good manners and a healthy diet. Future stars such as Peter Lorimer and Norman Hunter were sent back to their lodgings with provisions to help build up strength. Though, as Eddie Gray dryly notes, not all made their way into the mouths of United's young hopefuls: "Sometimes the steaks on the plates of the landladies were bigger than ours."

Revie's fatherly concern for his players was encouraged by his wife Elsie, who also realised the importance for footballers of a happy and settled home life. From the moment her husband had been appointed Leeds manager in 1961, Elsie had looked for practical ways in which she could help. Remembering how lonely it could feel as the wife of a recently transferred footballer who was offered little help in adapting to her new surroundings, Elsie endeavoured to try and create a more welcoming environment. Peter Lorimer, who went on to become Leeds' record goalscorer with 238 in all competitions, says: "Elsie played a big part in the family atmosphere that existed during Don's time and it was always my impression that she was the one behind sending out flowers to the players' wives on their birthday or when someone was ill. I remember once telling Don my Mum wasn't too well in Scotland and the next time I rang home she told me, 'Mr Revie has sent me flowers'. It was a little gesture that made a big impression on the entire family and I am certain it was down to Elsie. They worked as a real team and I always thought of Elsie as more than a wife to Don. It is true what they say about every successful man needing a strong woman behind him as that is exactly what Don had in Elsie."

Elsie was behind a pre-season party being held in a city centre restaurant during her husband's first year as Leeds manager where all the directors, staff, players and their wives were invited. Revie's speech that night vividly illustrated his thinking as he stressed just how integral everyone in the room was to the long-term success of the club. Backed up by the subsequent delivery of flowers on birthdays and so on, it was no surprise that the family atmosphere Revie craved at Elland Road was soon evident.

As time wore on, players' wives would also receive a bouquet after the birth of a child. Revie also acknowledged the travelling demands he placed on the players by, before a Cup final, getting the wives and girlfriends together in a hotel and saying, 'I've had your husbands all season long, so choose what you want from the menu or the bar and it's on me'. This attention to detail, in particular when dealing with the parents of his younger players, continued throughout Revie's time in charge at Elland Road. Gordon McQueen joined for £30,000 from St Mirren in September, 1972, as the successor to Jack Charlton and was quick to notice how attentive the new manager was to all his family, and especially the impression it made on his father. McQueen recalls: "Don was great with my Dad, nothing was ever too much trouble. He used to get him down from Scotland and put him up in a hotel so he could come and visit me. My Dad used to love Don and I did notice that when I signed for Manchester United, he never had the same interest as he did at Leeds. And I always put that down to how Don made him feel special. In a way, Don was very clever as by getting your parents, girlfriend or whoever on side, it meant when things like contract negotiations came round that they were sorted very quickly. Players would just sign because they were so happy."

Revie's attempts to foster a close-knit atmosphere throughout the club proved so successful that even today when many of his old players are at or around pensioner age, they still enjoy each other's company. Peter Lorimer says: "Don was our mentor and we all turned out to be not bad lads, so he must have done something right. We had no troublemakers or anything like that. Even now, we all hang out together as friends and enjoy spending time with each other, playing golf and the like. That isn't always the case in football. I still speak to some of the Manchester United and Liverpool lads from that era, and while one or two are pals, the same cannot be said about the whole team. The Leeds lads are all genuine friends, to this day." The Earl of Harewood also believes Revie's paternal guidance left a lasting impression on his young players. "I had a birthday party a few years ago," he recalls, "and someone who works at Harewood House suggested they should get the old Leeds team together as a surprise. It was a wonderful evening and what I noticed was how they were all still married to the same girl from their playing days and how happy they still are in each other's company."

Another trick Revie used to foster a sense of togetherness among his players was to introduce carpet bowls and bingo sessions on overnight stays. The thinking was that all the players should stay together ahead of a big game, not drift off in small groups, as any bond formed in private would inevitably be taken out on to the pitch. To introduce a competitive spirit to the bowls and an element of fun, Revie asked a couple of his players to fill the role of squad bookmakers. Eddie Gray was one who answered the call. "Peter Lorimer and I ran the book on who would win," says Gray. "We made some useful money, though there were times when we got stung as well. There was one particular golf day when the manager backed Mick Jones to win. Mick had just arrived at the club and, unknown to either me or Peter, was a good golfer. The manager knew, though. In the end, there were three players in a play-off – the manager, Mick and Jimmy Greenhoff. Now I am not saying the manager got to Jimmy but someone did because he was hopeless. Peter and I followed them around and couldn't believe what we were seeing. The manager cleaned up and we were well and truly done."

Revie's carpet bowls and bingo sessions may have not proved popular when later introduced to the England squad, but, at Leeds, they were viewed as not only a way of alleviating the inevitable boredom that comes with long nights away from home in a hotel but also a source of banter. Mike O'Grady, who spent four seasons at Leeds, recalls: "I remember Peter Lorimer trying to pull one particular stroke. When betting tax was introduced to the betting shops, Peter turned round to us all one night and announced he would also be putting the 10 per cent tax on the bets the lads were placing with him. He got short shrift!"

Revie's approach to fostering team-spirit and togetherness was rewarded by not only the development of a truly united team, but also one that few wanted to leave. At one time, he had 16 international players at his disposal. Revie could only pick 11, plus one substitute, so the potential for fall-outs was huge, especially as most of the squad reached their peak at a similar time. The reality, though, was a largely harmonious existence where those players out of the side were willing to stick around even when a transfer away would have brought the first team football they craved. Mick Jones says: "It is a tribute to Don that, during my eight or nine years at Leeds, not one player wanted to leave. Even the lads who were not in the first team did not want to move on. Mick Bates was on the touchline most weeks but he never wanted to leave. None of us did. I still go to Elland Road for matches and bump into a few of those who were mainly in the reserves. I ask them 'why didn't you move on?' To a man, they say it was because of the manager. He had this knack of being able to make everyone feel involved. Today, even the biggest clubs have players who want to leave, but this was never the case at Leeds under Don."

Revie's determination to put his players' needs first was a big factor in his squad remaining so loyal. John Wray, of the *Telegraph & Argus*, recalls: "Don made sure his players were looked after and they all appreciated it. There was one game in London when some idiot threw a brick through the window of the team bus as we pulled away from the ground. A replacement bus would take ages to arrive and Don did not want his players to have to sit around when they could be at home. So, he paid the driver a bonus to wrap up warm and drive the bus all the way back to Leeds."

It was not just in helping the players' families settle quickly at Elland Road where Elsie played a huge part in her husband's success, but also in the Revie family home. The life of a football manager is inevitably a demanding one with the pressures that accompany the role often becoming all-consuming.

Opportunities to switch off are few, and without the love and support of a close family, the job can swallow up the most level-headed of managers. Even the most routine of family tasks can see thoughts turn to what team should play on Saturday or when a star player is going to be back from injury. Daughter Kim recalls: "I only realised it later in life but my Mum did so much for Dad. She kept the family going seamlessly and was the one who helped with homework and things like that. Mum had a great understanding of the pressures that came with Dad's job and, subtly, she would make sure we didn't drive Dad crazy as kids. This was particularly the case on a matchday. She also made sure Dad was allowed to have a lie-in on a Sunday, the one day off he had in the week. It was a real partnership and Dad could not have been as successful without her. I think it helped that Mum was quite out-going and sociable. When you are married to someone famous, there is a danger of being lost in their slipstream but that was never the case with Mum. She was never happier than when chatting away to whoever, whereas Dad was much quieter."

Within a few months of Revie being appointed manager at Elland Road in 1961, there was little doubt who was in charge. The moniker 'gaffer' became wholly appropriate throughout his 13 subsequent years in charge. Few decisions, if any, were made without his say-so and stories of the power he wielded across the club and the city are legendary. Whether it be knowing exactly what his players were doing at night thanks to a team of spies keeping an eye on the pubs and clubs of Leeds or conducting contract negotiations, Revie was in charge and the man everyone went to for a decision. Within the family, however, it was a different story with many who met the couple socially suggesting Elsie was the one who ruled the roost. Bill Bridge spent 30 years as the sports editor of the *Yorkshire Post* and recalls one particular incident on the golf course when it became clear the Leeds United manager was not necessarily always the boss of his own home. "There was a Pro-Am tournament at Bradford Golf Club in Hawksworth," he says. "For some reason, Don didn't play so, instead, he caddied for Elsie. They were on the 14th tee when she asked Don what club to use. It is a difficult hole where you play uphill so have to judge the shot perfectly or it will end up rolling back towards the tee. Don was used to playing off the men's tee so he suggested using a 6-iron. Elsie followed the advice only for the ball to fall well short and end up more or less back at her feet. Well, she tore into Don and called him every name under the sun. As a footballer and a manager, he had always struck me as someone who was frightened of no-one. But I think he was of Elsie." Revie's son Duncan also recalls his mother often getting her own way when the couple had a disagreement. "Mum was very much a Scottish matriarch figure," he says. "She was a very, very strong character. I would not necessarily say she was the boss of the house as Dad gave as good as he got. But she could insist on getting her own way. One such time came when I was 15 and at Leeds Grammar School. Leeds United were top of the league and I was basking in being Don Revie's son, and all the attention that came with it. It meant my school work was suffering, so much so that despite having a high IQ I was consistently bottom of the class. In the end, I was relegated out of the top stream at Leeds Grammar and Mum, who was a teacher of course, was not happy at all. She said to my Dad one night, 'Don, this is not right – we have to send him away to boarding school'. My Dad pointed out they couldn't really afford to at the time because it was expensive but Mum insisted and got her way. I ended up going to Repton, a school in Derbyshire that Doug Ellis had recommended because it was good for football as well as education. I will always remember Dad dropping me off there for the first time and crying. I was crying as well, but Mum just shouted, 'Get in the car, Don, it will do him the world of good'. And you know what? She was right, as being away from Leeds meant I retrieved my academic career and eventually went on to Cambridge University, where I qualified as a lawyer."

Sending their son away to boarding school to keep his mind on studying rather than events at Elland Road may have been a necessity, but there is no doubting the all-consuming love the couple had for football.

Elsie's family had been steeped in football from an early age so she was a keen student of the game, an interest that was only strengthened when she met her future husband. Later, at Leeds, she was so keen on debating the whys and wherefores of a game that many believed, with tongue firmly placed in cheek, her influence stretched beyond supporting the manager. Peter Lorimer says: "Elsie knew her football and a few of us at Leeds used to think she picked the team some weeks."

Picking the team may have been stretching things a tad but, as son Duncan recalls, his mother certainly didn't hold back when discussing football matters with her husband. "Football was something they would debate furiously," he says. "Having grown up in a football environment and with two of her Grandads' brothers having played for Scotland, she was very knowledgeable. Mum and Dad would have some great arguments on a Saturday night about the game they had watched in the afternoon. They could get quite heated, and if I had to pick a winner I would say they finished as score draws. All sorts of things would be discussed – who should be tracking back, who should be doing more in possession and whether someone should be kicking with their other foot. The best thing is they were arguing about all this stuff when Leeds were winning everything. I dread to think what Saturday nights would have been like if Leeds had been losing every week."

Revie, perhaps remembering a childhood that saw his mother die when he was just 12 and his father often out of work, had craved stability both at work and home long before moving to Leeds. Team-mates at Manchester City and Sunderland in the 1950s speak of a man whose family was all-important to him. He also realised many of the younger members of the squad were miles from home on their own, so would often take them under his wing in an attempt to offset bouts of homesickness. John McTavish, a native Scot who signed for Manchester City in 1952, was just one of several who were co-opted into Sunday night card sessions at the Revie house.

Marrying into the Duncan clan meant Revie was suddenly part of a huge family, something he loved and, for the rest of his life, he would constantly be inviting relatives down from Scotland to stay. Elsie's brother David Duncan recalls: "Don loved nothing more than spending time with his family. When he was manager of Leeds, I lived in Manchester and he would constantly be asking, 'Are you coming over this weekend?' Basically, he liked it to be open house. I was not married so Don thought I would be available all the time. We would often go golfing for a few days to allow him to switch off from being Leeds manager." Eventually, an annexe was built so the Scottish relatives could permanently move south to Leeds – much to the delight of the Revie children.

By then, son Duncan and daughter Kim were at or approaching their teenage years. Dad may have been one of the most familiar faces in the country but both speak today of a home life that was a world away from the glamour of footballing offspring from the modern game such as the Beckhams' three children. Duncan recalls: "Dad had been a bricklayer before going into football and had his feet on the ground, as did my Mum's side of the family who had all come from mining stock. So, he was not someone who courted the limelight and we had a very ordinary family life. Dad was such a private man and so keen not to draw attention to himself that when we played golf at our local club, he would insist we got changed in the car park. I was always asking why we couldn't go in the clubhouse like everyone else? But it was just a case of Dad not wanting to get mobbed as we went in and be the centre of attention. He just wanted to play golf." This desire to stay out of the limelight when away from Leeds United was also picked up by family friends. Sheila Silver, now happily married to former Elland Road chairman Leslie, got to know the Revies in the 1960s through her late husband, Gabby Harris. She recalls: "Don was a very modest man and quite private. I always noticed when my late husband and I would go out to dinner with Don and Elsie that Don would always choose the seat with his back to the rest of the room. It seemed to me a way of making sure people would not recognise him and cause a fuss."

Managing is a demanding role at any football club. But with Leeds being among the most successful - and newsworthy - in the land, demands on Revie's time were huge. Don rarely turned down an interview, as John Helm, now a leading football commentator but for the final four years of Revie's reign the Sports Editor of *BBC Radio Leeds*, recalls: "Don understood the media had a job to do and because he always wanted to promote the club, he would make himself available. Even when the story was a difficult one, such as the year Sunderland tried to poach him away from Leeds to become their manager. I had only just started at the BBC and tracked Don down to Moortown Golf Club. Don could not really say anything, but knew I had a job to do so he gave me a few minutes because he knew it would please my bosses." Mike Morgan, who since 1970 has covered the Yorkshire football patch for a variety of national newspapers including the *Daily Express* and *The Sun*, backs up the notion of Revie always trying to find time for the media. He recalls: "I remember first meeting Don shortly after moving to Yorkshire from London. I was only 20 and completely in awe of the man but the first thing that struck me was how courteous and down-to-earth he was. I introduced myself as the *Daily Express*'s new man in Yorkshire and, despite having a million and one things to do, Don invited me into his office. We had a chat and, at the end, he handed over his home telephone number. And when I rang, he always took the call. It is very different to today where managers are protected by an army of press officers and the relationship between reporters and the clubs is 'them and us'."

Along with having to deal with the voracious appetite of newspapers who recognised how a strong Leeds United story on the back page could boost sales, Revie also had a number of other time-consuming duties as United manager. Along with the inevitable travel and overnight stays that surround matches was the wooing of parents when trying to bring the latest promising youngster to Elland Road and the detailed planning that went into preparing for each and every game.

Once all these time-consuming tasks are taken into account, it is a wonder Revie found the time to return home to do anything other than sleep. However, daughter Kim recalls: "Mum kept the family going but Dad did his best to be around. Funnily enough, it was on one of our first father-daughter outings that I started to realise that maybe my Dad was a bit different. He had taken me to the fair and was watching me on the dodgems when people would come up and ask for his autograph. I remember thinking, 'Why do they want to talk to my Dad and get his signature?' There was another night where we went to the circus. Duncan and Mum didn't come, so it was just me and Dad. I was only four or five and we had seats in the front row. The elephants were walking round when the ringmaster said, 'Do we have any celebrities in tonight?' They wanted the elephants to walk over someone famous. Someone pointed to Dad, who said he couldn't take part as I would have been on my own. Eventually, though, they persuaded him and I just remember being terrified watching these elephants walk over my Dad. I couldn't understand why he was being singled out." Kim also has a vivid memory of being upset one Christmas as a small child that her Dad, unlike her friends' fathers, would not be around – though, this time, it was enough to earn a stern telling-off. "Dad was going to be away because Leeds were playing and the team were staying overnight," she recalls. "I was not happy and said, 'I hate bloody football'. Dad pulled me up pretty sharpish and told me never to speak like that again."

It was an example of how Revie, just as he did with his young players at Elland Road, put great store by good manners. Another trait that Revie brought home with him from Leeds United was a competitive streak. Daughter Kim again: "Even family parties became a contest between two teams. We would be playing charades and everyone would be split into two teams, usually boys and girls. And the boys, Dad mostly, always cheated to win." The competitive streak that made Revie's Leeds United such a feared opponent also surfaced when he played golf with wife Elsie, as the couple's son Duncan recalls: "Golf was a big passion for my Mum and Dad. Mum was a very good golfer who got down to a handicap of 7 at one stage. She also played for Scotland at Under-19s level. But, when it came to playing together they ended up being so competitive that, in the end, they had to stop taking part in mixed foursomes because they would just spend the time rowing."

Revie's public persona may have been similar to that of his Leeds team, dour with little warmth. He may also, again like the players who looked up so adoringly to him, be forever damned as one of the bad guys of English football. But to those who shared his life either professionally or privately, he was a very different character. Daughter Kim recalls: "Dad was a very caring man and incredibly thoughtful to everyone. Over the years, I have met quite a few people whose ill relatives Dad visited along with a couple of the players after hearing about them. Friends of friends and people like that. No fuss was ever made, so much so that even the rest of the family didn't know Dad had been on the visits. Dad didn't do them for publicity or anything like that, he just wanted to try and cheer someone up who was ill."

Football was, unsurprisingly, a major bonding tool for Revie and his family. With Mum Elsie having been steeped in the game and Dad such a high-profile figure, a love of football was inevitably passed down to both the couple's children. Duncan still works in the sport as chief executive of Soccerex, the organisers of the largest convention for global football business that includes major players at FIFA and UEFA among their delegates every year. Daughter Kim's interest may have waned since Revie retired but she is in no doubt as to how integral football was to family life when Leeds were in their pomp. "A lot of the talk was football-orientated, especially when we had visitors," says Kim. "My Mum really knew her football and loved to sit down and discuss it with whoever was there. I was as immersed as anyone. When we lost a game, I would be upset because I knew how disappointed Dad would be. I went to the home games and also the ones in London, but the old folk and my Gran would go everywhere. She continued doing that well into her 70s, always wearing a rosette and scarf."

A deep desire burned within Revie for his children to have the chances he had been denied earlier in life. He had been born a year after the General Strike and his upbringing had been tough in depression-hit Middlesbrough. Revie's football skills were the only means of escape. Kim recalls: "Dad had it tough as a child due to his Mum dying. Because of that, he was always determined we should have the best in life – but also that we appreciated it properly. He used to drive home to us both how important a good education would be if we were to get on in life."

Revie regretted his own lack of education as a child in Middlesbrough, when finding enough food for the table was the priority in a family where his widowed father was often out of work. He was determined his children would fare much better so Revie was delighted when Duncan graduated from Cambridge University with a law degree. Sending his son away to Derbyshire all those years before to take him away from a life where Leeds United's fortunes were the be all and end all had paid dividends. Duncan recalls: "Dad once said, very touchingly, when asked what his proudest moment was that it had been 'seeing my son graduate from Cambridge'. He came down to the graduation and it was a world totally alien to him. We had a punt on the river and things like that, but he loved it. Mind, he was not overly impressed when

I also showed him around my college room, which was like a hovel. Dad looked around and said, 'You haven't been living here, have you?'"

To his critics, Revie was a man motivated – and, to an extent, obsessed - by money. His departure from the England job to take up a lucrative offer to manage in the Middle East is often cited as evidence of a grasping attitude towards cash along with his decision to sell the story exclusively to the *Daily Mail*, pocketing a substantial payment in the process. Generosity, either financially or in spirit, was certainly a word never associated with Revie during his time in charge of Leeds or England. Once again, though, those who knew him best paint a very different picture to what the public saw. Johnny Williamson, who had struck up a friendship when the pair were players at Manchester City that would endure even after Revie left for Sunderland and subsequently moved into management, insists: "Don was a world away from how most people in the street viewed him. Our families stayed in touch after Don had left Manchester City and he was forever inviting us over to Leeds. We would also go on holiday together to places like Spain or Portugal where we could all play golf. Don and Elsie would put £100 in, as would me and my wife Lorraine. Then, if anything else was needed for the cost, Don, who always booked the trip, would make up the difference. He was a very generous man. I always remember one particular trip when Don's son Duncan and his wife came along. We went out for a meal to what seemed like a really expensive restaurant and Duncan insisted on paying. Don agreed but, because he knew how expensive the bill would be, he secretly went to the waiter during the meal and said, 'When you bring the bill to the table later, make it for only half the cost and I'll sort the rest out'. Unfortunately, it rebounded on Don as Duncan was so happy at the price of what was a lovely meal that he said, 'This is the best place we've been and it is so reasonable – we'll have to come back'. I think Don came clean in the end and confessed what he had done!"

The final word on the difference between the public and private Don Revie goes to daughter Kim. She says: "My brother and I were really lucky. I know everyone loves their parents but we enjoyed spending time with them so much that, even in our 20s as others were trying to get away from their parents and strike out on their own, we loved nothing better than spending time with them both. We were very fortunate and I always tell people who ask what Dad was like the same thing. He was a great football manager, but an even better Dad."

Chapter 15

King Billy

After 11 years in the job, Don Revie had Leeds United running exactly as he wished. The family atmosphere he had so carefully cultivated at Elland Road had blossomed and the young boys he had watched mature into men had grown into one of English football's finest teams. The silverware he felt their efforts had deserved may not have been forthcoming with five runners-up spots in eight seasons underlining just how difficult Leeds had, their 1968-69 League title success apart, found that final step to take. But, the football played in 1971-72 as Manchester United, Southampton et al were humbled on home soil had still been a joy to behold. As Leeds prepared to embark on another season, Revie was happy with his squad. And central to that satisfaction with his lot was the captain. Billy Bremner, who Revie had worked so hard to keep at Elland Road in his early days in charge when the homesick Scot yearned for a return north of the Border, was the heartbeat of Leeds United. Named Footballer of the Year a couple of years earlier and by now captain of his country, Bremner had come a long way from the callow youth Revie, then senior pro at Leeds, had roomed with ahead of the teenager's debut at Chelsea's Stamford Bridge in January, 1960. A bond was formed that weekend in London as Revie laid all his footballing knowledge in front of the teenager, in the hope it would help settle nerves before his league bow. Over the years, that bond had strengthened and now, more than 12 years on, captain and manager were considered to be as one. Revie's son Duncan admits his Dad was especially fond of Billy Bremner. "Dad loved all the young lads but he had a special bond with Billy," he says. "It was very, very strong. They were both winners and Dad saw Billy as his leader on the pitch. Dad knew that Billy would go through a brick wall for him and vice-versa. They had an implicit trust."

During the early years of Revie's reign, Bremner had been played in the forward line – a tactic that largely worked with the young Scot netting 21 league goals in the new manager's first two full seasons. Moved into midfield in the summer of 1963, Bremner's determination and will-to-win had then helped the club to the Second Division title 12 months later. Revie had always felt Bremner was ideal captain material, and the chance to prove his hunch right came in the wake of the broken thigh bone suffered by Bobby Collins against Torino in United's first trip abroad in Europe. He had been the true inspiration behind the promotion success that was followed by a second placed finish on United's return to the top flight, but the injury meant he would miss most of the 1965-66 season. Jack Charlton was initially handed the captaincy, only for the defender's superstitions to get the better of him. "I always wanted to come out of the tunnel last, which was not possible as captain," he explains. Revie, therefore, turned to Bremner late in 1966 and his faith would be rewarded by the Scot going on to become the most successful skipper in the club's history. John Helm, then a budding journalist in West Yorkshire, recalls: "It was a masterstroke of Don's to make Billy captain. Until then, Billy had been a bit of a problem for the management. But, after the captaincy, he behaved fine and his disciplinary problems only resurfaced once Don had left the club in 1974. That was when Billy clashed with Kevin Keegan at Wembley. Don had known exactly how to handle Billy and his rebellious streak. He channelled it in a positive manner."

As with most decisions made by Revie, tremendous thought had gone into when would be the right time to make Billy Bremner his captain. It was always the long-term goal but an incident before United's trip to Holland to take on DWS Amsterdam in the Inter-Cities Fairs Cup second round may well have forced the hand of Revie, who felt the responsibility of the position may well bring a bit more of the maturity he felt Bremner was still lacking. Revie had been left furious when Bremner arrived at Manchester Ringway Airport ahead of the flight to Amsterdam without his passport. A search could not find the missing item, meaning a mad dash to Liverpool for Bremner to get another passport issued before returning to Ringway to catch a later flight on his own. Revie was not best pleased with the midfielder, though, in his ever-practical way, he would eventually act to ensure there was no repeat. Son Duncan recalls: "Dad knew how forgetful Billy could be so, in the end, he took his passport off him. Billy had kept turning up without it before European trips so, eventually, Dad confiscated it. Dad felt it was the only way to make sure his captain could be guaranteed to be available for the big European games."

The relationship between manager and captain could, even allowing for the tremendous bond that existed between Revie and Bremner, also be a volatile one. Bremner, for instance, continued to enjoy a pint and a game of dominoes with Jack Charlton in the Woodman Inn on a Thursday night even though he knew Revie disapproved. Then, there was the Friday when the pair had a major fall-out after Bremner had turned up late to catch the train south to London ahead of a game at West Ham. Peter Lorimer recalls: "Billy's wife Vicky had gone home for a few days so Billy went out with his pals on the Thursday night and had a few beers. Come Friday morning, everyone was at the train station waiting to set off but there was no sign of Billy. We knew where he was, he had got pissed and had stayed at the Griffin Hotel nearby. Don, who was such a powerful man in Leeds at that stage that he could order the station master to delay the train, sent Les Cocker off to get him. Ten minutes later, Les walked back down the platform with Billy behind. Billy's tie was all over the place and he looked the worse for wear. All the lads were laughing, but Don was not amused and he sulked about it all the way to London. Normally, he would play cards with us but this time he refused and sat on his own instead. Billy tried to get him to play but Don wouldn't budge. Eventually, Billy shouted across the carriage, 'If I let you down tomorrow, you can fine me or do whatever you want – but I'll tell you now, I won't let you down'. Sure enough, Billy was outstanding and we won the game. Afterwards, Don and Billy had their arms around each other and there were big smiles across their faces. They were the best friends in the world and you would never have known anything had gone on the previous day. But that's how their relationship was – very close but also capable of being volatile."

Under Revie's care and tutelage, Bremner became a mainstay of the Leeds side and was voted the finest player in the club's history by supporters in a poll at the turn of the Millennium. His statue proudly stands on the corner of Lowfields Road and Elland Road outside United's home, just 100 or so yards from the stand that bears Revie's own name. Both men's instrumental role in the rise of Leeds United has never been forgotten in West Yorkshire and supporters still sing their tributes to Revie and Bremner during home matches. It is doubtful whether Leeds could have dominated English football as they did for the 10 years that followed promotion in 1964 without the pair and Lorimer believes Revie's man-management, as in many cases, was crucial in getting the best out of his flame-haired captain. He says: "Billy was a totally brilliant footballer but Don had to manage him carefully. In my mind, Johnny Giles was our main man on the field but Don had to make Billy think he was. It was how he got the best out of him. I am certain Don told Billy in his last few years as Leeds manager, 'I want you to manage the club after I leave', when, as we all found out later, it was Johnny who he recommended to take over in 1974. I think Don kidded him along, which is why Billy bollocksed it up by going in to see the directors when he found out Johnny was going to get the job. The directors lost their nerve and brought Clough in instead."

It was not just with his captain, however, that Revie proved himself astute in his handling of players. Recognising that the youngsters he had helped nurture had grown into men with minds of their own, he faced a challenge to keep them together. It was a point that had been driven home during the near-mutiny that followed his decision to keep the players away from their wives in the wake of United's Inter-Cities Fairs Cup final first leg against Juventus in Turin. The way several had questioned his authority had upset Revie at the time. But he was pragmatic enough to recognise that a re-establishing of his authority was needed. And in many cases he did so during contract negotiations. Unlike today when the task of thrashing out a new deal for a player would be conducted between a chief executive/chairman and an agent, Revie held the talks himself. Peter Lorimer recalls: "Anyone who wanted a wage rise had to go see Don and none of us looked forward to it. The whole experience was a daunting one because none of us wanted to fall out with Don, but we also wanted to stand up for ourselves. I am not a big fan of player agents but in this respect it is a welcome development. I went in to see Don after the 1971-72 season. I had scored 29 goals and been voted Player of the Year, so felt I deserved a rise. I was on £130 per week at the time and said I wanted £200. Don's reply was 'no-one at this club is going to get £200'. The saga dragged on over the summer and, eventually, he rang me at home in Alwoodley. He called me down to the ground and asked if I had thought any more about it. I repeated that I wanted £200. In the end, he offered me £196 per week. I wasn't going to accept. But then my brother in law said, 'You know what he's doing, don't you? He is showing you who is in charge'. My brother-in-law also pointed out that, after tax, it didn't make much difference anyway and I signed for £196. Don had to show me who was boss. The funny thing is that, as I left the office, he said, 'Don't go telling anyone about this or they'll all want the same as you'. I found out years later he said the same to everyone. It was his clever way of man-managing us."

What Lorimer may not have realised was that anyone stepping into the manager's office at Elland Road was subjected to a bit of amateur psychology on Revie's part, as respected football commentator John Helm explains: "I used to go into Don's office from time-to-time when working for *BBC Radio Leeds* and could not work out why I always felt so small in there. After a few visits, I plucked up the courage to ask, 'Why do I feel about 5ft 2in tall when in your office and yet you always look about 6ft 11in?' Don winked and told me that his chair had been raised significantly higher than the sofa that visitors sat on. It showed how thoroughly professional he was when it came to Leeds United. He ran that club with a rod of iron and everyone knew he was there. It was a deliberate ploy to say 'hello' to everyone from the tea ladies to the groundsman every morning. People may have thought he was just being friendly, which in one respect he was. But it was also Don's way of letting everyone know he was at the club and that no-one had better be caught slacking."

With Lorimer's contract saga resolved, the 1972-73 season got underway with United determined to go one better than their runners-up finish of the previous three years. Revie, aware the clock was starting to tick on some of the older players in his squad, had eased Joe Jordan into the squad during the ultimately fruitless hunt for the League and Cup double the previous spring and felt the striker, recommended to his former club by Bobby Collins, was ready to play a more prominent role this time around. Promising defender Gordon McQueen was also in the process of swapping Scotland for Leeds, while Revie brought in Trevor Cherry and Roy Ellam from Huddersfield Town. Ellam, a £35,000 signing, would last just two seasons and make 19 starts, while Cherry, who joined for £100,000, went on to captain both Leeds and England before leaving to become Bradford City manager in 1982. Cherry had handed in a transfer request at Huddersfield amid rumoured interest from Birmingham City and Tottenham Hotspur so, when manager Ian Greaves called him down to Leeds Road and said, 'An offer has been accepted', he was expecting to meet either Freddie Goodwin or Bill Nicholson. "I asked Ian who it was but he wouldn't say over the phone," recalls the defender. "Whether he thought I had been tapped up and was just playing dumb, I don't know. But I really had no idea. I lived 15 minutes away from Leeds Road so jumped in the car and walked into the old offices. I was stunned when the person waiting was Don Revie. I thought, 'He must be here to see someone else?' I couldn't understand why the manager of the best club in England would want to sign me. Don sat me down and explained how he saw me initially as a full-back, which was a position I had never played, and then as a long-term replacement for Norman Hunter. I wasn't sure about the full-back part but, I reasoned, if Don Revie thinks I can play there then maybe I can? The deal took two minutes to sort out."

Cherry had played against Leeds during Huddersfield's two seasons in the top flight that had preceded their relegation just a few weeks earlier. There was little love lost between the two neighbours with Cherry's abiding memory being the furious reaction of Jack Charlton after Town had had the temerity to claim a point from a goalless draw in April, 1971. Unfortunately for the new signing, he fell foul of United's veteran defender almost immediately after moving across West Yorkshire. Cherry recalls: "I had a run-in with Big Jack on my second day. At Huddersfield, we had tackled in training and kicked each other. But at Leeds, they didn't and no-one told me. Before I knew what I was doing, I had clattered into Big Jack and he was on the floor looking distinctly unhappy. He got up, held the ball out and said, 'Any time you want this fucking thing, just tell me and I'll give it you – but don't clatter me like that again'. Don pulled me aside after training and said, 'I should have told you but we don't steam in like that during training, save it for Saturday'. Leeds played that many games that Don wasn't really too interested in training – match-days were what mattered to him."

With Cherry in for broken-leg victim Terry Cooper at left-back, Revie's side travelled to Chelsea on the opening day hoping to repeat the trick of the past four seasons when they had started with a win. Four goals without reply later, it was a chastened Leeds party that returned north by train - even though there had been mitigating circumstances, with Peter Lorimer forced to take over in goal after David Harvey suffered concussion. Mick Jones had also left the field with a twisted ankle as the ten men slipped to the club's worst opening day defeat since just before Revie's arrival as a player 24 years earlier. Normal service was resumed in midweek with a 2-0 win at Sheffield United as Leeds embarked on a ten-game unbeaten run that included the club's debut in the European Cup Winners' Cup. The 1-1 draw in Turkey against Ankaragucu marked not only Trevor Cherry's own European bow but also an indication he had been accepted at Elland Road. "I had a decent game in what turned out to be a bit of a kicking match," says the defender. "At the airport on the way home, Les Cocker put his arm around me and said, 'You're going to be all right here'. I felt 10 feet tall as it meant I had been accepted. I am sure Don must have spoken to Les and sent him over. His man management was second to none like that."

Cherry also realised within a few months of moving to Elland Road how his new manager had earned the unflinching support of everyone at the club. "The way he tried to look after everyone was amazing," says the former England defender. "I found out in my first season how he would go that extra yard for his players. My wife and I had moved house to Mirfield a few months after I joined Leeds but we had a few problems. There was a gas strike on and the water was coming down the walls. My son was only three months old so there was no way we could stay there. I went in to training the following day and, as usual, was one of the first in. Les Cocker saw me and said, 'Hello'. I must not have been my usual cheerful self because he asked what was wrong.

I explained the situation and he told me to go see the gaffer. But because I had not been there that long, I didn't go. The following day Les pulled me aside and said I had to go see the gaffer, so this time I went. Don immediately said, 'Fetch me this gas fella's number and leave it with me'. Later that day, the bloke from the Gas Board rang up and said, 'I'm terribly sorry, Mr Cherry, we can't sort your problem out until the weekend but, as a special favour, I can put an emergency pipe in now that will see you through'. I couldn't believe it – Don had somehow got round a nationwide gas strike. Once I had got to know the gaffer better, I asked him how he had sorted it out. It turned out he had rung the Gas Board bloke up and asked him if he liked football. He said 'yes' so the gaffer immediately offered him four tickets for the semi-final against Wolves and that was that. My wife loved Don from then on. Don knew the importance of keeping a player's family settled if he is to perform at the top of his game."

Leeds won the Cup Winners' Cup first round second leg against Turkish side Ankaragucu thanks to a Mick Jones goal, though setbacks in the league came either side of the 1-0 triumph as Newcastle United and Liverpool both inflicted defeats on Revie's men. Murmurings began to grow on the terraces and in the press that Leeds were a team in decline, a feeling only strengthened when Bill Shankly's Liverpool triumphed 1-0 at Elland Road in a League Cup fourth round replay. The response from within Revie's squad was impressive, losing just twice in the next 22 league games to maintain a push for the title. Progress was also made in the Cup Winners' Cup as a trip behind the Iron Curtain to take on Carl Zeiss Jena brought a goalless draw that was followed with a comfortable two-goal win over the East Germans in the return. The help of Bill Nicholson was sought ahead of the quarter-final meeting with Rapid Bucharest, his Spurs side having beaten the Romanians 5-0 the previous season. A thick dossier, showing how the rest of English football was catching up with Revie's methods, duly arrived and Bucharest were again left humbled by English opposition as United went through 8-1 on aggregate. As winter gave way to spring in 1973, the FA Cup was also proving a profitable competition for United. It may have taken two replays to account for Norwich City in the third round but routine wins over Plymouth Argyle and West Bromwich Albion put Revie's side in the quarter-finals for the sixth time in nine years. Reigning champions Derby County and Brian Clough, who by now was publicly venting his hatred of Leeds, were then beaten by a Peter Lorimer goal to set up a meeting with Wolves in the last four. Once again, United were chasing three major prizes as the season entered its decisive final month. Trevor Cherry had been at Elland Road for less than a year but already he had an insight into how Revie's side had maintained their challenge at the top of English football for so long. "The thought of losing never entered our minds," says Cherry. "Teams like West Ham had loads of ability but were renowned for not travelling well. But the Leeds lads used to look forward to every game with this inner belief that we would win. Thoughts of losing never even entered our heads."

Despite this overriding belief that success was their destiny, United would stumble once again at the vital time. The first trophy to disappear off their radar was the Championship. Injuries and suspensions had started to take their toll and a 1-0 defeat at Manchester City on March 31 meant Liverpool were able to steal a march on their rivals. Three points from a possible four at Coventry City and West Ham kept Leeds in touch only for arch-rivals Manchester United to inflict a damaging one-goal defeat at Elland Road. Revie's men now trailed Liverpool by eight points with five games to play. Fittingly, it was Bill Shankly's men who finally killed off any hopes of claiming the title with a 2-0 win at Anfield that clinched the home side's first trophy in seven years. Leeds would eventually finish third, seven points behind the champions.

By the time of the defeat to Liverpool, United had already booked their third FA Cup final appearance in four years courtesy of a 1-0 win over Wolves. Billy Bremner's strike midway through the second-half was the first goal the Midlands club had conceded in the Cup all season and a major source of satisfaction for Revie following the previous May's defeat at Molineux that had proved so costly. In the Cup Winners' Cup, Hajduk Split stood between Leeds and a place in the final with AC Milan being drawn against Sparta Prague in the other tie. As with Wolves at Maine Road in the FA Cup, the Yugoslavs adopted a defensive approach that was clearly designed to frustrate an opposing side playing their 70th competitive game under Revie in Europe. As a result, Leeds found chances hard to come by in front of a 32,051 crowd as the disciplined visitors stuck to coach Zebec Branco's plan. The breakthrough came on 21 minutes when Allan Clarke glided past sweeper Dragan Holcer and drilled a low shot across Radomir Vukceric in the Hajduk goal. The visitors, even though behind, refused to alter their game plan and there was no further score. There was, however, a sting in the tail for Leeds when goalscorer Clarke dished out his own retribution after being fouled by Mario Boljat and was promptly sent off by Hungarian referee Gyula Emsberger. Clarke had become the fifth Leeds player to be sent off in European combat and, come the final whistle, it was the Yugoslav players who celebrated on the field at the prospect of taking Revie's men back to Split with just a one-goal deficit to overcome. The return, a fortnight later, was preceded by the home fans driving past the Leeds team's hotel blasting their horns in an attempt to disrupt the sleep of those inside. One player unlikely to have got much shut-eye that night, anyway, was Terry Yorath whose wife had given birth back in Yorkshire as the United party flew out. Yorath's daughter, named Gabrielle Nicole, would go on to become famous as a sports presenter and marry Scottish rugby international Kenny Logan.

The players and fans of Hajduk Split were confident ahead of kick-off that the one-goal advantage of the visitors would be overturned. Leeds, who had been beaten at Anfield two days earlier, were taunted on their way into the Plinaric Stadium as to how many goals the home team would score. As veterans of European combat, however, Revie's men just shrugged their shoulders as if to say, 'We'll see...'.

With Clarke missing after being handed a two-game ban for his dismissal at Elland Road, Joe Jordan was paired with Mick Jones up front as Leeds went in search of the draw that would guarantee progress. Hajduk, roared on by a passionate 30,000 crowd, did create the game's two best chances only for David Harvey to deny Micun Jovanic with an early save and Ivan Surjek to head wide late on when it seemed easier to score. But, in truth, Leeds produced such a polished performance that Revie was later moved to compare it to his own favourite in Europe – the goalless draw in Budapest against Ferencvaros that had been enough to clinch the 1968 Inter-Cities Fairs Cup. United did get the ball in the net at the death through Johnny Giles, only for referee Robert Helies to rule he had already blown for time. The 'goal' Leeds didn't need was ruled out but it was purely academic as news filtered through that AC Milan had won 1-0 in Prague to seal a 2-0 aggregate victory and reach a final that would prove so controversial, an attempt would be made to overturn the result by a member of the European Parliament 35 years later.

Before the Cup Winners' Cup final in Salonika, however, United had the far from insignificant matter of an FA Cup final. Revie's former club Sunderland had, against all the odds, battled through to their first final in 46 years. Only a stunning save from Jim Montgomery had kept the Second Division Wearsiders in the Cup at Notts County in the third round before a goal by Dave Watson had earned a replay back at Roker Park that was won 2-0. It also took a replay to deal with Reading in the next round before a memorable 2-2 draw at Manchester City in front of more than 50,000 fans was followed by a 3-1 victory over Malcom Allison's side back in the North East. Luton Town and then Arsenal followed City out of the competition as, unbelievably, Sunderland reached Wembley. Leeds were immediately made overwhelming favourites, a feeling only reinforced when Brian Clough declared, 'There is no way Sunderland can beat Leeds' in his role as television pundit ahead of kick-off. This was a true David v Goliath encounter in every sense of the phrase with no club from the Second Division having won the FA Cup since West Bromwich Albion in 1931. Leeds just could not lose, even when it became apparent as the two teams strode out at the tunnel end of Wembley that the neutrals in the 100,000 crowd were backing Sunderland.

One man who did believe the apparently impossible was possible was Bob Stokoe. The Sunderland manager had previous with Revie and probably despised him more than any other figure in football. The pair had been on opposite sides in the 1955 FA Cup final as Newcastle United beat Revie's Manchester City but it was seven years later when their paths crossed for the first time as managers. Just four games remained of the 1961-62 season when relegation-threatened Leeds travelled to Bury for the first of a double-header against Stokoe's Shakers inside four days that would go a long way towards whether Elland Road would be hosting Third Division football for the first time the following campaign. Stokoe went to his grave in 2004 insisting that Revie offered £500 for Bury to forfeit one of the games. It was an allegation that did not come to light until the 1977 *Daily Mirror* investigation into Revie that also included claims about United's title-losing defeat at Wolves in 1972. So, while the millions watching at home tuned in to watch Sunderland take on Leeds at Wembley, few knew the depth of the resentment burning inside Stokoe towards his Elland Road counterpart. There were, admittedly, clues during the build-up as Stokoe launched a verbal attack on Leeds' approach during their semi-final win over Wolves. He added: "I was staggered during the semi-final at the way Bremner went the whole 90 minutes disputing every decision given against his team. My message to Mr Burns (the Cup final referee) is I want him to make the decisions and not Mr Bremner." The response from Bremner was to tell the *Yorkshire Evening Post*, "It is like Wilfred Pickles have-a-go week", Halifax-born Pickles having been the host of a BBC Radio show *Have A Go*.

Bremner's flippant remark was the last made by a Leeds player before the final as Revie ordered there to be no display of public confidence during the last few days. The result was taut, monosyllabic replies when the United squad were interviewed on television during the traditional Cup final morning build-up. In contrast, the Sunderland players looked relaxed and determined to enjoy their big day out – as Barry Davies found out when interviewing Dave Watson.

After asking the centre-half about his attacking talents, Davies was left puzzled by an explosion of maniacal cackling as team-mate Billy Hughes activated his new toy, a laughter box. Sunderland's relaxed attitude was also illustrated by the television cameras being allowed to film on the coach to Wembley, something that was unheard of at the time.

Once at the stadium, the contrasting mood within the two camps was still evident as the Wearsiders, who had just finished sixth in the Second Division, continued to milk the occasion. Leeds were intent on treating the final 'like any other game', though that is not to say Revie's men were not feeling confident. Trevor Cherry, the only member of the team not to have played 12 months earlier when Arsenal were beaten in the FA Cup final, recalls: "It was a big day for me, personally, but I felt, just like the rest of the lads, that we would win and set us up nicely for the Cup Winners' Cup final a week or so later."

Despite being the overwhelming underdogs, Sunderland settled quicker on the slippery, rain-soaked surface and went close when Mick Horswill hit a 20-yard shot that flew just past David Harvey's post. It was a let-off for Leeds, though only a temporary one as Ian Porterfield showed tremendous poise on 31 minutes to cushion a Dave Watson header on his thigh before thrashing a shot with his weaker right foot past Harvey and two defenders on the line. With almost an hour to play, though, United remained undaunted and had the ball in the net shortly after half-time through Cherry only for referee Ken Burns to, quite rightly, rule goalkeeper Jim Montgomery had been fouled. Leeds continued to pour forward and then, midway through the second-half, came the moment that prompted commentator Brian Moore to shout 'it's a goal' as a Peter Lorimer shot arrowed towards the net. Trevor Cherry had created the chance with a diving header from a Paul Reaney cross that Montgomery could only palm into the path of Lorimer. To ITV's Moore and the 100,000 fans inside Wembley, the equaliser had arrived. Only it hadn't as Montgomery, in one motion, got to his feet and threw himself in the path of the speeding ball, which was diverted on to the crossbar. Cherry, still on the floor inside the six-yard box, stuck out a leg but the ball bounced to safety. In that instance, the Cup was on its way to Sunderland. Cherry recalls: "I still can't believe Jim Montgomery saved that shot, it just didn't seem possible. Ninety-nine times out of a 100 it would have gone in. I thought my header was going in but that was nothing compared to the shock I felt when Peter's shot stayed out. I still watch it now and think it's going in."

The final whistle saw Bob Stokoe race from the Sunderland bench and on to the field, destined to embrace his hero goalkeeper. As Stokoe sported a trilby and overcoat over his red tracksuit bottoms, his jig of delight became such an iconic image that Sunderland replicated the look when erecting a statue in honour of their former manager outside the Stadium of Light in 2006. In the immediate aftermath of the final, Stokoe could not resist one last dig at his Leeds counterpart, famous for wearing a lucky blue suit to every game, when telling television viewers at home: 'I hadn't a lucky suit like Don Revie so I just came as one of the lads.'

Revie, for his part, refused to rise to the bait and remained magnanimous in defeat by insisting the better team on the day had won. Trevor Cherry agrees: "Sunderland out-fought us, which was unusual as it rarely happened to Leeds United. It was their day and just not meant to be for us. We realised that afterwards, though it did nothing to ease the sense of disappointment."

Chapter 16

A Greek Tragedy

When the English anarchist band *Chumbawamba* wrote the seminal tune *Tumbthumping* in the late 1990s, it was intended as an anthem to celebrate ordinary people's ability to have a good time despite being constantly battered by the effects of poverty and inequality. The line 'I get knocked down, but I get up again, you're never going to keep me down' may have seemed frivolous and shamelessly contagious. But the band, whose base for their early years was a communal house in the rough but proud Leeds district of Armley, was actually trying to get across a serious message about the working classes' ability to overcome adversity. It could also have been a lyric written with the fortunes of Don Revie's Leeds United in mind. If any club personified the character of being able to bounce back from potentially demoralising body blows, it was the one from the city that *Chumbawamba* later adopted as their home. No matter if it was a Cup final defeat or missing out on a league title by the slimmest of margins, the mantra coming out of Elland Road almost immediately after a setback would be, 'We will re-group and try again next time'. It was this attitude that led to Leeds being among those challenging for honours, season after season, for 10 years despite suffering far more heartache than happiness during their quest for success. In the wake of the FA Cup defeat to Sunderland in 1973, supporters were expecting a similar message with the European Cup Winners' Cup final just 11 days away. Initially, that was just what they got as Revie spoke about making amends for such a major disappointment by beating AC Milan to claim a third European trophy. This time, however, the words would soon take on a hollow ring after it emerged Everton wanted the Leeds manager. And, most worryingly of all for the Elland Road players and supporters, it seemed Revie wanted to go. Harry Catterick had left Goodison Park and Everton, after being rebuffed by Bill McGarry of Wolves and Ipswich Town's Bobby Robson, had turned their attentions to Revie. A five-year contract worth £100,000 was dangled in front of him, a substantial rise on the £17,500 per annum deal he had at Leeds. Revie had long held the belief, shared by many at Elland Road, that the board did not truly appreciate him. Not since the 1967 departure of Harry Reynolds, the chairman who had backed Revie both financially and emotionally in his early years in the job, had the United manager enjoyed anything more than cordial relations with the board. Reynolds' successor, Albert Morris, had died just a few months after stepping up to chairman and been replaced by Percy Woodward, who had remained in charge until 1972. Manny Cussins then stepped into the role but such had been Revie's power at Elland Road since the late Sixties that few decisions had been taken on club matters without his consent. Revie's value to Leeds was, of course, underlined by the decline that set in after his departure. But, at the time, some directors felt their manager was guilty of over-stepping the mark with an often autonomous approach, which led to resentment festering. The Earl of Harewood, who as club president since 1961 shared in all the highs and lows of the Revie reign, is adamant the board never truly appreciated what they had. "When Don left to manage England, the club took his club car off him," reveals the Earl. "It seemed a very mean thing to do to someone who had done such wonderful things for Leeds. I felt at the time – and still do to this day – that the club should think the same. But it seemed they didn't. They were very, and I mean this in the very worst sense, 'West Riding' in their attitude. I valued what Don did for Leeds so much that I wanted to give him a house, but unfortunately I didn't have any to spare. But I did give him some land that one could build on and he built a house on that."

Revie had been the subject of several offers during his time as Leeds manager, Sunderland being the first to try and lure him away from Elland Road in 1964. Birmingham City attempted the same several years later, while there were also tempting offers from abroad, with intermediaries from Torino and Juventus both contacting Revie to say a salary of £30,000 per year was on offer if he was willing to switch to Italy. All had proved unsuccessful but, this time, the attraction of Everton and an offer that had now been increased to include a £50,000 tax-free signing on fee was, it seemed, just too good to turn down. Revie's apparent attitude to money had long been a source of disquiet in football. In an era when footballers would often see out their entire career with one or two clubs, he had played for five. Revie had been taught an important lesson at the first of those clubs, Leicester City, and it was one he never forgot. John McTavish, who played with Revie at Manchester City for four years, recalls: "Don once told me about a chat he had with Ken Chisholm, one of his team-mates at Leicester. Ken had said that the only way to make money as a footballer was by moving clubs regularly. Don was a young lad at the time but he never forgot and did the rounds early in his career. He didn't even stay that long at City, considering how well he fitted in. At Maine Road, we used to get a £4 bonus for winning and £2 for drawing. My weekly wage was around £14, while our bonus for reaching the Cup final was just £20. Don always pointed to that as proof Ken Chisholm had been right all those years before."

Jack Overfield, the former Leeds wide man, was another who saw how much store Revie put by money, hearing first hand how he had deliberately engineered transfers earlier in his career. Overfield recalls: "The wages were not good for players. When I was at Leeds, most of us earned between £15 and £18 per week. But the one time you could earn some decent money was if you moved clubs but did not ask for a transfer. Then, you would get a payment as part of the move. Revie had been at a few clubs by the time he came to Leeds so I asked him one day how he had gone about moving clubs. He said, 'Start to cause trouble and you'll be gone in no time'. He said that was how he had got out of Manchester City. Revie was cute like that. He must have been strong-willed, though, because it was not something I could do. I was probably too soft."

Revie's determination to maximise his earnings as a player was understandable. He had a young family to support and the life of a footballer could be a precarious one. One bad injury, such as the broken ankle he suffered at Leicester when still only 18, could leave a footballer on the dole with no support from the game. The football clubs' attitude towards their players was also one that hardly engendered loyalty, some going so far as to show a complete disregard for them. Jack Overfield recalls: "Players were kept in the dark by the clubs in those days. I had a few injuries at Leeds but it was only a few years ago that I discovered I have no cruciate in one leg. I was having an operation on my knee and the doctors told me afterwards. Leeds had never said a thing when I was operated on as one of their players. They probably just wanted to sell me to Sunderland so kept it to themselves. I played on for three years and felt quite bad about it when I heard the news as Sunderland had been very good to me as a club."

With the 1973 Cup Winners' Cup final approaching fast, the rumours about Revie and Everton were growing by the day but the United manager remained steadfast in refusing to comment on the story. Eventually, though, the Goodison Park board made a formal approach to their Leeds counterparts and Revie called his players together a couple of days before the final against AC Milan to deliver the news personally. Many, though, had already worked out what was going on for themselves, as Trevor Cherry recalls: "Bill Mallinson of the *Daily Mail* was big pals with Don and because he had run the original story, we knew it must be right. It meant we flew to Greece on the Monday before the final feeling a bit low." Any hopes Revie may stay were dispelled further the morning after his confirmation to the team when it was revealed in the newspapers that the Leeds manager had been spotted in his yellow Mercedes asking for directions in the Freshfield suburb of Merseyside that was home to Everton's wealthy owner, John Moores. Unfortunately for Revie, the local he had stopped was an Everton fan who took great delight in revealing, 'There is no doubt the driver was Revie. It simply had to be him, unless he has a twin brother'. Tellingly for those clinging to the slim hope the Leeds manager did have a double, it then emerged Revie had joined his players at Manchester Airport for the flight to Greece rather than, as was usually the case, travelling across the Pennines with them on the team bus. The switch to Goodison Park seemed a fait accompli.

The timing, especially for a man notorious for his fastidious preparations for even the most minor of games, was shockingly poor. Nevertheless, Revie remained confident his players were capable of beating Milan and ending the season with at least one trophy. Soon after the Leeds party touched down in Salonika, however, rumours began circulating as to whether the final would be a fair fight or not. Peter Lorimer recalls: "Johnny Giles was not playing due to being injured so was doing some work for either television or radio. It meant he went along to the press conference and, afterwards, he headed straight for our hotel where he told us, 'The word is we can't win this game'. We all wondered what he meant and he said the referee is supposedly in Milan's pocket. We didn't believe it – until the game started and it became all too clear he was right."

Johnny Giles' suspicions had, in the eyes of the United players, been confirmed within four minutes of the kick-off when Greek referee Hristos Michas awarded a free-kick for an innocuous challenge by Paul Madeley on Alberto Bignon just outside the penalty area. It was a poor decision, made even worse when the resulting free-kick by Luciano Chiarugi clipped Madeley in the defensive wall and spun beyond David Harvey in the Leeds goal. The turning down of a United penalty appeal after Mick Jones had been clearly hacked to the floor during the first-half then turned the Greek fans against their own official, whose rejection of a blatant handball inside the area after the break brought more jeering from the vast majority of the 40,154 crowd in Salonika. Then, when a third appeal was rejected in the wake of several wild challenges going unpunished, Leeds' frustrations boiled over when Norman Hunter's response to being fouled with a minute to go was to push the miscreant, Gianni Rivera, to the floor. The inevitable dismissal followed to cap a miserable night.

Revie was distraught, unable to come to terms with the manner of such an unjust defeat. Peter Lorimer remembers looking across at his manager in the dressing room and seeing the pain etched across his face. "Refereeing decisions like the Milan final were something Don could not cope with as it was out of his control," he says. "You don't mind losing to the better team but when something happens like that night, it is a horrible feeling. Don could not handle it."

The fall-out from the final was huge with referee Michas being immediately suspended by his own federation and UEFA, though the latter stopped short of launching a full investigation. It is a decision that still rankles in Leeds, as was proved 35 years on from the final when Richard Corbett, one of Yorkshire's members of the European Parliament, launched a petition calling on UEFA to overturn the result. More than 12,000 signed, only for UEFA to inform Corbett that, due to the considerable time delay, an investigation could not be launched. Corbett followed up with a visit to UEFA's headquarters in Switzerland but, despite a sympathetic response, the outcome was the same. *Sunday Times* football correspondent Brian Glanville, who a year after the final in Salonika would publish a damning investigation into the bribing of officials by Italian clubs in the 1960s, called The Years of the Golden Fix, insists Leeds never stood a chance. "I worked with Keith Botsford on the investigation and we uncovered widespread corruption involving Juventus and AC Milan," says Glanville. "The Leeds v AC Milan final was not included in our remit but I could see Leeds were never going to win."

The United camp's thoughts about the referee in Salonika were even less complimentary as they flew back to England straight after the game. With Revie seemingly destined for Everton, the bitterness was also tinged with sadness at the ending of an era. The manager himself headed off on holiday, though not until he had grabbed a quiet word with one of the younger members of his Leeds squad. Trevor Cherry recalls: "The gaffer called me into his office soon after we got back and gave me the biggest compliment when he said, 'I'm going to Everton and I want to take you with me'. I had only been at Leeds a year so it really took me back."

United fans prepared themselves for the worst as Revie vowed not to comment until his return from holiday with wife Elsie. What few in Leeds realised, however, was that a bizarre twist lay just around the corner in the form of controversial MP Dennis Skinner. The previous year, the Government had brought in strict legislation designed to curb inflation, which by then had soared to ten per cent en route to a peak of 25 per cent in 1975. Passed by a majority of 79 votes in the House of Commons, the anti-inflation White Paper stated that no new recruit to an existing job could be paid more than his predecessor in the role. Millions of workers would be affected by the new law, though by far the most high profile would turn out to be Revie. Skinner, the MP for Bolsover, chose to raise the matter of Everton's offer in the House of Commons on May 24 by asking if the Pay Board were investigating. The matter soon escalated beyond the control of either Revie, Leeds or Everton. Whitehall moved quickly following Skinner's question in the House to announce a probe was now underway, an official statement later the same day adding that 'both clubs have been reminded of the Pay and Prices Code'. By 9am the following morning, Revie had telephoned Leeds secretary Keith Archer from his holiday near Athens to reveal he would be staying at Elland Road after all.

Publicly, it was claimed a desire to finish the job had kept Revie at Leeds, though many on Merseyside or in West Yorkshire suspected what had been the real deciding factor in the move breaking down. Whatever the truth behind the about-turn - and maybe part of it was, after all, a desire to stay at Elland Road as later that same summer he would turn down another big money offer, this time to manage the Greek national side – the players were delighted. Even those Revie rated so highly that he had been planning to take them with him to Goodison Park. "We never mentioned it again," says Trevor Cherry. "It was nice to know he had been happy with my first season, but just like the rest of the lads I was pleased the gaffer was staying. We had not won anything in my first year but I still fancied our chances the following season." Cherry's optimism would prove well placed.

Chapter 17

The Charge Of The White Brigade

Leeds United's players had, over the years, got used to their manager setting demanding pre-season targets. There had been the vow to chase an unprecedented treble of European Cup, League Championship and FA Cup in the summer of 1969. Five years earlier, Revie had told his newly-promoted squad that the First Division title was not beyond them. None, however, of his pre-season challenges would be as outlandish as the one set at the end of the summer in which Revie had twice considered leaving Elland Road when Everton and the Greek national team came calling. 'Right lads,' said Revie to the players assembled before him. 'We've been the best team for the last decade. I know we haven't won as much as we should have, but that's in the past. Now I've had a thought this close season – can we go through the whole campaign unbeaten?'

It was a bold statement. Only one club had ever gone through a top flight season without losing so much as one game and that was Preston North End in the first year of the Football League. The Lancashire club won 18 and drew four of their 22 games in 1888-89 to finish 11 points clear of runners-up Aston Villa. But, since then, the football world had moved on. Not only would Leeds be playing almost twice as many games and against far superior opposition, but Preston's Invincibles had only faced teams from the Midlands and their own native Red Rose county. The often chaotic nature of that inaugural season was also underlined by the points system of two for a win and one for a draw only being finalised more than two months after the Football League had got underway. One other club had remained unbeaten across a full season, but Liverpool's feat had come in the Second Division and, again, before the turn of the century. Arsenal would, of course, emulate Preston by going through the 2003-04 Premier League campaign without losing any of their 38 games. But when Revie set his Leeds side a similar target, it seemed an unattainable goal. Trevor Cherry, the defender Revie had planned on taking to Everton before performing a U-turn and rejecting the Merseysiders, recalls: "After Don had asked, 'Can we get through the whole campaign unbeaten?' we all just looked at each other as if to say, 'Did he really just say that?' But, soon, he had us believing it was possible and we were determined to give it a good go."

One United stalwart who would not be part of the push for footballing immortality was Jack Charlton. Now 38, the former England defender had featured in just 25 of the club's 64 games the previous season. He had decided before the FA Cup final defeat to Sunderland it was time to realise his ambitions of becoming a manager and went to see Revie. The Leeds manager tried to tempt his one time team-mate into staying at Elland Road but, quickly realising the defender's mind was made up and that a vacancy at Middlesbrough was of particular interest, Revie jotted down a list of conditions that Charlton should demand at his interview. The main stipulation was making sure he had total control of the football side. Armed with the handwritten list, Charlton travelled to Ayresome Park and turned the tables on his interviewers by asking them the questions. He was duly appointed and Boro went on to win promotion to the top flight in style, finishing a phenomenal 15 points clear of runners-up Luton Town in his first season. Charlton recalls: "Don had offered me a two-year deal at Leeds, with the possibility of me moving on to the coaching staff. But I wanted to step out on my own and, eventually, I went to Middlesbrough. The last thing Don said to me when I walked out of Leeds for the final time was 'if you ever need any advice, just pick up the phone'. I really appreciated that. He was the same with the other lads later on, such as Billy Bremner. We were all his lads even though we were no longer at Leeds and he wanted the best for us." Charlton would go on to enjoy a hugely successful career in management, following Boro's promotion success by leading Sheffield Wednesday out of the Third Division and then taking the Republic of Ireland to the 1990 and 1994 World Cup finals.

In his absence, Leeds got down to the business of making Revie's dream of remaining unbeaten a reality. The initial omens, however, were not good, as Trevor Cherry admits: "We played a couple of friendlies in pre-season against Bradford and Huddersfield and were awful. We drew one and lost one, and I remember saying to my wife Sue, 'Maybe they aren't the players they used to be any more?'"

Cherry needn't have worried as, once the real action got underway, Leeds hit the ground running. With Gordon McQueen having admirably filled Jack Charlton's boots, the first seven games were won. Revie had again resisted the temptation to dip into the transfer market, instead choosing to show faith in not only his experienced players but also youngsters such as McQueen, Cherry, Joe Jordan and Frank Gray who had been gradually introduced to the team over the previous 12 months or so.

United had ended the 1972-73 season under something of a cloud with the two cup final defeats and the drawn-out saga that saw Revie announce his departure to Everton only to back-track a few days later. There had also been a return to the disciplinary problems that had made Leeds so unpopular a couple of years earlier, the Football Association's response being to hit the club with a suspended £3,000 fine and a warning to improve their behaviour. Revie responded with a press conference and a charm offensive, but it was the actions of his players on the pitch once the new season was underway that started to win over their critics once again. After beating Everton 3-1 on the opening day, United faced back-to-back visits to north London to face Arsenal and Tottenham Hotspur. Crowds in the capital – and journalists, for that matter - had a notoriously poor view of Leeds, leading to a siege mentality being adopted by Revie and his men. Nothing would be allowed to disrupt the players during their trips to London. Former *Telegraph & Argus* football writer John Wray recalls: "There was always an edge to the games in London, not least because the press down there didn't like Leeds and Don knew it. He was so focused for every trip, and even a traffic jam would not be allowed to cause problems. On the rare occasions when the team bus did not have any police out-riders, Don would always be concerned about the heavy traffic. Because he was rarely off the BBC in those days, he would lean out of the front door and bellow, 'BBC coming through' at nonplussed drivers as the team bus did a nifty piece of queue-jumping. The ploy always succeeded." Leeds duly won both games in north London with the manner of the 2-1 win at Highbury and the 3-0 triumph at White Hart Lane being so impressive that Revie's team drew applause from the home fans. Not only that, referee Roger Kirkpatrick sought out the United manager after the Spurs game to congratulate him on how well behaved Bremner, Hunter, Giles et al had been. Leeds, it seemed, had put long-held feuds with bitter rivals aside and, most unbelievably of all to their arch-critics, stopped haranguing the officials throughout the entire 90 minutes. In its place, was a return to the free-flowing football of two seasons earlier when United had won not only the FA Cup but also many friends. Leeds, playing under the new giant floodlights that had been installed at Elland Road during the summer, were in danger of eclipsing the whole First Division. Peter Lorimer, for one, was delighted with the new approach. "I don't honestly think Don believed in us until that last year or so," says Lorimer. "He was quite a negative man, probably because he hated losing so much. For a lot of his time, everything was geared towards making sure we didn't lose. It was only when he was thinking of moving on that he said, 'Get out there and show everyone what a great team you are'. It must have been quite a wrench to let us off the leash like that because, deep down, he would have been worried it might all go wrong."

The 100 per cent winning start came to an end in the eighth game of the season when Manchester United claimed a point from their late September visit to Elland Road. Victories over Norwich City and Liverpool then came either side of dour draws against Stoke City and Leicester City before Leeds travelled to Manchester City. Top of the league, the United players were happy with their start only for Revie's pre-match team-talk to shatter any illusions they had of having pleased their manager. Trevor Cherry recalls: "We had gone 12 games unbeaten and nine of those had been won, including a 1-0 victory at Liverpool a week earlier. But because we had drawn two of the last three, Don was not happy. He sat us all down at Manchester City and launched into us. He said, 'I want to go unbeaten this season and win the league but if you lads are not going to do it for me then I'll go out and get someone who will'. We were unbeaten and just looked at each other stunned. But we did step it up, went out and beat Manchester City, and remained unbeaten right through until February."

The United players had long since got used to Revie's threats during team-talks, either before a game or at half-time. Eddie Gray, who started seven of the opening eight league games in 1973-74 but managed just one more appearance due to injury, says: "We could always tell when Don was upset at half-time. Every time, he would walk into the dressing room and go straight to the mirror to comb his hair. He wouldn't say a word. But we would know if he was unhappy because he would be combing his hair so hard that it was almost being ripped out. All we could do was watch and fear the worst. Then, in one move, he would turn round and bring his fist down on the table in the middle of the room so hard that everything on it would go flying. He would then shout, 'The chequebook is coming out on Monday morning'. We had the same team for ten years but he still kept saying the same thing, it became almost comical."

Revie, so determined to win a second league title, had learned from the lessons of the past. He decided very early in what turned out to be his final season at Elland Road that United would not become bogged down by chasing success in the Cups. A weakened side had been sent to Ipswich Town in the League Cup second round and been duly beaten 2-0, while Revie had also let his senior players know that progressing in the UEFA Cup was not a priority. Norwegian amateur side Stromsgodset included in their side a 5ft 7in goalkeeper whose daily job was as a postman so Leeds made light work of a 7-1 aggregate victory in the opening round to set up a meeting with Scottish club Hibernian at the next stage. Peter Lorimer recalls: "Don wanted us to get knocked out but Hibs were so incompetent we still went through on penalties. We drew 0-0 at home and then Don rested a lot of the lads and played the rest out of position, such as Billy at sweeper, in the return. Don dressed it up to the press as wanting to give the Scottish lads a chance to play in their own country but he told the senior lads he wanted out. He told me before kick-off, 'Keep out of any tackles, I don't want you getting injured'. John Shaw, who was still only a teenager, played in goal but, unfortunately for Don, had a blinder. Hibs just couldn't get past him, no matter what they tried. John saw it as his chance to really impress and was taking it. Thanks to him, there was still no score at half-time. We returned to the dressing room and it was almost comical to watch Don shake John's hand and say, 'I've never seen a performance like that, John. Brilliant. But I'm taking you off, son, so get in the bath'. Glan Letheran, our youth team keeper, was on the bench so Don brought him on. But the ploy didn't work as Hibernian still couldn't score and the game finished goalless, meaning the game would have to be decided by penalties. Don, who looked absolutely gutted, came up to a few of the senior lads and said, 'You might as well win it now, we'll just have to go out in the next round'."

Leeds won the shoot-out 5-4 only for Hibernian to immediately complain to UEFA that Revie and trainer Les Cocker had, contrary to competition regulations, passed on instructions to the players during the shoot-out. So incensed were the Edinburgh club that two directors flew to Switzerland to press for either United to be thrown out of the competition or the game replayed. As it was, UEFA's Control and Disciplinary Committee settled for banning Revie for one game and fining Leeds £400. The decision meant Revie could not enter the dressing room area or go near the dugout for the third round first leg tie against Portuguese side Vitoria Setubal at Elland Road. With Les Cocker instead taking charge of the team, Leeds laboured to a 1-0 victory on a snow-covered surface with Trevor Cherry scoring the only goal from a Frank Gray cross. Perhaps sensing their manager's indifference to the UEFA Cup, just 14,196 fans watched the encounter on November 28. Revie was back in the dugout for the return a fortnight later and even more determined that United should go out. Lorimer again: "Don told us we could take our golf clubs to Portugal and that definitely wasn't him. We were even out on the course the day before the game. Don had realised by then that because we were getting involved in every competition, we were constantly coming up short. Don's one aim was to win the league that season and nothing else mattered. Personally, I wish he had done it sooner as I am sure we would have won more trophies."

A United team featuring youngsters Peter Hampton and Jimmy Mann were still ahead on aggregate at half-time in Portugal only for three goals in 22 second-half minutes to put the home side in control. Gary Liddell, who replaced Gordon McQueen with 10 minutes remaining, did pull a goal back but Revie got his wish as Vitoria held on to progress to the quarter-finals where they lost to Stuttgart.

As Revie had hoped, the exit from Europe allowed his players to concentrate all their efforts on maintaining what had been a scintillating start to the league season. The weekend before flying out to Portugal had seen Leeds win 3-0 at Ipswich Town to equal Liverpool's record of 19 games unbeaten from the start of a campaign. A 2-1 win at Chelsea a week later, courtesy of goals from Mick Jones and Joe Jordan, meant a new record was established as United continued to close in on Revie's ambitious pre-season target. Just after Christmas, they did come within a whisker of the run ending when Birmingham City, with Gary Sprake now in goal for the Blues following his £100,000 move two months earlier, led 1-0 with just three minutes remaining. Joe Jordan saved the day by converting a Peter Lorimer cross to ensure the year ended with United's record reading played 23, won 16, drawn seven and, most importantly of all for Revie, lost none. It seemed a case of when and not if Leeds would win the title, though the one person who didn't seem to share the growing confidence at Elland Road was the manager. A fear of it all going wrong continued to gnaw away at Revie. Bill Bridge, former sports editor of the *Yorkshire Post*, recalls: "It was my first season at the paper and Don would always phone up at 11.15pm if there had been any midweek Division One games to find out the results. I could sense his nerves every time as he worried over how even teams in mid-table such as Spurs and Newcastle had got on. To me, it smacked of insecurity. Leeds were comfortably clear at the top and unbeaten but Revie was still afraid it would all go wrong."

The unbeaten run continued in the New Year as Frank Gray, who had made three league starts the previous season, came into the side briefly as injuries started to take their toll. Gray, who started the January games against Southampton and Everton, could have been forgiven for feeling daunted by the pressure of keeping the run alive. However, he insists: "Funnily enough, the team wasn't feeling the pressure in terms of remaining unbeaten because it wasn't something that was being talked about by the players. We left that to others outside the club. Our only incentive was to get the points that would keep us clear at the top. All the rest didn't matter and was only something the lads thought we might look back on at the end of the season."

Frank Gray may suggest today the unbeaten run was not becoming burdensome but United's displays were suggesting otherwise, Bristol City having knocked Revie's side out of the FA Cup fifth round after a replay. Revie had made just three changes from the line-up that had won 2-0 at Manchester United in Leeds' last league outing – Terry Cooper for Paul Reaney, Roy Ellam for Gordon McQueen and Johnny Giles for Terry Yorath – so could not be accused of taking the Elland Road replay lightly. Nevertheless, the Cup exit did mean that Leeds, whose unbeaten run in the league now stood at 29 games, had no further distractions in the quest to clinch a second league title.

Normal service seemed to have been resumed four days after Bristol City's shock Cup upset as goals from Billy Bremner and Allan Clarke put Leeds 2-0 up inside the first quarter at Stoke City. Bremner's 14th minute strike had left Stoke particularly incensed, the Leeds captain having been allowed to take a quick free-kick after being fouled on the edge of the area. It was taken so swiftly that goalkeeper John Farmer never moved as the ball curled into the net but referee John Homewood was unmoved by the inevitable protests that followed. Joe Jordan then thought he had made it 3-0 with a diving header at the far post only for the 'goal' to be ruled out for offside. Stoke, still furious at Bremner's goal being allowed to stand, regained a foothold in the game with a curled shot from Mike Pejic before Alan Hudson ensured the sides went in at the break level, with his first goal since joining from Chelsea. Leeds, who had lost Johnny Giles to a groin injury when two goals up, were rattled and duly fell behind on 69 minutes when Dennis Smith capitalised on a bout of head tennis in the visitors' penalty area to power the ball past David Harvey.

The Stoke players were overjoyed, as goalscorer Alan Hudson readily admits: "Everyone hated Leeds then, no matter what club you were playing for at the time. So, whenever you beat them, it was party time. I had just joined Stoke when Leeds came to the Victoria Ground with that long unbeaten run. They were the team everyone wanted to beat that season, even more than usual. But, before we knew what was happening, Leeds had gone 2-0 up. It looked like we were heading for a bit of a hiding, only to tear back into them and win 3-2. After the game, we were celebrating in the dressing room when one of the apprentices came in and said, 'Leeds are smashing up their dressing room'. He would then keep us updated with things like, 'The door is damaged now' and, 'The table's gone over'. But all we did was cheer that bit louder. That day at Stoke proved Alex Ferguson and his tea-cup smashing had nothing on Leeds under Revie."

To Jimmy Greenhoff, sold by Revie midway through the 1968 Inter-Cities

Cup final victory over Ferencvaros, the victory was particularly sweet. He recalls: "Everyone knows playing against your old club feels special and I was no different. You want to prove them wrong for letting you go, and because I was captain the day Stoke ended Leeds' long unbeaten run it was that little bit more special."

United's proud run was over and, despite still being eight points clear at the top, doubts started to creep into the mindset of a club who had suffered more than their fair share of heartache over the years. Home draws against Leicester City and Newcastle United were followed by a much-needed 1-0 victory over Manchester City to set up the March 16 trip to Liverpool. Such was the anticipation ahead of the meeting between the first and second placed sides that the gates at Anfield had to be locked more than an hour before kick-off. The majority of the 56,003 crowd went home happy thanks to Steve Heighway netting the only goal eight minutes from time, leaving Liverpool six points behind Leeds but with two games in hand. United's fate was still in their own hands but the destination of the league title was, by no means, the formality it had appeared at the turn of the year. Worse was to follow as Burnley came to Elland Road a week after the Liverpool defeat and won 4-1, a result the triumphant club's directors missed after the Leeds board had taken exception to a comment Clarets chairman Bob Lord had made earlier in the season about 'the Jews who run television'. Lord was banned by Leeds from Elland Road and his fellow directors boycotted the game in protest.

The 4-1 reverse, captured by the television cameras, was a catastrophic result whose potential significance was not lost on the players. Trevor Cherry, who featured in all but four of United's league games that season, recalls: "The Stoke defeat had been put down to being nothing more than a bad day at the office, the sort of which can happen in football even to the best teams. What was far more worrying, though, was losing 4-1 at home to Burnley. I was coming off the field afterwards and Mick Jones said, 'I can't remember us losing two in a row before'. He looked stunned, as if he could not take in what had just happened. So, you can imagine what the mood was like when we went to London for our next game and lost that as well to West Ham United."

The 3-1 defeat at Upton Park a week after the humbling by Burnley meant, for the first time that season, United's fate was now in another club's hands. Even if Leeds won their final six games, Liverpool could still pip them to top spot by finishing with a 100 per cent winning record of their own. Revie's nightmare scenario was unfolding in front of his very eyes and something had to be done. He knew all his powers of inspiration and persuasion were going to be needed to turn round the slump in form that was threatening to bring yet more heartache to a season's end for Leeds. Thankfully for United, they had a master in the art of man-management at the helm. Peter Lorimer says: "There was no-one better in coaxing a performance out of his team than Don. He had proved that time and time again in getting us to bounce back from setbacks in the past. His great trick was not to launch into the players after a game, Don felt conflict achieved little in the immediate aftermath. So, he would just come in and bang the table before saying, 'Get off for the weekend because on Monday morning we will be having a meeting about this – so think about what went wrong'. It would ruin our weekend because, inevitably, it would mean the lads mulling over in their minds what they could have done differently. But it was clever man-management as, often, anything said in the heat of the moment straight after a match is forgotten by the following game. Don's way was to get us all together on the Monday and let everyone have their say. He wouldn't shout us down, he would instead listen to what the lads had to say. It meant the meeting was constructive and we all left it determined to make amends the following game. He was a very clever man." Trevor Cherry, who would go on to be a manager himself and be in charge of Bradford City on the day of the Bradford fire when 56 supporters lost their lives, was another who appreciated the approach taken by Revie. "Don was not a ranter and raver," he says, "and waiting until the Monday to get his point across was a clever tactic. I took note and, when I went to Bradford, I tried to do the same. I was never one for running the players into the ground as punishment for a bad performance. My focus was always on looking forward, not back. It was an invaluable lesson I learned from Don."

The Monday morning inquest into the West Ham defeat behind them, Leeds were ready to welcome Derby County to Elland Road five days later. England were due to play Portugal in Lisbon on the Wednesday but Paul Madeley and Norman Hunter withdrew, citing injury. Alf Ramsey, in what would be his final game in charge of England before being sacked, was not amused but Revie was unmoved. He had made a habit of persuading his players to pull out of international squads to remain fresh for upcoming Leeds games, with only Billy Bremner choosing to defy his manager by joining up with Scotland as often as possible. Such an attitude meant he remained Leeds' most capped player with 54 appearances for many years until being overtaken by South Africa captain Lucas Radebe (58) and Ian Harte (54) of the Republic of Ireland.

With Hunter and Madeley making swift recoveries from injury to take their places in the starting XI, Leeds looked to get their season back on track against

Dave Mackay's Derby. Peter Lorimer, back in the side after being dropped against West Ham, settled nerves with a lobbed goal before Billy Bremner, who had been without any international commitments in midweek because World Cup-bound Scotland had no game, added a second. Any United fans hoping the tide had turned were to be disappointed, though, as Revie's team could only grind out goalless draws against Coventry City at Highfield Road and Sheffield United on home soil in their next two fixtures. The damage was not, however, as bad as first feared as Liverpool also dropped points. Nevertheless, the return fixture at Bramall Lane, just 24 hours after the meeting in Leeds, had taken on monumental importance. At half-time, the deadlock remained in Sheffield, while in Liverpool the home side were already 4-0 up against Manchester City. Revie's worst nightmare beckoned. He urged his side forward during the interval and was rewarded with a 2-0 victory, Peter Lorimer netting twice to continue his late season renaissance. Lorimer then scored again as Ipswich Town were beaten 3-2 in front of 44,015 fans at Elland Road to pile the pressure back on Liverpool, who had been held to a goalless draw in the Merseyside derby at Anfield. Bill Shankly's men could only now prevail by finishing the season with three straight wins against Arsenal, West Ham and Tottenham, while also needing Leeds to lose their final game at Queens Park Rangers. As it was, Liverpool fell at the first hurdle as a Ray Kennedy goal was enough to earn Arsenal both points at Anfield the following Wednesday. Coincidentally, a 'This Is Your Life' tribute to Revie was broadcast the same night on ITV after Eamon Andrews had surprised the Leeds manager four days earlier at a Variety Club dinner in the city's Queens Hotel. Far more important than the famous big red book, however, was the second league championship that was now in Revie's grasp. He was ecstatic, as were the thousands of fans who travelled to Loftus Road three days later to watch Allan Clarke clinch a 1-0 victory. Leeds ended the season with a five-point advantage over Liverpool who, by way of consolation, lifted the FA Cup at Wembley a week later courtesy of a comfortable 3-0 win over Newcastle United.

Gordon McQueen, signed only the previous season from St Mirren, had made 36 appearances and proved to be an admirable replacement for Jack Charlton. "Winning the league was a tremendous achievement and the thing that stands out most from my time at Leeds," remembers the former Scotland international. "Little Billy Bremner used to say it was the best Leeds team he had been involved in, so to be part of that is something that makes me very proud. The club had had a bit of bad press over the years but I think even the media finally realised during that season just what a special team we had."

The title's return to Elland Road had been vindication of Revie's decision to stick with a group of players who many had questioned just 12 months earlier in the wake of the FA Cup final defeat to Sunderland. His side had led the First Division table from day one and were worthy champions, something even his critics in the London-based media were forced to accept. John Helm, Sports Editor of *BBC Radio Leeds* during the title-winning season, recalls: "Don had a very good working relationship with all the northern-based journalists on the nationals, but less so with those from down south. He felt they had an agenda against the club and were always trying to trip him up. Don thought they would favour the London club, no matter how well Leeds played or what he said. He was probably right. I always felt Leeds were only the most unpopular side around because they were winners. The southern press didn't like Leeds and that is a big part of why that team never gets the credit it deserves. But in that final season under Don, even the critics had to say Leeds were deserved champions."

Revie, despite the lambasting he often had in the national press, was not one to bask in the personal glory after leading United to the title, as then *Daily Express* football reporter Mike Morgan recalls: "I interviewed Don after the 1974 title win and all he wanted to do was talk about the players and his staff. He said, 'Those lads are the ones who won the championship, not me. Them and people like Syd Owen, Maurice Lindley and Les Cocker – I am just the figurehead'. It was typical Don, who was such a modest man. After what happened with England, he had a reputation for being deceitful and less than honest. But, in my dealings with him at Leeds, he was the complete opposite. He also had a great sense of humour. There was one occasion towards the end of that season when David Harvey was presented with the Player of the Year award by the Scarborough branch of the official Supporters Club. The *Daily Express* sent me along but, after we'd enjoyed a few drinks and a good night, it turned out there had been a mix-up and I had no room booked in the hotel. 'Suave', we called him that because he was a scruffy sod and not because it rhymed with Harv, rang Don once we realised what had happened and Don just said, 'Let him kip in your room'. Unfortunately, we got up there to find only one double bed and had to spend the night in it together. Don thought it was hilarious when he found out the following day."

As the minds of United's Scottish contingent of players turned towards the World Cup in West Germany, thoughts in Leeds were focused on the impending return to the European Cup. Only Jack Charlton and Gary Sprake of the 14 players who had featured in the 'Battle of Britain' semi-final double-header against Celtic in 1970 had left Elland Road, meaning it surely represented one last chance for Revie's great team to emulate Real Madrid and be crowned the best in Europe. In the end, United would go incredibly close to fulfilling that dream with only Bayern Munich and a couple of questionable refereeing decisions denying the Yorkshire club victory in the 1975 final. By then, however, the man who had built Leeds up from almost nothing had been gone for almost a year.

Chapter 18

The Short Goodbye

'Kevin, get stripped,' was the curt instruction from Alf Ramsey. England were drawing 1-1 in a vital World Cup qualifier against Poland at Wembley on October 17, 1973, that had less than five minutes still to run. The home side, needing a win to book their place at the 1974 World Cup finals, had created and missed more than a dozen chances as Jan Tomazewski performed heroics in the Polish goal. Ramsey, the manager who had led his country to World Cup glory seven years earlier, was coming under increasing pressure from within the Football Association and knew the repercussions of failing to claim the two required points would be serious. In one last throw of the dice, Ramsey turned to the substitutes sitting behind him in the Wembley dugout area and barked his order. Kevin Keegan immediately stood up and Ray Clemence, in his eagerness to get his Liverpool team-mate into action as quickly as possible, pulled the striker's shorts down to his knees. Keegan was left red faced, but it was nothing compared to the embarrassment that followed as Ramsey made it clear the 'Kevin' in question was Derby County striker Kevin Hector. By the time Hector got on the field there was a little over a minute of normal time remaining but he still found time to head the best chance of the match wide of the post. The course of history for English football could have been changed in that instant, but, instead, the miss meant Ramsey was already living on borrowed time. Sir Harold Thompson, then the FA's vice-chairman and a figure Don Revie would come to hate with a passion during his own reign as England manager, had been campaigning for Ramsey's removal for several months so the failure to qualify for the World Cup was an opportunity Thompson seized upon. Six months later, the axe fell and Ramsey was sacked. Joe Mercer, the avuncular former Manchester City manager who had brought the league title to Maine Road in 1968, stepped in for the seven internationals scheduled for May and June but made it clear he was not interested in the job on a permanent basis.

With England having failed to qualify for the World Cup, the national newspapers filled their pages with speculation about the identity of Ramsey's successor. There was only one obvious candidate, a man whose club side had been at or around the top of English football for a full decade. They had won the league title twice, two European trophies, an FA Cup, a League Cup and reached countless finals. Despite such an impressive CV, Don Revie was, initially, not mentioned among the front-runners for the post that the press speculated included Leicester City's Jimmy Bloomfield and Gordon Milne of Coventry City. With the prospect of a second tilt at the European Cup on the horizon, it was felt within Lancaster Gate that Revie would be reluctant to give up one last chance of fulfilling his long-held dream to emulate Real Madrid and be crowned champions of Europe. Revie had flirted with switches to Everton and Greece the previous summer, but surely nothing would tear him away from Elland Road this time and the lure of taking on football's elite?

Revie himself, though, was in a quandary. Remaining loyal to the team he had seen grow from promising teenagers into one of the finest teams in the land was a big pull. But so was the chance to fill the highest office in English football management. Several years earlier, Revie had confided to the *Yorkshire Evening Post*'s Mike Casey that he planned to retire at 52. With this in mind, he had negotiated a nine-year consultancy role with the Leeds United board that would begin on New Year's Day, 1980. In return for attending four board meetings a year, he would pick up £10,000 per year – effectively a payment for services rendered in turning Leeds into a footballing force. The deal was still six years away from getting underway but, as he looked back on a reign at Elland Road that had begun in 1961, Revie appreciated more than most that time moved fast in football. And if he was ever going to make the step up to international management, this was the time.

There were other considerations that came into play, too, with many of the United squad edging towards the end of their careers. There was still plenty of football in the legs of Bremner, Hunter, Giles et al, as they would subsequently prove by reaching the 1975 European Cup final. But the clock was undeniably ticking on many of his star players. Revie had shown himself capable of dispensing with players before, Mike O'Grady being sold to Wolves just a few months after being an almost ever-present in the title-winning team of 1968-69 and Jimmy Greenhoff allowed to leave for Stoke City despite being popular with both the Elland Road crowd and his team-mates. But there was a sentimental side to Revie, as revealed the previous summer when he offered a two-year deal to 38-year-old Jack Charlton. The thought of having to show the door to the lads he had nurtured for so long was not appealing, as Revie's son Duncan confirms: "I never asked him outright about this, but I have always had the suspicion that Dad took the England job because he could not bear to break up the Leeds team he had built. The lads were all growing old and I just don't think he could face the prospect of moving them on after 10 years together. He would have to dismantle a team he loved so, to me, I think when the England job came along it was a case of 'problem solved'." Trevor Cherry, who would go on to win 12 of his 27 England caps under Revie, agrees: "If Don had a problem, it was being too loyal to that team. No-one wants to break their family up and that was why he wanted the England job. He couldn't bear the thought of that conversation when he would have to tell Billy, Johnny or Norman that they were no longer part of Leeds United any more. He was just too close to them."

Whether it was this reluctance to break up the team he had built or an ambition to prove himself at international level, Revie decided he wanted the England job. Feelers were put out to the newly-appointed secretary of the FA, Ted Croker, who immediately saw the appeal of a manager with the best record in the domestic game. Following the failure to qualify for the World Cup, English football had sunk to a low ebb and was badly in need of a lift. What better way to provide a much-needed boost than by appointing a manager with such a proven track record? FA chairman, Sir Andrew Stephen, and Dick Wragg, the chairman of the international committee, were similarly enthusiastic. Crucially, all three also noted the vastly improved disciplinary record of Leeds during the previous, title-winning, season. Talks were quickly organised where Revie outlined his vision to revive English football before an official approach was made to the Elland Road board. Typically, they initially tried to extract substantial compensation out of the FA for a manager still tied to a long-term contract before, in the face of an adverse reaction from both their manager and the public, settling for a much more realistic sum.

On July 4, 1974, Don Revie was confirmed as the new England manager and, within 24 hours, he had cleared his desk at Elland Road. The Leeds board had wanted Revie to remain until his successor was found but, despite 13 years as manager and another three as a player, the man charged with bringing pride back to the Three Lions proved, after all, that sentiment only went so far in football. Nevertheless, the players and staff were sad to see Revie go. Groundsman John Reynolds, then in the 18th season of a working life at Elland Road that has now stretched into a sixth decade, says: "I was very sad to see Don leave for the England job. Of course, I understood why he wanted to take the job but the club was never going to be the same. Don had never changed in all the years I had known him. All the success had made not a jot of difference to him, every morning he would still say 'hello' to everyone and thank all the staff for their efforts. I got the impression the staff meant as much to him as he did to us."

The club staff were not the only ones sad to hear of Revie's departure. Mike Morgan, then of the *Daily Express*, says: "Don had been brilliant for the press lads so we were sorry to hear he was leaving. As England manager, I knew Don would be out of my league because all our main writers in London would deal with him from now on so I knew I was going to miss him. At Leeds, Don had provided the press with great access to his players and, before every big game, we would be invited into the players' lounge and given carte blanche to interview whoever we wanted. It is very different now with all manner of obstacles put in the way to keep the players separate from the journalists. It is a real shame because, without the access we had back in the 1970s, the staple diet has become rumour and speculation. The clubs may complain about it but they have caused the 'them and us' attitude by putting the barriers up in the first place. Don, and Matt Busby for that matter, appreciated that access to the players was important, knowing it would more than likely lead to positive coverage." The local press were of a similar mind about Revie's departure. "Don was brilliant with us," says John Wray of the *Telegraph & Argus*. "There were three of us who regularly covered Leeds - myself at the *T&A*, Barry Foster at the *Yorkshire Post* and Don Warters of the *Yorkshire Evening Post*. Don was always available when we wanted a chat or an interview. We also used to travel on the team bus to games. Revie was always welcoming and I will always be grateful to him for one afternoon at Arsenal when Don Warters and I arrived to find our press tickets were not at reception. We explained to the steward who we were and that we had travelled down with the team but he just said, 'I don't care who you came with, you're not coming in without a ticket'. We were both getting worried as I had to file live copy for the *T&A* Saturday tea-time sports paper and Don Warters had to do the same for the *YEP*. Suddenly, Don Revie appeared at the entrance and told the steward in no uncertain terms to step aside and let us in. Somehow he had found out we were having problems and taken the time to come and find us to sort it out. I even think the team-talk was late that day at Highbury because of the problems. It was Don all over, always wanting to help the local press out." As Revie's 13-year reign came to a close, there was one last illustration of the special bond that had existed between the Leeds manager and the journalists who covered the club for the three local papers. John Wray explains: "Don wrote me a lovely letter just before leaving, saying how he had enjoyed working with me. I still have the letter at home and it is something I am very proud of."

Revie's last act at Elland Road before leaving for the England job was to recommend Johnny Giles as his successor. Unbeknown to the departing manager, however, Billy Bremner had got wind of the board being on the verge of appointing Giles and staked his own claim for the job. Eddie Gray remembers the day vividly. "Peter Lorimer and I were standing on Fullerton Park before training when Johnny came up to us and said, 'I'm the new manager'. But it turned out Billy had also applied, which he had every right to do as captain, and the directors panicked. They thought there would be a split in the camp, but they should have spoken to the boys as we would have told them that was nonsense."

Suddenly, Manny Cussins and his board were faced with a major decision to make. Common sense would suggest trusting the judgement of the man who had brought unparalleled success to the club over the past decade. However, the resentment felt by some over how it was the manager and not the board who wielded the true power at Elland Road during Revie's reign had not gone away. Nor would it have done several years later, if the comments of Cussins in the wake of Don Revie overturning a 10-year ban imposed by the FA are anything to go by. Part of Revie's defence in the High Court action against the FA was how the ban, for walking out on the England job to take up a lucrative post in Dubai, precluded him from taking up the nine-year consultancy role at Elland Road that was due to start in 1980. After the verdict, Leeds chairman Cussins, when talking to the *Yorkshire Evening Post*, did not sound like a man overjoyed at the prospect of possibly working with Revie again. He said: 'There is an obligation to Mr Revie and we shall carry out that obligation. We have a contract with him as a consultant. That doesn't mean we shall use him as a consultant. In any case, at the moment he is abroad for another two or three years but we shall honour our obligation.' Cussins, when talking to the paper's Mike Casey, then damned his former manager with faint praise: 'I have no axe to grind over the court case. Don may be very financially minded but he did a great job for Leeds United and all the players loved him.' But not the board, clearly.

If this attitude was prevalent among the directors at the time, it is no wonder the Cussins-led board went against Revie's recommendation and handed the job instead to Brian Clough. History shows the appointment was a disastrous one with Clough lasting just 44 days before being sacked and replaced by the much safer hands of Jimmy Armfield.

The choice of Clough, on the basis of his achievements as a manager, looked a sound one. But to go for such a vehement critic of Leeds United smacked of a deliberate affront to Revie. Clough had famously called for Leeds to be relegated the previous year, while, in his guise as a television pundit, he had described one particular win by Revie's men as, 'A bad week for football - the goodies lost and the cheats won'.

Whatever the true motivation behind Clough's shock appointment, what followed became one of the most infamous episodes in English football. Paul Trevillion, who had been brought in by Revie two years earlier to inject some US-style razzmatazz to Leeds United, says: "Brian was a complete one-off. Peter Shilton once told me how Brian strode into the dressing room at Nottingham Forest one day and made him take off his goalkeeper's jersey because, in Brian's words, 'I'm the fucking number one round here'. It was why Brian always wore green in the dugout at Forest. The problem was Brian was bigger than Derby before going to Leeds and bigger than Forest afterwards. But, at Leeds, it just wasn't the same and to go in like he did was all wrong. I did once say to Brian, 'Those lads had over 500 international caps between them and you should have respected that'. He accepted mistakes had been made."

So turbulent was life under Revie's immediate successor at Leeds that Clough would be gone a full month before England's new manager had taken charge of his first game against Czechoslovakia. Telling the players to, 'Chuck your medals in the bin because you have won them all by cheating' was Clough's first mistake and the relationship between manager and players, so strong in Revie's days, never recovered. Revie may have been in London preparing for his Wembley bow as an international manager but his shadow continued to be felt at Elland Road. So much so, that on the day Clough left Leeds, Revie was back in West Yorkshire taking part in the memorable Yorkshire Television special *Goodbye, Mr Clough* sitting alongside his bitter rival. Clough had been persuaded to take part by John Helm, then of the BBC but a good friend of YTV's Keith Macklin. He recalls: "The day Cloughie was sacked, I somehow got locked inside Elland Road with him. I knew Keith well so asked Brian whether he would take part. He could not understand what it would achieve but, in the end, he decided to do it. What neither of us knew at the time was Don Revie would be appearing as well."

A clearly indignant Revie rounded on Clough almost as soon as the live cameras were rolling, even going so far as to suggest, 'Brian is a fool to himself'. After 13 years, Revie was understandably finding it hard to let go of Leeds – a point reinforced when he spoke of 'our players' when discussing Clough's treatment of the team he had left behind several months earlier.

The YTV special was recreated for *The Damned United*, the 2009 film that charted Clough's controversial reign at Elland Road. Many fans from the modern era found it difficult to believe such an encounter had really taken place. Later, Revie would reveal in a television interview his bitterness at being paid by Leeds '£15,000 a year when Clough walked away with £44,000 tax free after just 44 days'.

Eventually, the Clough furore died down with the appointment of Jimmy Armfield bringing a much-needed calmer aura to Elland Road. Eight months later, pipe-smoking 'Gentleman Jim' had achieved what even Revie had not managed as Leeds reached the European Cup final. Unfortunately for Armfield, and just as it had so many times when Revie was in charge, luck would desert Leeds at the vital time as Bayern Munich won a controversial final in Paris on a night when United supporters rioted at the injustice of the Germans' victory. The trouble in the streets outside the Parc des Princes would lead to Leeds being handed a four-year ban from Europe by UEFA, a punishment that would later be cut in half after a personal appeal from Armfield. It would, however, not be until 1979 when Leeds next competed in Europe. And by then, not only had Armfield left Elland Road, Revie had effectively been kicked out of English football for good.

Chapter 19

A Legacy Squandered

When Brian Clough took his place in the Elland Road dugout for the first time, the evidence of what 13 years with Don Revie at the helm had done for Leeds United was laid out in front of him. Of the 11 players starting against Queens Park Rangers on the first Tuesday of the new league season, only three – Mick Bates, Trevor Cherry and Clough's own signing Duncan McKenzie - were not full internationals. It was not just on the pitch where the fruits of Revie's labour could be seen, either, with Elland Road standing almost as a monument to his work. To the left as Clough looked out from a dugout that, by today's standards, looked ridiculously small, was the North Stand terrace. Built four years earlier at a cost of £250,000, it had since been connected to the West Stand by a covered corner section. A similar corner stand was built on the opposite side, which under the grand masterplan to develop United's home would eventually be linked up to a new stand planned for the east side of the ground. To the right of Clough as he watched his home bow end in a shock 1-0 defeat to QPR, were the beginnings of the structure that would fill what used to be known as the Scratching Shed. Built at a cost of £400,000, the new South Stand opened early in 1975 and housed standing spectators in the paddock with seats behind. Its construction had finally allowed Leeds to move the pitch up to the front of the North Stand, ending the practice of supporters behind each goal being 30 yards from the nearest goalline. It was an anomaly that left one particular visiting manager confused, as groundsman John Reynolds recalls: "There was one funny incident when Freddie Goodwin and his Birmingham City team came to Leeds. He had played for us alongside Jack Charlton in the early days but, it turned out, had not been back to Elland Road for some time. After the game, Freddie travelled back to Birmingham and reported us to the Football League for having one half of the pitch bigger than the other. He had never said anything at the time. If he had I could have put him straight because, basically, he had been confused on coming out of the West Stand tunnel. In Freddie's day, the tunnel had been right on the halfway line but now, due to the new stands at either end, the tunnel sat midway inside one half of the pitch. He had not noticed the pitch had moved 60 yards to the north since his last visit. I had to show someone from the League round a few days later before they were satisfied."

Underneath this new pitch that left Birmingham manager Goodwin so confused was further evidence of the legacy Revie had left behind with a state-of-the-art undersoil heating system having been installed three years earlier. The final stage of the plan to transform Elland Road was to fill in the corner between the South Stand and the east side but, after spending £1m demolishing half of the Lowfields Road Stand in the late 1970s, work had to be abandoned due to lack of money. Without Revie at the helm, United had gone into decline.

Jimmy Armfield had initially proved an astute appointment after Clough's sacking, steadying the ship in the wake of such a turbulent chapter in the club's history to such an extent that Leeds reached the European Cup final. The following season also brought a fifth place finish in the league as Revie's side began to break up, Mick Jones' retirement in October, 1975, coming just a few months after Terry Cooper had moved to Middlesbrough. Norman Hunter would soon follow suit to Bristol City, while Billy Bremner joined Hull City. Armfield took the chance to blood some of the club's youngsters, while he also brought in Burnley's Ray Hankin. But the rot had set in. So much so, that any player hoping to challenge for honours no longer saw Leeds as their ideal club – a point reinforced when Gordon McQueen and Joe Jordan moved to Manchester United early in 1978. Less than four years after Don Revie had left Elland Road, Leeds United had returned to the level of also-rans, though a fifth place finish in 1979 and a brief re-appearance in the UEFA Cup did lift spirits. Relegation followed within three years, however, to leave Leeds exactly where they had been when Revie had taken charge in 1961 – skint and in the Second Division. Gordon McQueen, for one, is adamant when the slide began. He says: "Don leaving was the beginning of the end for Leeds. The club made some ridiculous decisions almost immediately afterwards, and just kept on making them. Even a couple of years later, the board could still not get it right. Leeds had a lot of good players when Don left but it all went wrong from that point and it was a real shame."

Much is made of how Revie's decision to leave was down to his reluctance to break up the team he had put together and it is true that many members of that great Leeds side were nearing the end of their careers in 1974. To some, this sentimentality is cited as a weakness and a factor in why the decline was so steep that, just seven years after competing in a European Cup final, United found themselves relegated. Peter Lorimer, however, refuses to pin the blame on his former manager, insisting there were sufficient talented youngsters already at the club to build a good side around. "People forget lads like Gordon

McQueen and Joe Jordan were only in their early 20s then and had been good enough to play in a team that reached the European Cup final," says Lorimer, who remained at Elland Road until 1979 before returning for another two-year spell in 1983. "Terry Yorath and Frank Gray were also there and played in the 1975 final so it is not as if the club had to start from scratch. The problem was some bad decisions were made, starting with the appointment of Clough instead of Gilesy." The Earl of Harewood concurs, citing how successful the policy of promoting from within proved to be at Liverpool – a club who also lost their talismanic manager, Bill Shankly, in 1974. United's club president says: "Don recommended Johnny Giles but the board went against that and gave it to Clough instead. We will never know if Johnny would have been a success but I, personally, feel he would."

The success that Brian Clough went on to enjoy at Nottingham Forest, taking a provincial Second Division club to two European Cups and one league title inside five years, as Leeds fell into decline was an irony not lost on anyone at Elland Road. Trevor Cherry remained with United until the club's relegation to Division Two in 1982 and admits to looking on enviously at what was happening at the City Ground. "I believe Leeds United's history could have been very different had the two managers that followed Don been the other way round," he says. "Clough was a great manager, his record shows that, but we got him at the wrong time. He came in to confront the players he had criticised in the past and it was never going to work. If Clough could have come along after Jimmy Armfield then I think Leeds would have been OK. Jimmy proved to be very good at breaking up that side. He did it gradually and with tact, so that there were no hard feelings on the part of the players. Well, apart from my own maybe! I played in every round of the European Cup run but was left out of the final so the old team could play. Syd Owen, one of Don's loyal staff, had a hand in it, I am sure about that to this day. Syd thought everyone who had been transferred to Leeds was tarnished in some way. He saw it as some sort of failure on his part that Don had been forced to go out and buy a player because he hadn't managed to bring a better one up through the ranks. Syd never liked Duncan McKenzie, for instance, because he had come in for big money. And Duncan didn't play in the European Cup final, either. I just wish Jimmy Armfield could have been appointed first and then, once Don's old team had been broken up, Brian Clough could have come in and done what he did with Forest at Leeds instead."

Revie had many strengths as a club manager, not least an ability to spot and nurture young talent. Eddie Gray, Peter Lorimer, Paul Reaney, Norman Hunter,

Paul Madeley and Terry Cooper were all handed their Leeds debuts by Revie before becoming mainstays of the success that followed. Likewise, Billy Bremner and Jack Charlton may have already been at Elland Road when Revie succeeded Jack Taylor in March, 1961, but both were never in any doubt as to the huge debt they owed their manager. This ability to improve the players under his charge meant transfer spending was relatively small, with any money invariably being used wisely. Eddie Gray says: "In that first eight to 10 years, he only brought in a couple of players for big transfer fees – Allan Clarke and Mick Jones. In fact, two of the best signings Don made, Bobby Collins and Johnny Giles, cost him buttons. It changed a little bit in later years with Trevor Cherry and so on but the way he built that side up for so little money is great testament to his managerial ability." As if to underline Eddie's point, club accounts show Clough spent more on transfers during 44 days at Elland Road than Revie managed in 13 years.

Following such a successful manager was always going to be a thankless task, no matter who was appointed. Clough did make mistakes, something even he admitted later in life. To Peter Lorimer, however, there is little doubt as to where the blame lies when it comes to how the tremendous legacy left behind by Revie was squandered. "If you had taken a couple of dossers out of Holbeck Moor," suggests United's all-time leading goalscorer about the district that sits near Elland Road, "and given them control of Leeds United, they couldn't have done as bad a job of running the club as what actually happened. Don left us as Champions and with £2m in the bank. Even in modern-day money, that represents quite a sum. But at a time when players were being signed for a maximum £300,000, it was a fortune and it beggars belief how the directors managed to blow it so quickly."

Chapter 20

The Three Lions

It is a time for optimism. As the man newly entrusted with the England football team emerges from the tunnel for the first time, all memories of the failure that led to the previous incumbent being sacked are forgotten. Lessons have been learned, a new era has begun and, this time, it really is going to be different. The Football Association, desperate to provide a helping hand, will invariably try to arrange a game against eminently beatable opposition for the new man's debut, usually a friendly and usually on home soil. The subsequent victory will then, so the blazers hope, cloud the fact that football managers, as with Prime Ministers, are essentially finite with all but a select few destined to end their careers in failure.

So it was with Don Revie as he walked around the greyhound track, that then still circled the Wembley turf, as England manager for the first time. Clad in a smart overcoat to keep out a chilly October night, he was 47 and a popular choice among supporters still reeling from having to watch the 1974 World Cup finals take place without the Three Lions just a few months earlier. Revie, as Leeds United manager, had won every domestic honour with the previous season having seen his side set a new Football League record by remaining unbeaten for the first 29 games. So, optimism was high. Not only that, but the free-flowing style Leeds had employed during their title success suggested that a return to the attacking approach the country craved after years of Sir Alf Ramsey's over-functional tactics seemed a distinct possibility. It was not only the fans who backed the appointment, either, with the press also being largely supportive. Brian Glanville, who has reported on England for *The Sunday Times* since the days Walter Winterbottom was nominally in charge of the national team, recalls: "Revie was the obvious choice, having built a quite brilliant team at Leeds, and I, initially, had very high hopes for what he could achieve." Jeff Powell, of the *Daily Mail*, admits to having similar thoughts on Revie's suitability: "In common with many, I pushed for Don to get the England job. There is no question he was the natural choice and it seemed the FA had made the right decision."

Enjoying the support of the London-based media was a new phenomenon to a manager whose side had ritually been criticised whenever they strayed too far from West Yorkshire and it was something Revie was determined to build on. Aware of how notoriously tetchy the relationship between Fleet Street and his predecessor had been, he quickly established a new level of co-operation by, just as he had at Leeds, handing out his home telephone number to journalists. Hospitality in the form of drinks and sandwiches were also laid on for the press at England get-togethers.

Among his players, Revie wanted to try and foster a similar spirit to the one he had created at Leeds. To that end, he gathered together 81 current and potential England players in Manchester soon after being appointed for a 'get-to-know-you' session. The intention of such a ground-breaking move was to make everyone feel included, while also proving to those on the fringes that, by working hard and impressing for their clubs, an England call-up was achievable. To some players, however, it smacked of the sort of indecision that would later characterise Revie's time in charge of the national team. Colin Todd, who made 18 of his 27 appearances for England under Revie, recalls: "To invite so many to what was just a get-together was odd. I could understand Don wanting to get to know his squad but to bring more than 80 along just suggested he had no idea who should be in the team." Todd's view would later be borne out by 47 of those invited to Manchester – including five of the half-dozen who travelled north from West Ham United - failing to make even one international appearance under Revie. Despite that, Sir Trevor Brooking believes the informal get-together did have its uses for the players. "As a footballer you never quite know if you are in the plans of a new manager," says the former midfielder who made 13 of his 29 England appearances under Revie. "So, in that respect, the gathering was meaningful. There were a lot of us there but Don made time to chat to every one of us individually. When it was my turn, he explained how he viewed the role of a midfielder and what he wanted from me. It was useful to hear his ideas."

To further try and get his players on side, Revie turned his mind to financial matters and negotiated improved rewards for anyone pulling on an England shirt. Where before a flat appearance fee of £60 had been handed over to the squad, now there was a sliding scale of an extra £100 for a draw and £200 for a win on top of the raised flat fee of £100. Older internationals were quick to condemn the move, insisting the honour of playing for your country should be enough. But to Revie the life of a footballer was a short and precarious one so, he felt, the players deserved financial reward. At the time, the players – none of whom earned the telephone number salaries of today – were grateful but, as with a lot that Revie did during his career, the introduction of incentive payments would be later used as a stick to beat him with. It was a similar story over the kit sponsorship deal the FA struck with Admiral shortly after Revie's appointment. Under the terms of the deal, England switched from their traditional all white shirts to ones with red and blue trims. The players also started to run out wearing tracksuits with 'Admiral' plastered across the front. Several FA councillors were horrified, branding the new gear tacky and distasteful. Debate continues to rage as to just who was behind the deal even though former FA secretary Ted Croker insisted several times before his death in 1992 that Revie was on the fringes and not the centre of negotiations. What is often lost in the rush to tag Revie as a mercenary is that whoever did strike the deal was clearly something of a visionary, as his son Duncan points out: "They called Dad greedy for selling the first sponsorship to Admiral, saying things like 'typical Don Revie'. But it was sensible and made commercial sense for the FA. No-one would bat an eyelid now as every club in the land has a kit deal. I believe it also made money for the players, though I imagine there will still be some who say they should play for their country for nothing. In my opinion, that is utter nonsense."

With the Admiral deal in place and the chosen 81 having met Revie in Manchester, the 1974-75 domestic season got underway with the new manager taking in as many games as possible. Along with Les Cocker, his right-hand man at Leeds and already on the England coaching staff, he kept tabs on both possibles and probables as the countdown continued to the visit of Czechoslovakia on October 30, a true baptism of fire that was given added significance by qualifying points for the European Championships being at stake. The turbulent goings-on at Elland Road did prove, understandably considering the effort that had gone into building Leeds United into such a force over 13 years, a distraction with Revie even finding time to appear in the Yorkshire Television special, *Goodbye Mr Clough*, on the day his successor, Brian Clough, was sacked. But, by mid-October, stability had returned to his former club with Jimmy Armfield installed as manager and Revie was free to focus fully on his impending international bow.

The sacking of Ramsey earlier in the year had led to Joe Mercer, the former Manchester City manager who had brought the league title to Maine Road in 1968, taking over the national side on an interim basis. Aged 59 and by now the general manager of Coventry City, he made it clear from the very start that he did not want the job long-term. Mercer liked his teams to play with a smile on their face so it was no surprise that the players should warm to him. In a hectic month at the end of the season, England played seven games and lost just once – a 2-0 defeat to Scotland at Hampden Park. There was just one other regrettable moment during Mercer's short reign and that came in his final game of a summer tour in Belgrade where England were due to play Yugoslavia. Unfortunately, a mix-up involving a local travel agent meant there was no-one from the British Embassy to greet the party at the airport so the players, who had been allowed to dispense with their FA blazers in favour of more casual clothes, had time to kill. Kevin Keegan chose to while away a few minutes by sitting quietly in what, unbeknown to him, was a restricted area. The retribution from the guards, who had no idea the interloper was a famous footballer, was swift and severe, leaving the innocent Keegan in tears after being beaten up. It was a horrible end to what had been an otherwise enjoyable interlude between Ramsey and Revie, and one that led some, admittedly with the benefit of hindsight, to later suggest Mercer should have been persuaded to stay on. Colin Todd, however, believes no amount of cajoling would have changed Mercer's mind. He recalls: "I played in all the games under Joe that summer and it was a good time. Joe was coming to the end of his career so felt no pressure. He made it plain from day one that he had no intention of staying in the job, which meant he could be more relaxed. He always had a smile on his face, but there was no way he wanted to stay on. What should not be forgotten by those who feel Joe should have stayed is that, back then, appointing Don Revie was the popular decision. I thought he was the right man to come in and sort us out. There was the big rivalry between Leeds and my team Derby – or, more accurately, Revie and Brian Clough - but his record after building that wonderful team showed he was the right man for the job."

Nine days before the European Championship qualifier against Czechoslovakia, the public got their first look at an England side under Revie when he took a strong XI to Sheffield Wednesday. Held in honour of the Owls' long-serving general manager Eric Taylor, who had died shortly before he had been due to retire, the game saw an experimental England XI selected with only three of the side that would start against the Czechs – Martin Dobson, Dave Watson and Frank Worthington - doing the same at Hillsborough. Trevor Brooking, who could come off the bench at Wembley the following week, was also named in the starting line-up along with Frank Lampard, Tony Currie, Rodney Marsh and Peter Shilton. England coasted to a 5-0 win thanks to goals from Currie, Brooking, Dobson, Worthington and Keith Weller, the Leicester City captain impressing so much that, within 24 hours, Revie had added his name to the 23-man squad he had intended selecting for the game against the Czechs.

The friendly at Hillsborough was a gentle warm-up for England's new manager, though any hopes the remainder of the build-up to the all-important visit of the Czechs would be equally straightforward were soon to be dashed by an old adversary. Alan Hardaker, as Football League secretary, had fallen out regularly with Revie during his time at Leeds but it was hoped within the corridors of power that the pair could now bury past differences. To that end, they held a six-hour meeting that was also attended by Dick Wragg, the chairman of the FA's international committee, to discuss how all parties could work together for the good of the national side. Revie wanted the League to postpone all Saturday games if England had an important international the following Wednesday, finding it ridiculous that Ramsey had only had a few days of preparation with his players before the fateful World Cup qualifier against Poland the previous year. Nowadays, FIFA insist all players selected for international duty should be available no less than five days in advance but in 1974 the managers were very much at the mercy of the clubs. Hardaker's response during this marathon meeting was to point out it was not within his powers to agree to such a request. He did, though, promise to go away and discuss the matter with the clubs, whose decision it would ultimately be. Revie, sensing an opportunity to get one over an old enemy, immediately decided to make the contents of the meeting public, telling a sportswriters' luncheon in London that a new era of co-operation between the League and FA had been established. Hardaker, on reading the comments the following day, was furious at what he saw as Revie's blatant attempt to corral him down a road he could not go down without seeking the permission of the clubs. A statement was hastily released on behalf of the put-out League secretary, reading: 'I have seen my name mentioned on numerous occasions by Mr Revie, concerning possible postponements of Football League matches. These are unauthorised statements and if Mr Revie wishes to reveal all his business with me to the press, then I wish it to be known I cannot co-operate.'

Revie, expecting such a response, continued his guerrilla campaign via the newspapers, the first salvo coming just a couple of days later with a warning about the dire consequences of an important player getting injured before the Czechoslovakia game. He went on to stress just how damaging this could be for England's qualification chances by revealing a dedicated phoneline had been set up at Lancaster Gate for managers to ring if any of their internationals had picked up an injury. Calls could be made from 4.30pm on the Saturday and Revie, again underlining how serious late withdrawals could be, vowed to man the line himself from 6pm, by which time he would have returned from

King Billy. Don Revie's on-field lieutenant, Billy Bremner, leads his team-mates out at Wembley ahead of the 1972 FA Cup final against Arsenal. Below, Bremner holds aloft the trophy after Allan Clarke's second half winner is enough to clinch a 1-0 win over the Gunners. (Yorkshire Post)

Returning heroes. Revie waves to the crowd as Leeds parade the Cup around their home city. (YP)

Facing the shareholders. Revie and Leeds chairman Manny Cussins prepare for the club's Annual General Meeting in January, 1973. (YP)

Heartache. David Harvey lays beaten on the floor as Ian Porterfield celebrates Sunderland's winner in the 1973 FA Cup final. (YP)

Serving a ban. A grim-faced Revie sits out a UEFA Cup tie against Vitoria Setubal in November, 1973, in the directors box. (YP)

In the public eye. Revie faces the media in March, 1974. (YP)

The main man. For 13 years, Revie ruled the roost at Elland Road. (YP)

Relaxing with the family. Revie joins daughter, Kim, and wife, Elsie, in the back garden at home. (YP)

The big red book. This is Your Life presenter Eamonn Andrews surprises Revie at the Queens' Hotel, Leeds, on April 21, 1974. (YP)

Opposite: Champions for a second time. Revie and his captain Billy Bremner parade the League Championship trophy in April, 1974. (YP)

A wanted man. Dick Wragg and Andrew Stephen of the Football Association board with Leeds chairman Manny Cussins and FA secretary Ted Croker at Elland Road. (YP)

England calling. Revie, pictured with Football Association secretary Ted Croker, accepts the offer to succeed Sir Alf Ramsey as England manager. (YP)

The boss. Revie finds time to share a joke with his England squad during a training session. (PA)

Leading by example. Revie shows Kevin Keegan, front kneeling, and his England team-mates how it is done during a training session. (PA)

Revie and wife Elsie arrive at the High Court, London, along with star witness
Lawrie McMenemy on the second day of his ultimately successful legal bid to
overturn a 10-year ban imposed by the Football Association. (PA)

Back home. After the lifting of a 10-year ban at the High Court, Revie is able to take
up a consultancy role at Elland Road. Here, he watches Leeds lose 2-1 to Aston Villa
on the opening day of the 1980-81 season. (YP)

In the desert. Revie watches from the bench as his team, Al Nasr, take on Al Sharjah in the United Arab Emirates First Division. Revie's side lose 2-0 but still remain top of the table. (YP)

No stranger to sand. Revie takes time out from managing in Dubai to play at Alwoodley Golf Club, Leeds, in July, 1982. (YP)

The final goodbye. Flanked by many of his former team, Revie pays one last emotional visit to Elland Road on May 11, 1988. (YP)

Billy Bremner, then Leeds manager, shares a word with his mentor ahead of the testimonial held in Revie's honour. (YP)

Mick Jones shakes hands
with the Boss in front of
former team-mates Paul
Madeley, Gordon
McQueen, Allan Clarke,
Billy Bremner and Jack
Charlton. (YP)

Bobby Collins, Revie's most
crucial signing in his early days
at Elland Road, greets his old
manager. (YP)

A proud father. Revie was delighted by the success enjoyed by son Duncan, here as the boss of Total Sport, and daughter Kim (opposite), who dad accompanied to the Yorkshire Television studios in Leeds for an interview about her first record, It's Come Back Again. (YP)

Don's widow Elsie continued to be a regular visitor to Elland Road after her husband's death, joining then Leeds manager Howard Wilkinson and the Earl of Harewood at a Gala Dinner in 1992. (YP)

A city mourns. Within hours of Revie's death on May 26, 1989, the main gates at Elland Road are adorned with flags and scarves. (YP)

watching Arsenal's London derby with West Ham. It would take the best part of two years but Revie would eventually win his battle with Hardaker as the League agreed to move a Saturday programme preceding an important international forward to the previous midweek just in time for the World Cup qualifiers.

As important as the issue was to Revie, a far more pressing concern in October, 1974, was the impending visit of Czechoslovakia. After missing out on the European Championship finals in 1972 and the World Cup two years later, sitting out another major tournament was not an option so it was important England started brightly. Knowing the effect a passionate Wembley crowd could have on the young Czech side, Revie implored the fans to join in with a rousing rendition of *Land of Hope and Glory* and lyric sheets were distributed in an attempt to stir up a frenzy of patriotism. In the end, the fans responded – though it took a double substitution in the 64th minute to kick-start the Revie era. Trevor Brooking and Dave Thomas were the two who made the telling impact from the bench. An inviting cross from QPR winger Thomas just eight minutes into his debut allowed Mick Channon to break the deadlock. The Southampton striker then turned provider by twice creating openings for Colin Bell to score, the first the result of an exquisite diagonal pass and the second coming from a flighted cross. The 83,858 crowd were elated and *Land of Hope and Glory* boomed loudly around Wembley in celebration of two qualification points secured. The reaction in the following morning's newspapers was equally positive as the influence of the new manager was heralded amid predictions that English football had found a new saviour. The man himself, however, was in a less optimistic mood, as Revie's son Duncan discovered the following morning. He recalls: "Everyone was delighted with the start England had made so I went to see Dad at his hotel. I went into his suite with a big smile on my face but could see straight away that something was wrong. I asked why he didn't look very happy after such a great win and he came down to sit next to me before saying, 'We haven't got the players – there is no Bremner and no-one like Giles'. He looked as miserable as sin, as he explained that it just wasn't going to work due to a lack of good enough players. No matter what I said, Dad was adamant. Even now, I can't explain it, he just knew."

In public, at least, Revie remained upbeat and seemed to be basking in the praise being showered on his team. But the forebodings expressed in private to his son would not go away and his mood darkened considerably three weeks later when Portugal visited Wembley. Again, qualifying points were at stake but, this time, there was to be no happy ending as England stumbled to a goalless draw against a side they had been expected to beat comfortably. Portugal had drawn 0-0 with England the previous April in Lisbon in what turned out to be Sir Alf Ramsey's last game in charge, but the manner of their 3-0 defeat to Switzerland just seven days before the trip to London meant few had given the visitors a chance. Revie had been in Berne, his candid response when asked by the English media about the spying mission being to say he would not allow his players to watch the film of the game as it may 'give them a false impression'. The Portuguese were incensed, manager Joce Maria Pedroto accusing Revie of belittling his players before adding: 'You can tell your Mr Revie that, when I was manager of Vitoria Setubal and he was manager of Leeds, he said the same things and we knocked them out of the UEFA Cup.' It proved a prophetic statement as, unlike the happy sounds of *Land of Hope and Glory* after the Czechoslovakia win, the only sounds as Revie walked towards the tunnel after his second game were jeers and slow-handclapping. On a hugely disappointing night, countless passes went astray and the midfield singularly failed to develop any understanding with the attack. All the old failings had returned and Revie's decision to make four changes from the side that had won so convincingly against the Czechs brought muted criticism, particularly as the recall of the fit-again Terry Cooper after two years out had backfired badly as the Leeds full back lasted just 24 minutes. Nevertheless, Revie's standing in the country as the man to lead England out of the international wilderness remained intact as the New Year began.

England's first assignment of 1975 was a home friendly with West Germany. The prospect of the newly crowned world champions coming to London caused great excitement - so much so that the March 12 meeting would attract Wembley's first capacity 100,000 crowd since the ill-fated World Cup qualifier against Poland 18 months earlier. With interest so high, the build-up was much more intense than would normally be the case for a friendly with Revie's decision to hand the captaincy to Alan Ball in place of Emlyn Hughes quickly becoming a major talking point. Ball, by now 29 and playing for Arsenal, had been sent off five times in his career, while his last international appearance had come 11 months earlier. Revie, though, would not be moved with the choice of Ball being made because he believed the midfielder was the closest English football had to a Billy Bremner. He also felt it was a nice piece of symbolism against the opponents Ball had helped beat in the 1966 World Cup final.

The second major surprise came when Revie announced his starting line-up 24 hours ahead of kick off as Leicester City's Steve Whitworth and Ian Gillard of QPR were down to make their debuts as a new full-back partnership. More intriguingly, Alan Hudson was named in midfield. The mercurial Hudson had, throughout his career, been the very antithesis of the type of team player Revie professed to admire. Hudson's inclusion was also controversial because, when a Chelsea player, he had been banned from international football by Sir Alf Ramsey for refusing to tour with the England Under-23 side. Hudson's selection left many baffled, though the player himself believes Revie chose the World Cup holders as the opposition for his international debut deliberately. "I had been banned for two years but had been playing well and was hoping to get back in," recalls Hudson who, by the time of his first international cap, was at Stoke City. "So, when Revie got the England job, I thought it was the worst possible thing that could have happened. I actually saw him as a racialist, but not in terms of colour, just whether someone was born in London or not. And if they had played for Chelsea then he particularly hated them. He didn't pick me for the first couple of squads so I was initially surprised to find out I was playing against West Germany. But then it dawned on me - they were the World Cup holders and we were expected to get thrashed. I am sure to this day he only picked me because he wanted me to fail. If I'd had a poor game, he would have had a ready-made reply to those saying I should be in the England squad."

Whether it was cunning subterfuge on Revie's part or simply wanting to see how Hudson would fare against the very best, the decision proved a sound one as the debutant inspired England to a memorable victory. With Hudson dove-tailing neatly with Colin Bell and Alan Ball, England tore into the West Germans to such an extent that Franz Beckenbauer was moved to comment afterwards, 'They were a revelation, playing a new and exciting style that we were not prepared for'. It took just 25 minutes for England's superiority to yield a goal, Hudson's free-kick from the right picking out Bell who scored with a volley that was deflected into the net. Bell then came close to adding a second by following in a Malcolm Macdonald shot that Sepp Maier fumbled before a quickly-taken free-kick midway through the second half allowed England to double their advantage. The ever-alert Mick Channon was the man who caught the Germans cold before Bell swung over a deep cross for Macdonald to score with a far post header. Kevin Keegan also found time to strike the crossbar with a chip from the edge of the area and, although the West German side had been an experimental one, there was no doubting the feeling among the crowd that they had just witnessed England's best display in years. Hudson was elated, though the nagging feeling that Revie had only selected him to fail could not be budged. "Unfortunately for him, I played well so his plan didn't work," he says. "Revie ignored me in the dressing room and never praised me or anything like that. I did wonder then if I would be in the squad for the next game or not, even after playing so well."

Hudson's fears about being axed straight away proved unfounded as Revie retained him for the following month's game at home to Cyprus. Ball, a player who Revie had once been desperate to sign for Leeds, also stayed as captain as Revie looked to put down a marker to the rest of the group. A 5-0 rout of the Cypriots followed as Malcolm Macdonald became the first international to score five goals at Wembley. His opener came after just two minutes with a bullet header that was followed by a mis-kick after being picked out by Keegan. A close range header then sealed Macdonald's hat-trick shortly after half-time before two further headers completed the one-man demolition job. Macdonald would later claim Revie had demanded – and received - money from journalists wanting to interview the striker after the game before pocketing it himself, but as England flew out to Cyprus for the return, the spirit within the team was high. Revie, in particular, was in a happy mood as the qualifier in Limassol would be the first of four in quick succession for England, meaning he had the players together for an extended spell for the first time. During the domestic season that had just finished, Revie estimated he had seen his players for just 15 days in total – and that included the previous summer's get-to-know-you meeting in Manchester. Now, here was a chance to get down to work with his players on the training field and learn more about their characters off it.

The display against Cyprus may not have been the best way of illustrating the value of time together but the 1-0 win courtesy of a sixth-minute winner from Kevin Keegan meant England topped their qualifying group with seven points from four games. Czechoslovakia were second with four points from one game less, while Portugal's solitary point came from the goalless draw at Wembley that had preceded a 5-0 thrashing by the Czechs. Three points from the autumn trips to Bratislava and Lisbon would, therefore, be enough to seal qualification to the quarter-finals, which in those days were staged on a two-leg basis. An extra incentive was that the host venue would be chosen from the four countries who then battled through to the semi-finals, and Wembley had already got the nod from UEFA if England made it through. To Revie, the prospect of competing for a major trophy with the added advantage of being on home soil was an exciting one.

That, however, could wait as the England party flew back from Cyprus with the Home Internationals about to kick-off. Revie had vowed to give several untried players a chance, though there was only one debutant, Ipswich Town's Colin Viljoen, included for the opening game as his side fought out a dull goalless draw with Northern Ireland in Belfast. It was the first visit to Windsor Park by an England side in four years due to the on-going Troubles in Ulster and the authorities sensibly tried to keep everything low-key, with only two soldiers stationed on the tarmac as the team's plane touched down. A military helicopter did shadow the bus ferrying the players to their hotel ahead of a pre-match meal but, otherwise, the game was little different to any other played by England in the 1970s. Nevertheless, the players were happy to be back on the mainland within hours of the final whistle, and able to start focusing on the meeting with Wales at Wembley five days later.

Revie was enjoying having his squad together for an extended period for the first time, but he was also mindful of how easily players can grow bored so a trip to the cinema was arranged for the Tuesday afternoon. Unusually, the following night's starting line-up was named en route to the film as Revie revealed five changes from the side that had drawn in Belfast. Kevin Keegan was among those not included and the striker's subsequent decision to go AWOL was the first inkling the public had that all was not as well behind the scenes as results were suggesting. Keegan felt let down by Revie failing to explain the reasons behind being dropped along with Malcolm Macdonald, Colin Bell, Emlyn Hughes and Dennis Tueart. The Liverpool striker fled to a cottage in north Wales before eventually being coaxed back to the team hotel on the Thursday morning. In his absence, England had been held to a 2-2 draw by the Welsh despite David Johnson giving the home side an early lead on his debut. Two goals in ten second-half minutes then put the visitors ahead only for Johnson to net an 85th minute equaliser that left England needing to beat Scotland to finish top of the Home Internationals group for the eighth year running, albeit with the 1972 and 1974 tournaments seeing them share pole position with the Scots.

With Keegan restored to the team, England tore into the visitors from north of the Border and were two goals ahead inside seven minutes through Gerry Francis and Kevin Beattie. Scotland, despite a brilliant performance from Kenny Dalglish, never recovered and Colin Bell brought Revie to his feet in celebration again five minutes before half-time with a fierce drive from outside the penalty area that flew past Stewart Kennedy. A Bruce Rioch penalty cut the deficit before Francis and Johnson completed the rout of the now dispirited Scots in the second-half. Revie was elated, though he still found time to sneak away from the jubilant post-match celebrations in the home dressing room to console a member of the defence that his side had just so ruthlessly exposed. Gordon McQueen recalls: "Along with all the Scottish lads, I was hurting badly but Don pulled me to one side after the game and told me to stay positive despite the result. It had been a marvellous day for Don but all he was bothered about was trying to console me, which was him all over."

The five-goal demolition meant Revie walked out of Wembley that night as happy and content as he could remember since leaving his beloved Leeds. There may not have been, as he had bemoaned to son Duncan several months earlier in a London hotel suite, a Bremner or Giles within the England ranks. But an eight-game unbeaten run and pole position in the European Championships qualifying group suggested Revie was already well on his way to restoring a sense of pride to English football.

Chapter 21

A Dysfunctional Family

'Don Revie's so-called family have more in keeping with the mafia than Mothercare.' So said Brian Clough, during one of his regular attacks on what he considered to be the blatant intimidation and cheating that was endemic in Leeds United during the early 1970s. That Clough, then manager of Derby County, should dislike someone many considered to be his polar opposite was not a surprise. Nor was it an accident that he should try to get under the skin of his arch rival by ridiculing the father figure persona Revie put so much store by. The truth, as even Clough recognised deep down, was that Revie had intentionally built not just a football team at Elland Road but a band of brothers so devoted to one another that if you made an enemy of one, you made an enemy of them all.

Revie, on being appointed England manager, understandably wanted to engender the same spirit within the players he now had at his disposal. What had worked at Leeds, he believed, would work with the national team and the get-together that saw 81 players join up in Manchester a few weeks after his appointment was just the start of the exercises designed to build and then harness team spirit. Players being conscripted into games of carpet bowls and bingo soon followed along with quiz nights as a whole host of initiatives that had proved successful and popular at Leeds were transplanted to the England camp. To Revie, it was a tried and trusted formula that would help create the type of bond more normally associated with a club side even though the players would only see each other, at most, for a few days every month or so. Almost straight away, however, his ideas were met with resentment as seasoned internationals rebelled against the initiatives that had been lapped up by the impressionable young men he had honed into such a formidable unit at Elland Road. It was a point that was immediately apparent to Trevor Cherry after being called up to the full England squad for the first time during Revie's second season in charge. He recalls: "I detected an atmosphere immediately and it was all very different to Leeds. Some of the lads just wouldn't buy into the carpet bowls and things like that. They were only meant as a bit of fun to pass the time but a few made a big deal of it and refused to take part." Alan Hudson, whose spectacular display on his debut had helped England beat West Germany in Revie's third game, was one of those who felt there were much more suitable ways for grown adults to spend their evenings. "What a waste of time they were," he says. "I remember looking across one night at Alan Ball, a World Cup winner, being forced to sit in a corner of the room so he could play bingo. What a joke."

Hudson's view was shared by many in the squad but it was, by no means, typical of everyone. Joe Royle, for one, enjoyed the diversionary social activities that were laid on. "A lot has been said over the years about the carpet bowls," says the former Everton and Manchester City striker who won back his England place under Revie after recovering from serious injury. "But I enjoyed them. They were certainly better than playing cards all night, which was the alternative. It was used as a stick to beat Don with at the time and I have always thought that was wrong." Revie's attempts to cajole his players into his team-building activities were not without their lighter moments. Sir Trevor Brooking recalls: "There was this one night when we were having an indoor putting competition. Mick Channon was one of those who didn't really care for things like that so he used to make sure he was one of the first to be knocked out. It meant his odds for the putting were something like 100-1 with the team bookies, who this particular night were Don and Kevin Keegan. I was queuing up to put my fiver on and Mick was in front of me. He put a tenner on someone else but then a fiver on himself. Straight away, I thought, 'He's up to something here' so I put my fiver on him instead. The lads were falling about laughing a couple of hours later when Mick won, while Don and Kevin's faces were an absolute picture."

For every supporter of Revie's attempts to build what he called 'the England family', there seemed to be a dissenter from within the ranks and it was a similar story with the dossiers that were also introduced. Just as at Elland Road, they were handed out on the eve of a match and tailored towards each individual England player. Everything from the strengths and weaknesses of the opposing team to how they lined up at set-pieces were included but, unlike at Leeds, from the very start there was a split within the squad between those who found them useful and those who felt the dossiers inhibited the natural game of talented players. Colin Todd, who would later manage in the Premier League with Bolton Wanderers, was firmly in the first camp. He recalls: "History has shown that Don was quite a visionary with those dossiers as they have since become the norm. I came into the England squad from Derby where Brian Clough wasn't bothered about the opposition. He just sent us out to play. But Don was the complete opposite and very thorough, which I feel is something that should not be held against him. Every manager in the Premier League uses Pro-Zone today in an attempt to analyse the opposition and what Don did in his dossiers was exactly the same. The problem was that most of the squad were not used to that sort of approach, whereas nowadays a player would not bat an eyelid on being handed a dossier." Others, however, were not quite so keen with a couple letting it be known they used the dossiers to keep score during card games, a revelation that greatly hurt Revie. Most did not go to such extremes with their criticism; instead pointing out that the dossiers were in danger of leading to self-doubt due to a tendency to go overboard in highlighting the quality of the opposition, even if the next game was against the minnows of Cyprus. Sir Trevor Brooking, whose international debut had come in Sir Alf Ramsey's last game against Portugal, says: "At West Ham, I only played for two managers – John Lyall and Ron Greenwood – and they were both keen to play to our strengths rather than focus on the opposition. There would be the odd little thing like working on beating the offside trap the week before playing Liverpool but, otherwise, they wanted us to impose ourselves on the other team. Don was very different in his approach and used to hand us these thick dossiers where the opposition were built up in terms of their strengths. I felt there was a real danger that the more we read them, the more inhibited we would become. Kevin Keegan and Ray Wilkins were of the same mind, thinking we should let the opposition worry about us."

The mistrust some in the squad felt for Revie's methods meant that as the players regrouped for the first game of the 1975-76 season, a friendly against Switzerland in Basle, the atmosphere was a muted one. The dropping of Alan Ball from the squad a few days earlier had mystified many in the England dressing room after the midfielder's impressive six-game stint as captain the previous campaign. Ball was certainly hurt by the rejection, making it clear right up until his own death in 2007 that he still resented how Revie had never attempted to explain the reasons behind his axing. Worse still, Ball had actually discovered he was out of the squad from a journalist calling to ask for his reaction.

There may have been no qualification points riding on the Switzerland game but that did not mean Revie and his backroom team were going to be any less thorough in their preparations as an 18-page dossier was compiled and duly handed out to the players. The squad had flown out on the Monday with one notable addition to the usual mixture of solidity and experience preferred by Revie as Sheffield United's Tony Currie was handed a recall after two years away from international football. Likened by Revie during the build-up to West

Germany's mercurial Günter Netzer, Currie started at the 30,000 capacity St Jakob's Stadium and was one of the few success stories on a night when England won a drab game as their manager tried to outfox the watching scouts from Czechoslovakia. Not only did Revie send out his team wearing numbers that paid little heed to their positions, he also instructed Mick Channon, the recognised penalty taker, to step aside if a spot-kick was awarded so as not to allow the Czechs to study his technique ahead of the following month's vital European Championships qualifier. Whether Revie's duplicity served any purpose is debatable but it was typical of the thorough approach he had brought to the England set-up with the flight to Basle seeing him once again sit next to a rather unusual consignment. Son Duncan explains: "Dad used to take all the players' boots in a big sack on away trips and buy a seat for them. His reasoning was that replacing a player's kit was easy but his boots would be a different story. Some players can't play if they don't have their usual pair. Dad likened it to a violinist getting to a concert and finding his favourite violin had gone missing. And, don't forget, in those days footballers only had one pair and not several like today."

Sporting his familiar pair of boots, Kevin Keegan opened the scoring on eight minutes before being handed a great chance to double his and England's goal tally when a penalty was awarded. Channon, mindful of his manager's pre-match instructions, duly stepped aside only for Keegan to see his effort saved by goalkeeper Erich Burgener. England made light of the miss in the 19th minute as Channon made it 2-0 before a blunder on the half hour by Ray Clemence provided the Swiss with a route back into the game as Kurt Muller headed into an empty net. Suddenly, the home side were causing all manner of problems and there was little doubt England were the more relieved side to hear the final whistle blow, as Gerry Francis, made captain in only his fifth appearance, admitted afterwards. Nevertheless, Revie flew home with the enviable record of having won six and drawn three of his first nine games in charge. Some in Fleet Street, however, were already looking beyond the unbeaten record in an attempt to assess whether sufficient progress was being made. Brian Glanville, of *The Sunday Times*, says: "I was having serious reservations. We were a year into his time, yet England looked nothing remotely like a good team. It was hard to resist the thought a year had already been wasted." If Glanville had misgivings about Revie as an international manager after the friendly in Switzerland, the visit to Bratislava the following month in October for a vital European Championship qualifier against Czechoslovakia served to make his mind up.

The trip behind the Iron Curtain was always going to be a tough one, as was made clear a week before the game when blatant anti-British propaganda started to appear in the local press. The Czech sports paper, *Gol*, led the way by printing a huge photograph of the X-rated tackle by Leeds United's Terry Yorath on Bayern Munich's Bjorn Andersson that had put the Swede out of the European Cup final just a few months earlier. Alongside the photograph was a caption that made it clear Revie, despite not having been in charge as Leeds lost 2-0 to the Germans in Paris, was the man who had built a team so capable of naked aggression. A few days later, and just as the worst of the anti-British feeling appeared to be dying down, Czechoslovakia coach Vaclav Jezek waded into the controversy by insisting, 'England today don't play football, they only destroy and go after the ball like a bulldog'. The attacks served their purpose and, come matchday, the England players were being jeered on to the field by the raucous 50,651 crowd packed inside the Slovan Stadium. The thick fog that had descended on Bratislava only added to the sense that England were walking into the unknown. That they were doing so employing an incredibly attack-minded line-up meant Revie was either bold or reckless, two characteristics that had seemed alien to him when in charge of Leeds. His clear intention had been to take the game to the Czechs with a forward line containing Allan Clarke, Malcolm Macdonald and Mick Channon playing in front of an equally attack-minded trio of Colin Bell, Gerry Francis and Kevin Keegan in midfield. Revie, on being questioned about his selection on the eve of the game, told his inquisitors, 'Perhaps this team will bamboozle them'. In his defence, England did start well, with those able to peer through the thick fog seeing Macdonald put the ball in the net after just seven minutes. Unfortunately, the linesman intervened to rule the 'goal' out for offside and it was the waving of the same flag just eight minutes later that brought a halt to the game as the official indicated to referee Alberto Michelotti he could no longer follow play. Several announcements were subsequently made over the PA system promising the Czech fans the game would restart once the fog had cleared but, eventually, Michelotti bowed to the inevitable. The abandonment came as major disappointment to the 300 fans who had made the arduous journey from England. In order to try and minimise the disruption, the game was re-arranged for the following afternoon but by then only 120 England fans remained in Bratislava, the rest having returned home on pre-booked travel. Those who stayed, as it turned out, were the unfortunate ones with Revie's attack-minded line-up - no changes having been made overnight - sliding to a 2-1 defeat despite going ahead through Mick Channon. The impetus in the qualifying group had swung inexorably the way of Czechoslovakia, who now trailed England by two points – or one win – but had a game in hand. Portugal, who were due to host the Czechs next, completed the trio of countries still hoping to reach the finals but there was no escaping the fact England's fate was now out of their own hands. Revie needed the fates to smile on him but, instead, he could only watch frustrated from the main stand in Oporto as Portugal and Czechoslovakia fought out a 1-1 draw a little under a fortnight later. England were still on top of the group with a game to play, but as Revie's side were due to travel to Lisbon where they had to better the Czechs' result against the group's whipping boys, Cyprus, few held out much hope of progressing.

Revie, realising qualification was likely to be beyond his men, spent the build-up to the trip to Portugal stepping up his campaign to be given more preparation time with his players before important internationals. He felt his team had been put at a distinct disadvantage in Bratislava due to Kevin Beattie suffering an injury playing for Ipswich Town at Manchester City as a full Football League programme took place the previous weekend. Revie, as a result of Beattie having to sit out the game, had been forced into a re-shuffle of his side and the England manager contrasted this with how his Czech counterpart had enjoyed a full three weeks with his players. With late withdrawals also proving a major headache ahead of the final qualifier against Portugal - England's tally of 15 fit players on the flight out to Lisbon included three goalkeepers – the manager's frustration was obvious as he told the press, 'At international level, we are looking like an amateur body seeking professional results'. On a lighter note, however, he did also point out how he had instructed the secretary of the FA's international committee, the genial but tubby Alan Odell, 'Not to drink or smoke so he is available for selection'.

England's spirits were lifted slightly when the Under-23s clinched a place at their own European Championships with a 2-0 win over Portugal. But, when the senior side got underway the following night, any hopes it would act as an inspiration were soon dispelled when Rui Rodrigues curled a 25-yard free-kick beyond Ray Clemence and into the net. Just 16 minutes were on the clock and although Mick Channon did equalise shortly before half-time, the night would end in huge disappointment as Portugal, thanks in part to England's abject failure to work out how to beat the offside trap, held on for a 1-1 draw. Revie's hopes of reaching the quarter-finals were all but over – the final act coming four days later when Czechoslovakia beat Cyprus 3-0 - and the recriminations began as soon as the England plane touched down. Among the first to have his say was Football League secretary, Alan Hardaker, the subject of Revie's thinly-veiled attack about amateurism on the eve of the draw in Portugal. Hardaker said: 'I am a cynical man and it sounded to me that we smacked of excuses before we even left for Portugal. We have got to face up to the fact that we weren't good enough. It is Revie's approach to administration that is amateurish. Revie wants it his own way, just as he wanted it his own way when at Leeds. I have a long memory and when Revie was at Leeds, he was probably the least co-operative of all the League managers.' Then, in reference to the bonus payments Revie had instigated on taking the England job that would have seen his squad receive £2,000 per man for reaching the European Championships, Hardaker added: 'If we had the same national pride as Wales (who had qualified for the quarter-finals) instead of playing for all these bonuses, we might get somewhere.'

Revie, his pride wounded by England's failure, could only take Hardaker's words on the chin as his squad went their separate ways. With no game scheduled until the following March, four months away, Revie started to take stock. A record of just one defeat in 11 games was decent enough but, even so, the nagging doubts that international management was not for him refused to go away. At Leeds, he had thrived on the intimacy of club management and relished the day-to-day involvement with his players. He had been so hands-on that Billy Bremner, Johnny Giles et al were massaged by Revie once a week, and the contrast with the more distant world of international management pained him. Colin Todd recalls: "He seemed to me like a manager who badly missed working with his players every day. We would only meet up once a month or so and it just didn't suit his approach. When we joined up with a squad, Revie was so enthusiastic and it rubbed off on me. But then, before we knew it, the game was over and we were back at our clubs. To someone who had been involved in every bit of his players' lives at Leeds, he found it difficult to adapt." John Helm, who by 1975 had moved from *BBC Radio Leeds* to join *BBC Radio 2 Sport*, agrees: "Don never had those individual relationships he had at Leeds. Being the England manager was a very different beast as he had to be a lot more political. He wanted to be with his players on the training pitch, but instead he had to attend this committee meeting and that committee meeting."

Even Revie's former players at Leeds were realising just how much he was missing the 24/7 lifestyle that came with managing a major football club, as Frank Gray recalls: "Whenever I played for Scotland Under-23s, Don would send me a telegram that simply said, 'Good luck – confidence and concentration'. He had left Leeds but they still came through every time before I played. I even got one before I played against England, six months after he had become their manager."

Revie's son Duncan is another who remembers how hard his dad found it to adapt to Lancaster Gate's slower pace of life. "He was bored rigid at the FA," he says. "Dad preferred the much more hectic environment of Leeds. The commute to London was also something he didn't like, but I think the biggest problem he had was the FA being the most antiquated organisation he had come across. The committee structure frustrated him a lot. At Leeds, he had been used to making all the decisions but with England it had to be done by committee members. It took forever. He could choose his own players but travel and the like was decided by other people. He hated that."

Revie's unease at how, 15 months into the job, his professional life had changed for the worse was not helped by the dissent and criticism coming his way following England's failure to qualify for the European Championships. He had stated from day one that the 1978 World Cup was his overwhelming priority, but being pipped to a place in the last eight by a Czechoslovakia side who would go on to win the tournament had been a major setback. The press, initially so supportive of his appointment, had started to turn against Revie, who was determined to fight his corner. Brian Glanville, of *The Sunday Times*, recalls: "Through his newspaper columns, he started to respond to his detractors and I found out from Jason Tomas, who was ghosting the columns, that he was mentioning me a lot. Eventually, I was contacted by the BBC who asked if I would take part in a live debate with the England manager during *Sports Report* one Saturday. I agreed, but could not believe it had been Don's idea. I told him so before we went on air but Don was so thin-skinned that he wanted to have it out with me and it was a lively exchange. Subsequently, Don asked Barry Davies how he felt the exchange had gone, to which he replied, 'I am presuming the second leg is at Elland Road.' Basically, I felt Don had become incredibly twitchy after England had failed to qualify for the European Championships and that he did not have the temperament to manage an international team. He needed the day-to-day involvement of a club to keep his mind busy. Once with England, he had too much time to think and that became apparent in his team selections. He would turn himself inside out in making a decision and, in my opinion, often panic. It came as quite a surprise to us all as, at Leeds, he had built a quite brilliant team by knowing his own mind. With England, he was totally different."

Revie's team selections, not least the 4-3-3 attacking line-up in Bratislava where Kevin Keegan was played in midfield for the first time since his days at Scunthorpe United, had already begun to raise eyebrows. The feeling that, by being starved of the contact he craved with his players, Revie had too much time to ponder was growing among those close to the England team. Under Sir Alf Ramsey, a player who had impressed in the last international would invariably find himself in the team for the next game regardless of how he had performed at club level in the meantime. Revie, in contrast, was much more susceptible to chopping and changing, so much so that it was not until his final two games that England fielded the same XI. Sir Trevor Brooking, who played under four international managers in the eight years from 1974, says: "One of the things we thought as players was that we were continually on a one-game trial. The side was changed a lot and it was very easy to find yourself out of the side. Of course, no-one should ever be able to take their place for granted but the success under Alf Ramsey was because he showed loyalty to his players and that gave everyone continuity. Under Don, no-one quite knew if they were his man or not."

Fundamental team changes had, the critics argued, played a major part in the failure to qualify for the European Championships. The dropping of two captains, Emlyn Hughes and Alan Ball, entirely from the squad was a particular bone of contention. Playing key members out of position was another accusation made of Revie, along with an alleged suspicion of flair players such as Charlie George and Alan Hudson. The latter had played in the impressive wins over West Germany and Cyprus but was destined never to feature for the senior side again.

Revie, perhaps mindful of the criticism, staged an about-turn in March, 1976, by handing Derby striker George a first call-up to the senior squad and Hudson a return to the fold, albeit as an over-age player with the Under-23s. Joining Hudson in the squad to face Hungary in Budapest was Jimmy Greenhoff, who had been sold by Revie midway through Leeds' 1968 Inter-Cities Fairs Cup final victory over Ferencvaros. The Stoke pair's return would, however, prove to be a brief one. Hudson explains: "It was a ridiculous decision to pick me for the Under-23s in the first place. I had played for the senior side against West Germany and I just thought it was a case of Revie pandering to the press again. It was the same for Jimmy. Revie didn't like flair players. The number he left out during his time as manager proved that, so we weren't expecting too much to come from being selected for the Under-23s. Despite that, we joined up only to soon fall foul of Revie. Due to watching our weight and not being hungry, neither of us went down for lunch one day so Revie sent

Les Cocker to get us. He then had a real go at me and Jimmy and, funnily enough, neither of us were included ever again. It was a real shame for Jimmy as it meant he became one of the best players never to win an England cap. The only bonus for me from being dropped was it got me out of all that carpet bowls and bingo." Greenhoff has a similar recollection of the trip to Budapest, adding: "He didn't want to play us but was pushed into it, which is why Huddy was put on the left wing despite only using his left foot to stand on – his right more than making up for it, of course. We knew then Don Revie didn't want us in the England set-up and resigned ourselves to that fact. I do believe if he hadn't become manager, I would have played for England. My big problem was Don had sold me at Leeds so didn't want to pick me because it would have proved he was wrong in the first place. The press picked up on it so maybe that influenced his thinking as well." Both Greenhoff and Hudson started in a strong Under-23s line-up that was captained by Gerry Francis, the QPR midfielder who would that season skipper the senior side in eight of their 10 internationals. Despite the experience on show, Hungary coasted to a 3-0 victory en route to a 4-3 aggregate victory in the last fixtures played at that age group before a switch was made to Under-21s.

As England approached their first senior international of 1976, Revie was preaching the need for patience as he built towards the World Cup qualifiers due to get underway the following summer. Following the failure to reach the last World Cup in West Germany, England had not been seeded in the draw so Revie was relieved to discover his side had been handed a group containing Italy, Finland and Luxembourg. The reasoning behind such optimism was the Italians had, like England, recently failed to qualify for the European Championships after finishing third behind Holland and Poland in Group 5, while Finland and Luxembourg had collected just one point between them from 12 games. The first qualifier against the Finns in Helsinki was scheduled for June so Revie had seven games to assemble a side capable of putting down a marker to the rest of the group. The first of those was against Wales in Wrexham, a friendly organised to celebrate the centenary of the Welsh FA, and Revie sent out an experimental line-up containing seven debutants. Among them was Trevor Cherry, who had pressed his claims by scoring the only goal a week earlier as the Football League beat the Scottish League at Hampden Park. He recalls: "Les Cocker came up to me after the Football League game and said, 'Don wants you in the main squad'. I couldn't believe it and I didn't sleep that night thinking about what it would be like to play for my country." Peter Taylor, fresh from helping Third Division Crystal Palace into the last four of the FA Cup with a 1-0 win at Sunderland in the quarter-finals, was another handed his international bow at the Racecourse Ground. "Suddenly, to find myself among all these big names was quite daunting at first but Don put me at ease," says the man who would go on to manage England Under-21s and take temporary charge of the senior side for one game. "Palace had knocked Leeds out of the Cup that season so I was relieved that Don wasn't going to hold it against me." Taylor, the first player from the Third Division to play for England since Palace's Johnny Byrne in 1961, enjoyed a dream start to international football by coming off the bench to double the one-goal advantage given to Revie's men by Ray Kennedy. It meant Alan Curtis's stoppage time goal for the Welsh proved no more than a consolation. The two countries met again just six weeks later, this time in the opening game of the Home Internationals and, once again, Taylor proved the difference with a low 20-yard shot that earned England a 1-0 win in Cardiff.

The trip to south Wales was, as had been the case 12 months earlier for the first of England's Home Internationals, a happy one for Revie. The domestic league season had ended so he was able to look forward to an extended period with his team. He could also detect a new-found spirit and determination among his players after no-one took up his offer for those not involved against Wales to go home and spend time with their families. Kevin Keegan, underlining this sense of togetherness, had also chosen to miss the celebrations that followed Liverpool's league title success, a decision that again delighted the England manager. A 4-0 thrashing of Northern Ireland at Wembley then further improved Revie's mood as his squad set off for the following month's World Cup qualifier in Finland via Scotland and a three-game tour of the United States.

England's visit to Hampden Park would settle the destiny of the Home Internationals as the Scots had also beaten Wales and Northern Ireland. With the memory of the previous May's 5-1 thrashing at Wembley still fresh in the mind, Scotland were in no mood for pleasantries. The point was underlined to Revie when his pre-match assertion that this was the best Scots side he had seen in 10 years was contemptuously dismissed by his managerial counterpart, Willie Ormond, with the reply, 'Your mother made a mistake at your Christening – you're Con Revie, not Don Revie'. The stage was set for a classic battle with the Auld Enemy who silenced the 85,165 crowd that had mercilessly jeered the National Anthem ahead of kick-off when Mick Channon opened the scoring in the 11th minute. Bruce Rioch equalised shortly after. Then, an almighty blunder by Ray Clemence early in the second-half handed the Scots victory as the Liverpool goalkeeper allowed a tame shot from Kenny Dalglish to squirm under his body. As the locals partied long into the Glasgow night, England's crestfallen players retreated to their hotel base in Troon where Revie quickly got to work in boosting confidence and stressing how collecting two points from the qualifier in Finland on June 13 was all that mattered.

Before Helsinki, however, there was a short tour of the US where England were due to pit their wits against Brazil in Los Angeles and Italy, the country who stood between Revie's men and a place in the 1978 World Cup finals, in New York. A match against a so-called Team America, featuring Pele and Bobby Moore, would then be followed by that all-important first qualifier in Finland.

The tournament was held as part of the bicentennial celebrations marking the United States' independence from the UK. Italy and England were both invited due to their failure to qualify for the European Championships. Los Angeles was treated to a fine opening game with England's performance against the Brazilians a vast improvement on their last effort against Scotland. Trevor Brooking's return from injury had given the midfield extra polish and with Gerry Francis also impressing, England dominated for long periods only to be let down by wasteful finishing. Brazil, in contrast, failed to hit their usual heights, only to snatch what the neutrals in the crowd considered an unfair victory with a last-minute goal from substitute Roberto. Even Revie's critics admitted his side had been hard done by as the travelling party moved on to New York where the city's sizeable Italian community was always going to guarantee a decent crowd at the Yankee Stadium. In the end, the 40,650 who turned out to see Italy take on England were treated to a classic that, once again, boosted Revie's belief that the coming World Cup qualifying campaign would be a successful one. Whether he felt the same 20 minutes into the game is, though, debatable as the Italians raced into a 2-0 lead. England were shell-shocked and clearly in need of a lift, which duly came during the half-time interval courtesy of their manager. Joe Royle, making only his second appearance under Revie, recalls: "Don came into the dressing room and gave the most inspirational team-talk I ever heard. It was amazing and we went back out thinking we could take on the world, never mind Italy." Buoyed by Revie's words, England took just seven minutes to turn a two-goal deficit into a 3-2 lead as two goals from Mick Channon, named captain for the day, sandwiched a header by Phil Thompson. The Italians, stunned at the manner of the turnaround, soon lost their composure and discipline. Watching from the bench as the tackles became more brutal was Peter Taylor, who remembers his manager being desperate to fight fire with fire. "As the Italians were kicking lumps out of us," he recalls, "Don turned to me on the bench and said, 'If this had been Leeds, I could have sent you lads out to kick them back – but because this is England, I'm not allowed'. I could see he was absolutely gutted at not being able to have a go back because of what the FA and the press would have said."

Any feelings of regret on Revie's part were, however, swept away at the final whistle as England celebrated a momentous 3-2 win. It may have only been a friendly but the potential psychological effect of beating a side England would face with qualifying points at stake just six months later was massive, not least because the win had come with a team missing many of Revie's more experienced players. Three days later, two goals from Kevin Keegan and another by captain Gerry Francis ensured a Team America side made up of players from the North American Soccer League were beaten 3-1 in Philadelphia. England finished the tournament second behind Brazil, who beat Italy 4-1 in another ill-tempered encounter that saw three sent off and future England manager Fabio Capello carried from the field. After the defeat to Scotland at Hampden Park, it was a major fillip for Revie but one of his former Leeds players still felt things were not quite right. Trevor Cherry says: "I still sensed the England lads weren't fully with Don. Every great manager makes one mistake and I thought Don's was to make Gerry Francis his skipper. Gerry was not his type of player and he certainly didn't believe in Don like Billy Bremner, Don's captain at Leeds, had. During the trip to America, Don told everyone to go out on the night of the Brazil game and have a good time but be in by 1am. Gerry got everyone together and said, 'He can't tell us what to do, we're grown men'. And this was Don's captain. At Leeds, if the gaffer had told us to jump in the river then we would have jumped in the river. That night in America told me the England lads did not really buy into what Don was trying to do."

Cherry's concerns aside, it had been an encouraging tour of the US to leave the squad in confident mood ahead of the opening qualifier against Finland. Before flying out to Helsinki, Revie arranged practice matches against Imperial College, London, and non-League side Uxbridge where both teams were asked to play in a style identical to Finland. The Finns may have contained nine part-timers but, typically, he was determined not to leave anything to chance against a side that had ground out a goalless draw in a European Championships qualifier against Italy the previous year. With that in mind, Revie also showed his players a film of what he considered their best performance in the US, the

1-0 defeat to Brazil, to boost spirits further. The upshot was a highly motivated England tearing into Finland, eventually winning 4-1 thanks to two goals from Keegan and one apiece for Mick Channon and Gerry Francis. It was a dream start to qualifying, as Italy manager Enzo Bearzot acknowledged later that night back at his hotel two miles from Helsinki's Olympic Stadium. Slumped in an armchair and surrounded by his staff, the man who would lead Italy to victory in the 1982 World Cup final admitted it had been a bad evening, with his side unlikely to win by such a convincing margin in Finland. The opening salvo had been struck and, as the England players celebrated long into the night with Elton John, Revie was able to reflect on an encouraging end to what had been, at times, a hugely trying season.

Chapter 22

The Italian Job

The position of England manager is often described as an 'impossible job'. Not only will the incumbent be judged on results and an ability to satisfy a demanding nation, he must also be able to handle a spotlight being shone on every facet of his life. History shows us questionable business dealings are a no-no, as is substituting the nation's favourite striker when he is just one goal short of equalling a long-standing record. And as for expressing any views on karma and reincarnation, forget it unless the Prime Minister taking time off from saving the world to call for your sacking particularly appeals. Potential enemies lurk around every corner, though one place they should not be found is within the corridors of the Football Association. For Don Revie, however, the new man at the helm of English football was proving to be a more hostile adversary than even his biggest critic in the press. Sir Harold Thompson was, by today's standards, an unlikely figure to be leading the FA. An internationally renowned chemist and a former Professor at Oxford University, he had taught a young Margaret Thatcher and was considered a formidable intellect. He had played football at University and been the driving force behind the setting up of Pegasus, the combined side of mature students from Oxford and Cambridge Universities that twice won the FA Amateur Cup. Thompson had, as an FA executive director, played a major role in the sacking of Sir Alf Ramsey in 1974, an act of revenge that many felt had its roots in an incident that occurred two years earlier in Prague on Thompson's first international trip. He had been asked to put a cigar out by the England manager as it was annoying the players during breakfast and although Thompson complied, he took huge umbrage at being told what to do by someone he considered a mere employee, a serf.

Revie's own relationship with a man whose pomposity and domineering manner upset many FA employees got off to a similarly bad start when, during dinner one night, Thompson, by now vice-chairman of the FA, turned to the newly appointed manager and said: 'When I get to know you better, Revie, I shall call you Don.' To which Revie replied: 'Well, when I get to know you better, Thompson, I shall call you Sir Harold.' Thompson had treated Revie's predecessor with similar disdain by only using his surname, something that riled the class-conscious Alf Ramsey enormously. Few who crossed

Thompson's path during his time at the FA remember him fondly. The Earl of Harewood, a former FA president, recalls: "Sir Harold was, in the very worst sense, a dour man. He knew his place and that place was at the very top. And he wanted everyone to treat him accordingly. He did not respect anyone but himself." Brian Glanville, of *The Sunday Times*, is another who saw few redeeming features in Thompson. "He was an Etonian buffoon and someone I never got on with at all," he says. "The problem with Thompson was he was completely paranoid. He was a quite brilliant man in his own field but wholly lacking when it came to being chairman of the FA."

Thompson's elevation to the top job at Lancaster Gate came when he succeeded Sir Andrew Stephen in June, 1976. It was, to put it mildly, a development that was not welcomed by Revie, whose son Duncan recalls: "Thompson treated Dad like some sort of servant. My Dad hated him with a passion, absolutely hated him. He was a Corinthian Casuals-type who did not realise the world had moved on."

Thompson's appointment as FA chairman came amid a rare air of optimism surrounding the team. England had laid down a marker to the Italians in the World Cup qualifying campaign by winning 4-1 in Finland and there was genuine hope that Revie had, at last, hit upon a winning combination. A forward line of Kevin Keegan, Mick Channon and Manchester United's Stuart Pearson had struck a good balance during the internationals that preceded the summer break, while the midfield had also functioned admirably with captain Gerry Francis in situ alongside Trevor Brooking. Unfortunately, by September, when the first international of the new season at home to the Republic of Ireland had arrived, injury had robbed Revie of his skipper and the subsequent reshuffle led to a poor display. Charlie George, in the squad again but this time handed his debut, was asked to play behind the front line rather than in his customary position and struggled. Revie had also opted for a sweeper system that was then largely alien to the English game and the result was Eire, managed by Johnny Giles, looking by far the better side in a 1-1 draw. Revie cut a forlorn figure at the final whistle, his subsequent comment to the press of, 'The door is still open to younger players' sounding more like a plea than an invitation.

One bright spot for the manager was that the following month's qualifier against Finland at Wembley would be the first of a new era of co-operation between the England team and the Football League. After much lobbying from Revie and despite the opposition of his long-time adversary Alan Hardaker, the League had that summer agreed to postpone games on the Saturday before an important international. Trevor Brooking felt the move was long overdue.

"Every international manager faces the same problem and that is not seeing enough of his players," says the FA's director of football development. "Moving the League programme was a sensible decision, though I would have gone even further and made sure the players did not set off back to their clubs until the Thursday lunchtime. That way, the manager would be able to sit everyone down the morning after a game and run through a few things when it is all fresh in the mind. Instead, what happens even today is the manager will say a few things in the dressing room straight after a game and then not see the players for at least a month."

The new sense of co-operation with the League meant Revie had his players for six days before England were due to take on the Finns, allowing him sufficient time to organise a practice match against Uxbridge that saw Joe Royle net four goals in an 8-0 win. With goal difference likely to be important come the end of the qualifying campaign, Revie also instructed his defenders to practice their shooting while the eve of the game saw the squad watch an American documentary on the powers of positive thinking.

Hopes of a resounding victory over Finland were raised just three minutes into the game when Dennis Tueart opened the scoring only for the expected avalanche of goals to fail to materialise. Instead, the Finns, whom Revie had likened pre-match to a good Third Division team, hit back with an equaliser through Kalle Nieminen early in the second half. Joe Royle restored the home side's lead in the 52nd minute but that was the end of the scoring as chants of 'What a load of rubbish' rang out from the 92,000 crowd long before the final whistle. The reaction was understandable with England's switch to a 4-2-4 formation having failed abysmally due to too much emphasis being placed on the inexperienced Ray Wilkins in the centre of midfield. With the vital qualifier in Rome just a month away, England seemed to have regressed alarmingly and Revie was in a quandary. Should he tweak his line-up, or should he go for wholesale changes in a game that may well define the whole qualifying campaign? He agonised long and hard for the next few weeks.

Even being involved in a train crash failed to derail his thoughts for too long. Revie had been on a train heading from Yorkshire to London when it somehow scraped against one travelling in the other direction, leading to the outside corridor windows being smashed and several door handles ripped off. Revie was unharmed by the accident, though when he announced his starting line-up for Rome there were many who wondered if the England manager was suffering from delayed shock. Not only were Emlyn Hughes and Stan Bowles, two players considered surplus to requirements for the best part of two years, in the team, but the back four of Hughes, Dave Clement, Roy McFarland and Mick Mills had never played together before. Revie had watched the Italians eight times, the most recent being an unimpressive 4-1 win over Luxembourg, and the suspicion was he had spent so long agonising over the best approach that he had managed to confuse even himself. Joe Royle, one of six players to be dropped from the previous month's win over Finland, recalls: "I only have one gripe with Don from his time as England manager and it was the game in Rome. I had played really well against Italy in New York when we came back to win 3-2 and Bill Taylor, one of the coaches at Manchester City, said Don wanted it to be known that I had done so well I would be definitely in the team for the qualifier. In the end, I didn't even make the bench – and I had scored the winner against Finland in our last game." Colin Todd was another to miss out in Rome despite having played the previous month and he was left equally bemused. He says: "When Don was at Leeds, he always had a settled side. Every week, you could name their XI without looking at the team-sheet. But once he took over England, it all changed and he never gave the impression of knowing what his best team was. It was his downfall in the end because the close team spirit he worked so hard to create was impossible to generate as the faces changed so much. If he had gone about the England job like he did at Leeds, I am certain he would have been a big success."

The inclusion of Bowles, in particular, had been a major gamble and completely out of character for a manager who in the past had rarely left anything to chance. It was as if the constant drip, drip, drip of criticism and advice from the press and public had finally pushed Revie into making decisions he would never have countenanced when ruling the roost at Leeds. The Italians made the right noises ahead of kick-off by suggesting they believed Revie could be bluffing with his named line-up, coach Enzo Bearzot even going so far as to outline what contingency plans Italy had prepared if Stuart Pearson started rather than Bowles. But there was no mistaking the confidence that oozed from the home side as they took to the field in the Olympic Stadium. Such belief turned out to be well-placed as the darting runs of Franco Causio, the artistry of Roberto Bettega and a stern, unforgiving back four all combined to great effect as Italy coasted to a 2-0 victory. Sir Trevor Brooking, who made his 15th international appearance that night in Rome, recalls: "To be honest, it could have been a lot more. We never got going. There was a lot riding on the game. Don made a few changes and played a few of the players out of position. He kept playing me on the left, a position I rarely played for my club West Ham, and I never really felt comfortable. If I wasn't seeing much of the ball in the first 20 minutes, I would drift inside and Don didn't like that. I had a couple of real rollickings off him as a result."

England had been well beaten and their players suffered one final ignominy on the way home as a strike by baggage handlers meant they had to carry their own luggage across the airport tarmac. A little inconvenience was, however, nothing compared to what lay in store for Revie once back home as even his allies in the press started to question whether any progress at all had been made since Ramsey's sacking two-and-a-half years earlier.

Three months later and things deteriorated even further as Johan Cruyff and his Holland team-mates gave their English counterparts a footballing lesson at Wembley. The Dutch won 2-0 but the margin of victory could have easily been doubled without flattering the visitors. Once again, Revie's team selection had looked flawed with a midfield containing Brian Greenhoff and 32-year-old Paul Madeley left horribly exposed by Holland's short passing game. The manner of the defeat had been so total that Stan Bowles' reply to team-mate Mike Doyle claiming afterwards it had been, 'Like men against boys' was to add, 'More like Muhammad Ali v Richard Dunn'.

Suddenly, Revie had enemies everywhere he looked. Some were real and some were imagined, though to a man now realising the clock was ticking on his reign it was often difficult to differentiate between the two. One man, however, who made no attempt to hide his disquiet was the chairman of the FA, Sir Harold Thompson. The Earl of Harewood recalls: "There was one particular game when my wife and I were in the Royal Retiring Room waiting to go into the Royal Box. Thompson and Lady Thompson were there and I said, 'Let's hope we win', to which Lady Thompson replied, 'Yes, or let's hope we lose and we can get rid of that man'. Her husband just nodded." Rumours started to reach Revie's ears that the FA had already started to look for a replacement, as he revealed to Trevor Cherry. "I got to know Don really well towards the end of his reign," he says. "We would sometimes have a drink after a game and I sensed in our chats that the pressure was getting to him. There were so many arrows coming at him from all manner of directions that he didn't know who he could trust. He knew certain people within the FA were out to get him and the problem was he didn't know how to stem the tide."

Chastened by the defeat to Holland, Revie soldiered on but now there seemed to be a potential banana skin around every corner. Luxembourg were the next visitors to Wembley in March for a World Cup qualifier and Revie, as he had done previously, organised a practice match. This time, his first-choice XI would take on a side made up of seven squad members and four players from non-League Uxbridge in what should have been a gentle warm-up. Instead, England lost the game. Even more embarrassingly, the same line-up then faced a reserve team featuring 49-year-old Revie plus coaches Bill Taylor and Ken Burton the following day and was defeated once again. The 1-0 defeat lost none of its amusement factor for the public when it was pointed out the second string side had featured 14 players against the ten of England in an attempt to replicate the likely packed defence England would have to overcome against Luxembourg.

Respite came courtesy of a 5-0 victory, a result that compared favourably with Italy's 4-1 win over the same opponents in Rome the previous year, but the upturn in fortune was not to last once the Home Internationals were underway. First up was a trip to Northern Ireland where Dennis Tueart snatched a 2-1 victory with a late winner against the run of play. England had been without five Liverpool players in Belfast due to a clash with the European Cup final, the Reds beating Borussia Moenchengladbach in Rome. Their return to international action proved an unhappy one as Wales claimed a first win at Wembley. Leighton James scored the only goal from the penalty spot a minute before half-time to leave Revie and England badly in need of a lift at home to Scotland five days later. It didn't materialise, tens of thousands invading London from north of the border as the English were overrun on and off the field. Kenny Dalglish and Gordon McQueen sealed a famous 2-1 win to trigger the biggest pitch invasion at Wembley since the 1923 FA Cup final as celebrating Scots tore down the goalposts and dug up the turf. The irony that it should be one of his former Leeds players who administered one of the killer blows as England lost consecutive games at Wembley for the first time was not lost on Revie, as McQueen recalls: "We had not been able to speak on the pitch as it was being invaded by thousands of Scots but Don came to find me afterwards for a chat. He was under a lot of pressure because the results were not going for England but he still managed to joke, 'What are you doing to me?' There was no malice on his part and he even explained how the England boys had been practicing all week in training how to deal with me at corners. Don considered me the big danger so got Joe Corrigan to stand in as me because he was the tallest. Thankfully for me, it didn't work."

For the second consecutive season, defeat to Scotland preceded a three-game tour that would kick off against Brazil. The destination this time, though, was not the US but South America with the game in Rio being followed by testing internationals against Argentina and Uruguay. Another major difference compared to 12 months earlier was that the manager would not be at the opening fixture due to what the players were told was a scouting mission to watch Finland v Italy. Several suspected something was amiss as Revie was not the sort to hand over the reins of his team, even to his trusted right hand man Les Cocker. Sir Trevor Brooking, who travelled on the tour but failed to make an appearance due to a hamstring injury, recalls: "At first, Les said the manager would be joining us later because he wanted to keep out of the firing line after what had happened against Scotland but then it was claimed he wanted to scout a game. It seemed strange." What no-one could have forecast, however, was exactly what Revie was up to as he began to negotiate an escape route from the England set-up by flying to Dubai for talks on becoming the new manager of the United Arab Emirates. In his absence, Cocker sent out the team Revie had selected to face the Brazilians and but for some wasteful finishing England would have been ahead at half-time. The hosts did improve after the break but some fine saves by Ray Clemence and a Trevor Cherry block on the line ensured the game finished goalless. The arrangement was for Revie to meet his team in Argentina and, to cover his tracks, he duly flew to Helsinki to watch Italy coast to a 3-0 win, a result that saw England drop to second place in the group. He then carried on to Buenos Aries on the same flight as the Scotland team, who were heading for Chile. After being updated with a report on how England had played against Brazil, Revie sought a meeting with Dick Wragg, the chairman of the FA's international committee. Here, he explained to Wragg how he believed there was a conspiracy to have him sacked and that, to avoid any fuss, the FA could pay up the remaining two years on his contract. The bill would be £50,000. Wragg declined, pointing out that if there was any behind-the-scenes collusion going on then he would know about it. He then stressed that only failure to qualify for the 1978 World Cup finals might change matters, a claim that the Earl of Harewood insists was not 100 per cent true. "I knew for a fact the FA were already negotiating with Bobby Robson to replace Don because the Ipswich Town chairman told me," recalls the Earl. "Moves were afoot to get rid of the manager and the FA were plotting against Don. I felt that was not right." The FA's unhappiness had also filtered through to the media, as John Helm recalls: "There were certain people at the FA who were making no effort to hide their dislike of Don's style of football and it wasn't long before Don was made aware of that."

The FA's patience may have worn thin but they remained ignorant of Revie's plans as England took on Argentina in an ill-tempered contest that saw Daniel Bertoni cancel out a third-minute opener from Stuart Pearson. Bertoni and Trevor Cherry were then sent off eight minutes from time. The England defender was particularly unlucky as his only crime seemed to be being punched in the face and losing two teeth. Cherry recalls: "It was a political decision to send me off. There was no way the referee was going to send just their lad off. It was the first time England had played in Argentina since Sir Alf Ramsey had called them 'animals' during the 1966 World Cup and it was clear the locals really hated us. That game was the only time I was sent off in my career, either at club or international level, and the fact that I was later exonerated and not banned shows I did nothing wrong. Don realised that and told me not to worry about it."

England moved on to Montevideo where a dull goalless draw rounded off a first unbeaten tour of South America, a feat that would usually be cause for celebration. It was suggested in the press that the three draws would keep Revie in the job at least until after the qualifier with Italy at Wembley in November, when England's fate would be known for definite. Unbeknown to everyone but Revie and his very closest confidants, however, a huge bombshell lay just around the corner.

Chapter 23

Desert Storm

The summer of 1977 was a notable one for English sporting scandals. In May, the cricket authorities at Lord's were sent into a tailspin when it was revealed England captain Tony Greig had helped sign up 35 elite internationals for Kerry Packer's World Series in Australia. In the furore that followed, Greig was forced to step down. A couple of months later, another high-profile figure was removed from office as the manager of FA Cup holders Manchester United, Tommy Docherty, paid the price for his extra-marital affair with the wife of the club's physiotherapist, Laurie Brown, being exposed. Both high-profile departures received blanket coverage in the media and were debated endlessly by a fascinated public. When it came, however, to the biggest story of the year, there was only one contender - Don Revie's defection to Dubai.

The news was broken by the *Daily Mail* on July 12, 1977, under the front page headline 'Revie Quits Over Aggro'. But it was the following day's revelations in the same newspaper that Revie had resigned to take up a £340,000 four-year contract with the United Arab Emirates that caused a huge storm and left his reputation, at least outside West Yorkshire, beyond repair. It was a sensational turn of events, leaving the powers-that-be at the Football Association fuming. The first they knew of either development involving their manager had been when reading the *Daily Mail*. For Jeff Powell, the newspaper's chief football writer, it was the scoop of a lifetime and one whose roots lay in a long-standing friendship that had begun almost a decade earlier in rather inauspicious circumstances. "My first real contact with Don had come when Leeds had played Ferencvaros in the European Cup in Budapest eight years earlier," he says. "Back then, the press guys socialised with the players and we went out to a nightclub after the game. We had a few drinks before asking for the bill. When it came, one of the lads thought the money they were asking was too much and then the bouncers got involved. It became heated very quickly and when Billy Bremner said, 'Everyone pick up a chair', I remember thinking, 'What have I got myself into?' We ended up having to fight our way out and a few of the lads suffered cuts and bruises. Unfortunately for us – and me, in particular - as we got back to the hotel, Don was standing at the top of this ornate staircase in his dressing gown. He pointed straight at me and said, 'You, what have you done with my boys?' It wasn't the best start to a relationship with a manager but, over the years, we did become more and more friendly. Eventually, we reached the stage where he would consult me over decisions and that was how I came to learn about his plan to quit as England manager a couple of weeks before I broke the story."

In the telephone call from Leeds that first made Powell aware of what was about to happen, Revie had calmly outlined the details of the offer. He also revealed exactly where he had been when supposedly on a scouting mission as England were drawing 0-0 with Brazil a couple of weeks earlier. The call ended with Revie inviting Powell to Turnberry, Scotland, for the Open Championship, where it was agreed they would discuss the matter further. The initial plan was for the *Daily Mail* writer to fly, only for Revie to then ask Powell to drive via Leeds instead. Powell recalls: "I arrived at his house and immediately saw the curtains were drawn, which struck me as very strange. At first, I thought someone in the family had maybe died and it might be a bad time. Thankfully, it wasn't and Don invited me in to explain in more detail what was happening. Basically, he wanted advice on things such as how to make sure the Arabs had paid the money, and how he could get there undetected. In the end, he just said, 'If you help me, you can have the story'. And that was that. We went to the Open together and, afterwards, I drove back to London."

Once back in the capital, Powell started to put the story together while telling his bosses at the *Daily Mail* only that he had a huge exclusive and that funds for unlimited travel would be needed. It had been agreed by Revie that Powell should also travel to Dubai, and that the newspaperman would make all the arrangements as, clearly, the England manager could not do so without arousing suspicion. Eventually, a plan was hatched that would see Revie fly out under the name of his son Duncan on a deliberately complicated route designed to ensure none of the *Mail*'s rivals could follow. Powell recalls: "The first stop-off had to be Switzerland as that was where we could check if the money had been paid into Don's account. The plan was to fly to Zurich first, then on to Geneva before returning to Zurich. It was only then that, if we felt safe, we would fly on to Athens before completing the journey from there."

The travelling odyssey duly got underway on July 11, the day after Revie had celebrated his 50th birthday. Powell had left behind two sealed envelopes in the London office of the *Daily Mail* with strict instructions for neither to be opened until he had made contact by telephone from Switzerland, where he and Revie were due to stay before continuing on to Greece the following day.

The first envelope contained the 'Revie Quits' story and a letter of resignation that was to be delivered to the FA's headquarters at Lancaster Gate that night. The second had the follow-up story detailing Revie's planned new life in the Middle East. Powell made the call at 7pm and his sports editor duly retrieved the envelopes from his locked drawer. A discussion then took place over whether to leave the story out of the first edition, a common practice until the advent of the internet and 24-hour news channels as it stopped other rival newspapers lifting an exclusive and claiming it as their own. "Eventually, it was decided we should run it," says Powell. "The thinking was there was no way the other newspapers could not credit the *Mail* with the story because they would be unable to check it for themselves with anyone. Don was with me, his family had gone back to Scotland to avoid the storm and Les Cocker had also been put up in a hotel to keep him out of the way. Later that night, I had dinner with Don at a restaurant overlooking Lake Geneva and he asked, 'What do you think is happening in London?' I knew all hell would be breaking loose." Happy everything was okay, Powell then checked the letter of resignation was on its way to the FA. It was. Unfortunately, due to the late hour, the FA's Lancaster Gate headquarters was closed so the letter had to be pushed through the door. It meant no-one found the envelope until the following morning, by which time every person in the land had read over breakfast of the England manager's decision to quit. Revie had told the *Daily Mail*: 'I sat down with my wife, Elsie, one night and we agreed that the England job was no longer worth the aggravation. It was bringing too much heartache to those nearest to us. Nearly everyone in the country wants me out. So, I am giving them what they want. I know people will accuse me of running away, and it does sicken me that I cannot finish the job by taking England to the World Cup finals in Argentina next year, but the situation has become impossible."

After digesting the news over breakfast, the FA's initial shock quickly gave way to anger. Dick Wragg, a big supporter of Revie and the man he had approached in South America the previous month about possibly having his contract paid up, told the press: 'The worst part of this miserable business was learning about it from reporters.' Speculation immediately began as to Revie's whereabouts and whether he had another job lined up. Suggestions he had been approached about a possible return to Leeds United were quickly scotched by the Elland Road board who assured manager Jimmy Armfield, on holiday in Spain at the time, his position was safe. In Fleet Street, the press had been caught on the hop by the *Daily Mail* and the search bordered on the frantic.

Reporters spent the day hunting for Revie, fruitlessly following up leads that all culminated in dead ends.

By now, Revie and Powell had reached Athens where the *Mail* enjoyed a major stroke of good fortune. Powell explains: "We touched down in Athens and an English football fan recognised Don and came over to ask for an autograph. The story had not reached Greece at this stage but, after learning later that everyone in England was asking where Don Revie was, this fan decided to telephone his favourite newspaper. Fortunately for us, he was a *Daily Mail* reader. The person who answered the phone in the office thanked the fan and then said, 'Please don't tell anyone else'. It was a slice of good fortune because, if he had been a reader of another national newspaper, then they would have been on to us." With Revie's whereabouts still a secret, the *Mail* staff back in London began preparing their second big exclusive about his new life in the Emirates. The details, when revealed the following morning, left the nation stunned. Revie would be paid £60,000 a year for four years plus a further £100,000 in bonuses. Not only that, he would be provided with free luxury accommodation in Dubai along with cars and other perks. The Revie family had also been promised they would always travel first class. It was a jaw-dropping deal. For Revie, however, there was now no hiding place. Despite that, he remained in defiant mood, telling the *Mail*, 'For years everyone seems to have believed I've just been feathering my nest, so perhaps the time has come to put myself first for once'. Any semblance of sympathy over his initial claims of being put in an 'impossible' situation disappeared immediately. Condemnation rained down, especially when it emerged that the *Mail* had paid what Revie later admitted in the High Court was a 'substantial' sum for the stories. The reaction of the newspapers left trailing in the wake of the exclusive was swift and vengeful. Reporters, many of whom already resented Revie's close relationship with Powell and Frank Clough of *The Sun*, lined up to lambast the now ex-England manager, who was variously accused of being a traitor, a mercenary and a liar. The FA's deliberate leaking of Revie's attempt to be released from his contract in return for £50,000 the previous month was also seized upon by a media scenting blood. The decision to sell his story to one newspaper for a reputed £20,000 had backfired spectacularly, as even Revie himself admitted later in life. Son Duncan says: "If there was one thing Dad would have changed had he been able to have his time again, it was his decision to sell the story to one newspaper. It meant the knives were out for him elsewhere. Having said that, the legacy of that time is Jeff Powell remains one of our family's greatest friends to this day. My Dad trusted him implicitly."

In the wake of the revelations, old adversaries seized the opportunity to have their say. Bob Stokoe, the Sunderland manager who had taken such pleasure in beating Revie in the 1973 FA Cup final, claimed, 'He should have been castrated'. A tad more measured was the response of Football League secretary Alan Hardaker, who said: 'Don Revie's decision does not surprise me in the slightest. Now I can only hope he can quickly learn to call out the bingo numbers in Arabic.'

Revie's reputation had hit rock bottom but there was worse to come in the form of the September 6 edition of the *Daily Mirror*. Under the front page headline of 'Revie – The *Mirror*'s disturbing dossier on his rise to fame', details were laid bare of his alleged attempts to fix matches. Bob Stokoe claimed to have been offered money to 'take it easy' before Leeds played his Bury side in 1962, while the game at Wolves 10 years later that cost Revie's side the League Championship was the subject of fresh accusations. Richard Stott wrote: 'Don Revie planned and schemed and offered bribes, leaving as little as possible to chance. He relied on the loyalty of those he took into his confidence not to talk, and it nearly worked.' Former Leeds goalkeeper Gary Sprake was the star witness. The publication brought a swift response from Revie's solicitors, Harrisons of Leeds, who said in a statement: "All the allegations in today's *Daily Mirror* concerning Mr Donald Revie are completely denied and action by Mr Revie is being considered." Revie did initiate legal proceedings, though he never, ultimately, sued the *Mirror*. It is a decision his daughter, Kim, bitterly regrets. "A lot of damage was done by Dad deciding not to sue over the match-fixing allegations," she says. "He wished he had done so later in life but I just don't think he wanted the hassle at the time. He was starting a new life with the United Arab Emirates. It is a shame because it means many of those who didn't know Dad personally have a distorted view of him. That is evident even now with things like *The Damned United*."

Revie, through the decision to swap Lancaster Gate for the Middle East, had quickly become public enemy number one. The reporter who wrote the original story for the *Daily Mail* insists, however, that his friend was a victim of England being a much more puritanical place than it is today. "The criticism that came Don's way was over the top," says Jeff Powell. "I don't think it would happen now because the world has moved on. No-one thinks any worse of Bobby Robson for sorting out a job in Holland with PSV Eindhoven when still England manager. Like Don, Bobby was struggling at the time and wanted out. In fact, if you look at how several England managers have behaved since Don left then you do wonder how it caused such a furore at the time."

One man who was determined Revie would not get away with such a blatant disregard for the FA was chairman Sir Harold Thompson. A statement from Lancaster Gate released three days after the first *Daily Mail* exclusive revealed legal advice was being taken, before adding, 'We unanimously deplore the actions of Mr Revie'.

On August 18, the FA announced Revie had been charged with bringing the game into disrepute. The grounds for the charge were threefold. First, he had announced his resignation without telling the international committee. Second, he had deceitfully asked for his contract to be paid up at the meeting with Dick Wragg in Argentina and, finally, by being in Dubai negotiating the move as England played Brazil, he had debased the position of manager. A suggestion the FA were seeking a four-year ban on Revie to cover the entire length of his deal with the United Arab Emirates was subsequently denied, though there was little doubting the appetite for vengeance that existed within English football's governing body. Sir Harold Thompson was particularly adamant Revie should be brought to book, so much so he went against FA secretary Ted Croker's advice by deciding to chair the five-man disciplinary panel himself. Revie's legal team had already intimated their client would not be appearing so the commission went ahead without him on September 17. Unsurprisingly, the outcome was that Revie be banned from all involvement in football under the jurisdiction of the FA until he agreed to face the charge in person. There was, however, to be no attempt to get FIFA involved – meaning, crucially, Revie was free to carry on coaching the United Arab Emirates.

A year later, Revie finally chose to respond to the FA's indefinite ban. He pledged to contest the charges and a hearing date was set for December 18, 1978. Revie won an early concession when granted the right to have his legal team present, something that was usually forbidden under FA rules. The hearing took place on the same day as Alan Ball had to answer his own charges for accepting illegal payments from Revie. Ball had revealed the three £100 inducements, which dated back to 1966 when Revie wanted to sign the then Blackpool midfielder, in his recent autobiography. Ball admitted the charges and was fined £3,000. Any hopes the FA might deal with Revie equally leniently had been quashed when it was confirmed the hearing would be chaired by Sir Harold Thompson. It was something Revie's QC, Gilbert Gray, protested against vehemently, arguing that the FA chairman could not be anything but biased against his client. Gray also claimed the FA had no jurisdiction over Revie but, as with the objection to Thompson's involvement, it was overruled. It meant the case proceeded with Thompson both asking Revie questions and giving evidence; a ridiculous state of affairs that, again, Ted Croker worried may come back to haunt the FA. The crux of Revie's argument was the belief that he was about to be sacked, while much was made of the tremendous pressure he felt his family had been placed under. Revie also stressed again the decision to take up the post in the United Arab Emirates had been to safeguard his family's future. On this last point, Gilbert Gray suggested this should be reason to praise, not pillory, his client. Revie spent four hours defending the charges against him but called no witnesses. Peter Swales and Dick Wragg, both members of the international committee, spoke on behalf of the FA before the five-man panel withdrew to consider its verdict. When it arrived the following day, Revie was not in court to hear the bad news. The Commission - and Thompson in particular – had been distinctly unimpressed by Revie's attempts to justify the move to Dubai and banned him for ten years. The suspension was back-dated to the day Revie had walked out of the England job. Clearly, the FA wanted justice to be seen to be done but the size of the ban shocked even those who were expecting a severe punishment. Trevor Cherry recalls: "I could not believe it when I heard. I thought the FA acted terribly, it had been an open secret Don was about to be sacked and yet they still went after him. It was wrong."

Such a draconian punishment meant Revie's solicitors were always likely to go to the High Court to try and overturn the ban. As he would discover a little under a year later, however, justice would come at a very high price.

Chapter 24

Victory – At A Price

Football and the courts are not natural bedfellows. The taxman may, from time to time, be forced to seek legal redress against miscreant clubs who choose to abide by deadlines of the transfer and not fiscal variety. Certain Premier League footballers may also find themselves hauled in front of unimpressed magistrates for exceeding the speed limit. But, on the whole, English football has largely managed to keep its own house in order, save for a couple of notable cases during the 1960s involving match-fixing and the Professional Footballers' Association's successful smashing of the retain-and-transfer system. So, when it was announced Don Revie planned to take the Football Association to the High Court in an attempt to overturn his 10-year ban, the news caused a sensation. For the first time, the working life of an England manager would be laid bare in front of the nation. No stone would be left unturned. From the moment November 26, 1979, was set as the start of the case, it became one of the most eagerly-anticipated dates on the football calendar.

Revie, by now, had been in Dubai for more than two years. Along with Elsie, he had adapted well to life in the Middle East. The lifestyle had been everything Revie had hoped for with the United Arab Emirates FA treating the couple like royalty. Nothing was too much trouble, with family and friends being regularly flown out to ensure there was little danger of either Revie or his wife becoming homesick. Son Duncan recalls: "People say Mum and Dad fled to the desert but they loved it out there. Dubai was not as built up as it is today but they had a fabulous villa and staff. The sunshine was fantastic and it allowed them both to play a lot of golf. I went out to see them twice a year, a fortnight at a time, and it was wonderful to see Mum and Dad so happy." As enjoyable as the lifestyle was, however, Revie appreciated if he ever wanted to return to English football in the future – and, in particular, take up his nine-year consultancy position with Leeds United that was due to begin in January, 1980 - then the FA ban had to be quashed. The only option was the High Court so, on a cold Monday morning a little under a month before Christmas, the Revies found themselves smiling for the photographers in central London before heading inside one of the capital's grandest buildings.

The crux of Revie's bid to overturn the ban was that Sir Harold Thompson, as FA chairman, had been unfit to sit on the FA Commission that had handed out the punishment. Revie's QC, Gilbert Gray, had argued the same point a year earlier only to be dismissed by Thompson. Now, however, it was hoped Mr Justice Cantley would find Thompson's role as 'prosecutor, witness, judge and jury' meant Revie had not received a fair hearing. The Earl of Harewood attended every day of the High Court case and he felt, from the very start, Revie had a strong argument. "The ban had been vindictive," he says. "Don simply had to go to court to get his livelihood back. After what the FA had done, it was the only way he would be able to work again in this country."

Gray's opening address outlined his client's case, with the first nugget of information for the media and public to seize upon being an accusation that Thompson had tried to interfere with team selection. Thompson, Gray alleged, had told Revie in November, 1975, that Malcolm Macdonald and Allan Clarke should not have been selected for the draw in Portugal that ended any hopes of qualifying for the European Championships. Once Gray's opening address was over, the FA's own counsel stood up and argued Revie's departure during a World Cup campaign had 'materially prejudiced the England team's chances of qualifying for the finals'. 'Exemplary damages' were also, it was confirmed, being sought due to the failure to qualify having cost the FA significant potential profits.

Day two brought graphic descriptions of the travails Revie had suffered as England manager; namely sleepless nights, fans throwing objects at him when walking down the Wembley tunnel and, above all, his 'hostile' relationship with the FA chairman. Thompson, it was claimed, had made Revie and assistant Les Cocker travel second class when on scouting missions abroad as opposed to the first class promised in their contracts, while he had also complained bitterly about an eight-day summer get-together of England players costing £8,000. Revie, under cross-examination, was forced to admit his own fallibility in charge of England and how he had made too many changes to the team. On his players' response to the fabled dossiers he put so much faith in, Revie admitted to the court: 'I found out later, after I left, that they were using them to keep scores when they played cards at the hotel.' By the end of the third day, Revie had made another string of revelations, including how he had lost his voice on the 1977 tour of South America due to nerves brought on by the pressures of the job. He insisted the decision to quit had been taken at a football conference in Bournemouth earlier that summer after rumour had reached him of the FA approaching another manager to take over the national team. He also admitted to having asked the FA to pay up the remaining two years on his contract, though he vehemently denied asking for an additional £5,000 'golden handshake'. And while he agreed the story of his departure had appeared in a national newspaper before the FA had received his resignation letter, he claimed in mitigation to have only given the story to the *Daily Mail* to prevent the newspaper divulging his plans even earlier.

Revie, who also claimed to have rejected advances from Barcelona and Saudi Arabia during his England reign, was not without support in court. Notable football figures such as Jimmy Hill, Jock Stein and Lawrie McMenemy all provided character witnesses. Johnny Giles also offered his support, while wife Elsie confirmed her husband's sleepless nights and how even taking prescribed tablets had not helped cure his insomnia. The Earl of Harewood was another to appear when the acrimonious relationship between Revie and Sir Harold Thompson came under the spotlight of the court. He recalls: "I told them exactly what Thompson was like and how he had wanted to sack Don. His behaviour had been wrong and I wanted the court to understand that. I also explained how the Ipswich chairman had personally told me the FA had approached him over the possibility of Bobby Robson becoming the new England manager when Don was still in the job." Thompson's attitude towards Revie was picked over in court for several hours. It emerged the FA chairman had, according to Revie's counsel, deliberately mis-pronounced the surname of his manager despite constant reminders. "It was a mistake a lot of people made," explains the Earl of Harewood. "They would pronounce it 'Re-vvie' and not 'Ree-vie', as it should have been. But Thompson seemed to take great pleasure in continually getting it wrong because he knew it wound Don up. It was typical of his attitude."

The start of the second week saw Thompson finally take the stand. The FA chairman had already received the backing of Bob Lord, the Burnley chairman and key decision maker within the Football League. Lord had insisted he had never been given the impression Revie would be sacked. But this was the real deal with Thompson's testimony expected to have a huge bearing on the case. Unlike Revie, he could recall only two instances where the pair had not been in agreement. The first had been in 1975 when Revie had wanted to pull out of England's game in Northern Ireland due to the on-going Troubles, which Thompson had over-ruled. The second disagreement had been over his fears that too much money was being spent on the national team. Asked about comments he was alleged to have made about certain England players picked by Revie, Thompson countered: 'I can't see why the chairman of the FA can't express his opinion on the performance of players.' Pressed further, he then flatly denied having tried to interfere with team selection. His evidence closed with a claim that Revie's resignation had caused 'enormous chaos' and 'damaged the image of soccer in Britain'. This point was reiterated the following day by the vice-chairman of the FA Commission that had banned Revie, Robert Strachan, who stressed how concerned the FA were at preserving standards. He said: 'There are some 30,000 clubs affiliated to the Association. I would have thought one would have expected a better example from the manager of England.' Revie bringing dishonour on the post was a theme the FA's counsel returned to throughout the case, Robert Johnson QC accusing Revie of 'bringing disgrace to the sport' on more than one occasion. Johnson said: 'Football is the most popular sport, and the numbers who go to watch other sports are trivial by comparison. The England team is the shop window of football. It is a sport - the purpose is the promotion of sport and not commercial gain.'

After both counsels had summed up their respective cases, Mr Justice Cantley retired to make his decision. It meant an anxious wait for the judgement, which arrived a week later. Neither Revie nor Thompson was in court to hear the ban lifted. Ted Croker's fears over Thompson's insistence on chairing the Commission had been realised as the judge, following legal precedent, ruled the FA chairman had not been able to take an objective view when imposing the ten-year ban. Revie, by now back in Dubai, was free to work again in English football. The £90,000 consultancy role with Leeds United negotiated on his departure from Elland Road in 1974 could begin, as planned, in the New Year. Any feelings of jubilation on the part of Revie's legal team were, however, soon to be dispelled as Mr Justice Cantley launched an astonishing personal attack during his own summing-up of the case. Revie 'lacked candour' and was 'greedy'. He had, in resigning, presented a 'sensational, outrageous example of disloyalty, breach of trust, discourtesy and selfishness'. The judge also branded Revie a 'prickly man' who had been brooding on 'imagined wrongs'. To illustrate the point, he added, 'It is easy to irritate a prima donna without having any hostility towards the lady'. Cantley also 'utterly' rejected Revie's claim that he had not asked for a golden handshake when attempting to get the final two years of his contract paid up during the fateful tour of South America. As character assassinations go, it could not have been much worse. Further financial insult was added to injured pride when the claim for damages was rejected and Revie ordered to pay two-thirds of his own costs. The FA, meanwhile, lost its own counter-claim for damages over missing the World Cup and was ordered to pay all the costs of the 1978 Commission hearing. The final bill for the game's governing body was believed to be around £150,000. Neither party had emerged with any credit from the episode, even if the judge did move to try and absolve Sir Harold Thompson of any blame by dismissing the accusations of hostility towards Revie and describing the FA chairman as 'an honourable man'. It is a description the Earl of Harewood still finds hard to accept today. "The judge rather took the sting out of Don winning the case by what he said afterwards," he says. "Cantley said, 'I must find for Mr Revie and I am disappointed to have to do that because Sir Harold Thompson is an honourable man'. He wasn't. And to say, 'Mr Revie is not an honourable man' was outrageous. Don had won the case." Asked whether he would have handled the saga differently had he still been FA president, the Earl adds: "Of course, though my problem would have been that the president of the FA was treated as a remote figure. One went to Wembley for matches and presided at the annual meeting, but did little else. There was also a lot of strange thinking within the FA. I had stepped down as president because Sam Bolton, who was on the FA Council, once came up to me and said, 'The Queen doesn't come to Wembley because you are divorced'. It was nonsense. She simply didn't like football. But he insisted that was the case, so I resigned. The thing is, after I had stepped down, she still didn't come to Wembley." Others, however, did not share the distaste of the Earl for Mr Justice Cantley's comments. Brian Glanville, of *The Sunday Times*, says: "The judge had no alternative but to find for Revie because Thompson had completely over-reached his powers and acted as both judge and jury at the original FA Commission hearing. The ban could not remain. But, tellingly in my opinion, the judge also described Revie as 'greedy'. It was an apt description for a man who had ratted on England by leaving to make more money elsewhere."

Revie's victory, as hollow as Mr Justice Cantley's scathing summing may have made it, was still a victory that brought a degree of satisfaction as it had come against his old foe, Sir Harold Thompson.

Back in Dubai, the news was greeted with a smile. Revie had much to be pleased about. Not only was he able to take up the consultancy work with Leeds United, he was also enjoying life in the Middle East. Crucially, progress was being made with the United Arab Emirates team. Revie had taken over with the Emirates in a sorry state, ranked fourth out of the five teams competing in the Gulf League. The players were undisciplined and lacking in motivation, something Revie quickly put down to the generosity of the Emirates FA. Son Duncan recalls: "Dad always used to say the players were very skilful but lacked professionalism and discipline. They won one of his early games and, the next thing Dad knew, the Sheik had bought all the players a Jaguar apiece. Dad didn't like that as it meant the players lacked hunger. He felt they should earn rewards like that, not be handed them on a plate."

If a lack of professionalism was evident to Revie on his arrival amid temperatures well in excess of 100 degrees, so was the lack of facilities. His new team had never played on grass, though the 12 clubs in the top division of the Emirates League had ordered artificial pitches. A new £25m national stadium was also under construction as Revie signed a five-year deal for the benefit of the world's media.

By the time Revie had won his High Court case in England a couple of years later, the facilities available to him were much improved. He also had much more control over his players than had been the case when in charge of England, Revie, displaying the same energy and enthusiasm that had characterised his career in management as he regularly took the squad away for training camps. He also quickly set about trying to improve standards. Central to his plans, just as had been the case when taking over Leeds United almost two decades earlier, was setting up a youth programme. Son Duncan recalls: "The standard of football was not very high when Dad got there but he worked really hard to turn it round. His legacy was that, 10 years on from Dad stepping down as manager, the United Arab Emirates qualified for their one and only World Cup. And the people in charge of the UAE FA put that down to the work my Dad had done." Revie's influence was such that, even now, the great work he did for UAE football is not forgotten, as a shocked Duncan discovered on a visit to Dubai in 2001. "I had not been for quite some time, probably since when Mum and Dad were living there," he explains. "Soccerex were looking at getting involved in Dubai so I flew out on a fact-finding trip. Dubai had changed enormously – where you used to drive five miles to the family villa and see nothing but sand, now everywhere was built up. I was talking to the Sheik about my Dad one day when he suddenly said, 'You must go to see your father's villa'. I said, 'It can't still be here after all these years and all this building work'. But he assured me it was. Later, we drove through a maze of streets before eventually pulling up at a big pair of gates with a padlock. The driver unlocked them and there was my Dad's old villa. It was overgrown but they had left the place untouched, as some sort of shrine. It was quite moving as it showed they had not forgotten Dad and that the Revie name still carried huge weight out there."

Revie left his job as national manager in May, 1980. It was an amicable split with his contract, which still had a year to run, being cancelled by mutual agreement on the pretext that the UAE wanted an Arab-speaking coach to run the team. With Revie free to work again in English football following the lifting of his ban, a return home was mooted. Instead, the Revies opted to stay in Dubai where they enjoyed such an enviable lifestyle. Sheila Silver, whose late husband Gabby Harris had been such a good friend of Revie that he used to travel on the Leeds United team bus to away games, recalls: "When my husband died, Don was very upset and I remember him crying at the funeral. Don and Elsie were living in Dubai and invited me out to stay. They had a fabulous lifestyle. Don was very highly regarded and the local people adored him. Don was also very friendly with the royal family and it was one of their happiest times. They had a lovely bungalow, and for the month I stayed I had my own wing. It was very kind of them both." The move had proved a happy one, with the Revies even managing to indulge their passion for golf in the desert. "Dubai was very different to today," says Sheila Silver, "and I did wonder how they would adapt to there being just sand and no grass. I didn't think there would be a golf course, for instance, but there was. Both Don and Elsie would each carry a piece of turf around to take their shots off."

After leaving his post with the national team, Revie quickly found employment with UAE First Division club, Al Nasr. Formed a little under 30 years earlier, the club had played at various locations in Dubai before settling at the newly-built Al Maktoum Stadium in 1978. Under Revie, Al Nasr finished as runners-up in the league and developed an impressive youth policy that, come the 1990 World Cup finals, would see four of the club's players feature for the United Arab Emirates in Italy. Unfortunately for Revie, however, he had left Al Nasr before the youth policy began to bear fruit. He was sacked in 1983 with the club sitting third in the league table.

Revie returned to England but, by the following year, was on the move again with ever-loyal wife Elsie once more by his side. Egyptian club Al-Ahly had offered Revie a two-year deal but, in the end, the couple only stayed a few months. Son Duncan recalls: "Unlike Dubai, they just didn't settle in Egypt and it quickly became apparent they never would. They had had enough of travelling so came home." The aborted stint in Cairo and the return to England did not, however, quell Revie's desire to return to management. He was 57 and five years beyond the time-limit he had once set himself for retirement. But his competitive spirit burned as brightly as ever. Revie was still being paid £10,000 per year as a consultant to Leeds United and had enjoyed passing on advice, when required, to Allan Clarke and Eddie Gray, two of his old boys who had since been appointed manager at Elland Road. He had played a part in the appointment of his two former players so had a vested interest in both doing well. But being on hand for advice was not enough to occupy one of the sharpest minds in football, as Eddie Gray quickly discovered during his own three years at the helm from 1982. "Don was always available if I needed a chat," he says. "We spoke about certain things and he would give me advice if I asked for it. But it was difficult for Don because he did not come to watch us very often. He had been living abroad when I first got the job so that made it impossible for him. But, even after he and Elsie had come back to England, Don didn't seem to feel comfortable being at Leeds. Basically, because of the way he left the club and then what happened with England, Don felt awkward."

With Elland Road containing too many ghosts, Revie looked around for a suitable vacancy to end his exile from English football. After seven years away, he realised so much had changed but still clung to the hope there would be a way back into club management. Revie was prepared to be patient but, almost straight away, a telephone call from a club in apparent turmoil seemed to offer the answer to his prayers. First Division Queens Park Rangers had finished fifth in the 1983-84 season, having built on the success of reaching the FA Cup final two years earlier. Terry Venables' reward for creating such an impressive team on limited resources had been the offer to manage Barcelona the previous summer. 'El Tel' became an immediate success in Spain but the same could not be said for the club he left behind in Shepherds Bush. 'Chaotic' is, instead, perhaps the best way to sum up what followed as Venables's successor, Gordon Jago, lasted just one week before being sacked and replaced by Alan Mullery. Even this appointment, however, had only come after Rangers had failed to lure David Pleat away from Luton Town. Results nose-dived and Mullery survived just six months, the nadir coming when a 6-2 first leg lead against Partizan Belgrade in the UEFA Cup was turned into an embarrassing exit on the away goals rule in Yugoslavia. Mullery's sacking meant Rangers, by now deep in relegation trouble, were looking for their fourth manager of 1984. Chairman Jim Gregory knew an experienced older head was required. Don Revie was at home when the telephone rang, as son Duncan recalls. "It was just an ordinary night," he says. "But then, when Dad had come back from answering the phone, he had a smile on his face. He said, 'That was Jim Gregory and he has offered me the QPR job, I am going to meet him in London tomorrow to sort it all out'."

It was an attractive offer, especially as QPR had only lost Clive Allen from the team that had been so impressive in qualifying for Europe the previous season under Venables. Revie knew that by restoring confidence and tweaking a couple of things, Rangers' season could be back on track within weeks. The trip to central London was spent mulling over what needed to be done at Loftus Road. By the time he met Gregory in a hotel, an excited Revie was certain QPR were the club for him. Within minutes, however, it became clear there would be no fairytale return to English football as Gregory reneged on the previous night's conversation over the telephone. Revie's son Duncan explains: "Basically, Jim Gregory withdrew the offer after, according to Dad, getting cold feet. He halved the offer and Dad realised he could not work for someone like Gregory and that was that. Unfortunately, Gregory then put out a press statement claiming Dad had asked for double the money. It was a really cheap trick and it made things uncomfortable for Dad once again." Gregory's subsequent claim that Revie had increased his own demands was, unsurprisingly, seized upon by the press. The 'Don Readies' headlines were dusted off and printed once again, leaving Revie disillusioned. The game that had been his life for almost 45 years had turned its back on him. Revie realised there would be no way back. He still loved football but it was no longer the be-all and end-all of life. Instead, he vowed to enjoy his retirement.

Chapter 25

Make Sure My Lads Get A Drink

Retirement is a time for reflection, rest and enjoyment. Some take to it immediately, relishing the chance to enjoy a slower pace of life and indulge the interests that the demands of work had often precluded. Others, though, find it difficult to adapt. They miss the prestige and power, and find filling the long days a constant struggle. Happily for Don Revie and his family, he found retirement suited him. Golf had always been a major passion, providing Revie with an invaluable escape from the rigours of football management. Those precious few hours when all that mattered was connecting sweetly with a little white ball had been something to savour. So, as retirement beckoned, regular visits to the golf course were always going to be high on the agenda. The family's villa in Spain had been bought specifically because of its location next to the local course, as had been the Wentworth home Revie moved into following his aborted stint in Egypt.

As enjoyable as he found golf, Revie was also determined to keep busy in other ways. His son Duncan had left the legal world to set up his own corporate entertainment business, Total Sport. The seed had been planted in Duncan's mind many years earlier when his father was still manager of Leeds United. "He once took me round Elland Road," recalls Duncan. "It was not in the best of conditions with the old Scratching Shed still at the end where the South Stand can now be found. But he turned to me and said, 'A time will come when fans will get here at lunchtime to enjoy hospitality before a game'. He also said there would be shops and bars for fans to enjoy. I looked around at what was, basically, a bit of a dump and thought, 'My Dad has finally gone mad'. The directors didn't even get to Elland Road until 2.30pm in those days so why would anyone else? But he was right. He was very clever in realising the direction football was heading." Once Duncan had set up Total Sport, his father worked as a part-time consultant. He enjoyed the work and, in particular, being able to see at close hand his son's success. Later, Duncan would set up Soccerex, whose Chiswick offices today boast a 'Don Revie Bar'. Revie had always believed there had been a need for the establishment of a forum for the global business of football. Jeff Powell says: "Don was always concerned about what would happen to his family so he would be delighted to see how well

Duncan has done with Soccerex."

Retirement also allowed Revie to travel the world watching major sporting events, a desire he had spoken of when revealing his decision to quit as England manager via the *Daily Mail*. Football, though, remained a major part of his life. The Queens Park Rangers episode had stung Revie but he still remained deeply in love with the game. As often happens in retirement, he loved nothing more than to reminisce about the old days – and, in particular, his time as Leeds United manager. He would sit for hours with Duncan, discussing his 13 years at Elland Road. "We had quite a few reflective discussions," says Revie's son. "A recurring theme was how he wished he had allowed his Leeds team to play more freely a lot earlier. Dad was adamant taking the shackles off before his last couple of years would have won Leeds more trophies. It was a big regret. With hindsight, he realised too much focus had been put on the opposition. The dossiers had been invaluable early on because Leeds simply didn't have the team to play any differently to the kick and rush Dad used - or just 'kick' if Bobby Collins was playing. But, once those young lads had matured, Dad wished he had given them a lot more freedom. It riled him that his lads did not win the medals he felt they deserved."

The seed of Revie believing his Leeds players had not been handed enough freedom until it was almost too late had been planted during his time as England manager. Trevor Cherry recalls: "We started to have a drink after England games because I think he just wanted someone friendly to talk to. He was under a lot of pressure and, as an escape, he would love to talk about his time at Leeds. Don once said, 'If I had my time again, I would have let you lads loose a lot earlier. I wouldn't have shut up shop once 1-0 ahead at places like Ipswich, instead I would have told you to keep going and win 5-1'. He had seen that the England lads were not as good as he thought they were when in opposition at club level. With England, he said he had two or three good players. But at Leeds, he had a team."

As much as Revie enjoyed a stroll down memory lane, he did insist on casting a keen eye over the modern game. Always a deep thinker, he continued to tell family and friends how football could be improved. Some of his ideas, such as the belief players should train at 3pm in order they were more attuned to kick-off time are yet to catch on. Others, however, have. Duncan recalls: "He campaigned for the introduction of professional referees for years. It was something Dad believed passionately in so he would have been delighted when they were finally brought into the Premier League. The preparation time available to international managers today would also have pleased Dad, as would how things like Pro-Zone have revolutionised the life of a manager. Pro-Zone has also vindicated the dossiers Dad used to put together."

Football fans love comparing different eras and asking whether greats such as Stanley Matthews or Tom Finney would have been able to thrive in the more defensive-minded modern game? It is the same with managers. What would Brian Clough and his ilk have made of the increasingly major role agents play? Or the exorbitant salaries that can turn a player's head so far his career soon begins to suffer? Many of the arguments are fatuous but one former player who believes Revie would have adapted to the demands of football in the new Millennium is Trevor Cherry. "Don would definitely be able to work in today's game," he says. "In many ways, football has caught up with many of the ideas Don introduced when managing England and Leeds. Certainly, I doubt the England players of today would make as much of a fuss over something like the dossiers as the lads did when Don was in charge. He was also a big believer in a player getting what he was worth so I doubt he would have been fazed by all the big salaries they get now. He always felt players were vastly under-paid. I don't think he would have liked agents very much, I certainly can't think of anyone at Leeds who had one during my time. But, as with all great managers, he would have adapted. The manager that reminds me the most of Don today is Sir Alex Ferguson. Just like Don, he is someone who is driven and determined to make sure his team is successful. If Sir Alex can thrive in the modern game, then I am in no doubt Don would have been able to do the same."

In 1986, Revie delivered on a long-standing promise to Elsie and moved to his wife's native Scotland. Their new home was in Kinross, not far from where she had grown up in Lochgelly. Golf continued to be a major part of the couple's life, even when Revie started to notice he could no longer hit the ball as far as he once had. Initially, he put it down to age. Being 59, he could not hope to match the long drives of his youth. Son Duncan recalls: "I had always been able to hit the ball past him but now he was dropping further and further behind. After one round, he said, 'I don't know what happened there, son, as I was really nailing the ball but it just wouldn't go anywhere'. It was frustrating for him, but nothing more."

A few weeks later, however, Revie started to experience pains in his legs during the final few holes. At first, it was just an irritation. A hot bath on returning home would usually ease the pain and he would be fine again. Gradually, though, the problem worsened and medical opinion was sought. At first, the doctors thought it may be a slipped disc. Revie, despite not being reassured, played on but his health continued to deteriorate. Duncan recalls: "When he started to get pain in his knees, it was clear Dad had a problem. But the doctors couldn't work out exactly what the problem was. For two years, it was mis-diagnosed as the sort of injury a lot of ex-footballers suffered from."

When Revie's hands started to go numb, the doctors finally accepted this could no longer be put down to the sort of injury suffered by former sportsmen. The simplest of everyday tasks had become a problem and his family were frantic with worry. Baffled doctors began exhaustive tests immediately. In May, 1987, Revie was summoned to London for a meeting with his consultant, who told him that he was suffering from motor neurone disease. Revie, in common with most people in Britain, had never heard of it. The consultant calmly explained how motor neurone was a condition where the delicate nerve cells leading from the brain and spinal cord to the muscles die. And how, without these cells, the muscles simply stop functioning. Sufferers, the consultant continued, experience increasing difficulty in speaking, swallowing, moving their limbs and, eventually, breathing. There was no cure and life expectancy, once diagnosed, was between two and five years.

For a man whose life had been based around football and sporting activity, it was the cruellest of blows. He was facing an inexorable slide towards disability. The entire Revie family were devastated. Little was known about motor neurone in 1987, other than that actor David Niven had been one of its victims a few years earlier. So, the family began an exhaustive and frantic search for help. There had to be someone, somewhere who could offer hope? A hospital in Texas offered the first chink of light. It was a leading centre of research into the disease, so the Revies immediately flew to America. Even a drug to alleviate the condition would have made the trip worthwhile but, instead, they returned to England dejected and disappointed after discovering Revie would receive no help because he was not a US citizen.

Revie's health was deteriorating at an alarming rate. Regular visits to the local hospital for exercise had failed to hold back the effects of motor neurone and he had started to lose full control of his limbs. A specially designed electric wheelchair was bought as standing for any longer than a few seconds had become impossible. The family home was also adapted to his needs. Revie, displaying the fighting spirit that had characterised his great Leeds United team, vowed not to be beaten. He bravely tried to keep his beloved family's spirits up, as daughter Kim recalls: "It was horrible to see someone who was so strong and such a big bear of a man become so frail. But, underneath, he was still the same Dad with a big competitive streak in him. He would say things like, 'If I can walk from this door to the other wall then I get 10 points'. He would then shuffle across the room on his zimmer frame. When he had managed it, he would look at me and smile."

When news of Revie's illness was made public, he was inundated with letters of support from well-wishers. Among the many hundreds of cards and messages that arrived at his Kinross home was one from Colin Grainger, his former team-mate at both Sunderland and Leeds. Grainger recalls: "I wrote to wish Don all the best. I reminded him of the time we used to play cards on Sunderland's away trips and how he won most of the hands. A couple of weeks later, a letter arrived signed by Don. It had been written by someone else, presumably because Don could not write it himself, and it read, 'Colin, happy memories – and you were always a better footballer than a card player'. It showed his sense of humour was still intact."

An emotional return to Elland Road followed in September, 1987, as Leeds beat Manchester City 2-0 in the Second Division. Revie, with the aid of a walking stick, had taken his bow on the pitch to applause from both sets of fans. Billy Bremner had, by now, returned to Leeds as manager. Just a few months earlier, he had led United to the FA Cup semi-final and the play-off final only to fall at the last hurdle. Revie was proud to see his old captain doing such a good job and left Elland Road that night believing Bremner and Leeds were destined for a return to the top flight. His spirits were lifted further a few months later when it emerged Russian doctors were claiming to have discovered a breakthrough in the treatment of motor neurone. A drug had been developed that would help repair the nerve cells being killed by the effects of the disease. As with the trip to Texas the previous year, the Revies had to go and see for themselves if a miracle cure had, indeed, been found. Unlike America, however, getting into the old Soviet Union was a laborious process. Here, though, a friend from the past proved invaluable as Revie's old boss at Al Nasr in Dubai, Sheik Mana Bin Khalifa Almaktoum, stepped in to help. The Sheik appreciated time was of the essence and started to pull strings, as Revie's son Duncan recalls: "The Russians claimed to have made a medical breakthrough so we wanted to see if it was right. Getting behind the Iron Curtain was not easy, though, and it took the Sheik's contacts getting involved to smooth everything over. As he had done with the trip to America, the Sheik also paid for all the transport to Russia and all the medication we needed. Dad had left the Middle East three or four years earlier and yet the Sheik still insisted on paying for everything. It was a wonderful gesture and showed how much they still thought about him." Unfortunately for the Revies, the trip to

Moscow ended in similar disappointment to the Texas visit the previous year. It was another hammer blow, and one made all the more painful a few weeks later when the *News of the World* ran a supposed exclusive story suggesting Revie had been cured. The Foreign Office's confirmation Revie had been to Moscow seemed to be proof enough for the newspaper but the reality was, sadly, very different. There was no cure and Revie's condition was getting worse by the day. Typically, however, this had not stopped him becoming heavily involved in charity work for motor neurone research.

To help with the fund-raising, Johnny Giles suggested to Revie a game be held at Elland Road in his honour. All the proceeds would be split between motor neurone research and the Leeds City Council children's charity 'Give a Life'. It would take an almighty effort on Revie's part to attend, not least as the effects of motor neurone had by now made walking impossible and his speech had started to become slurred. A private and proud man, he did not want this to be the final image the world had of him. Nevertheless, he agreed to Giles' proposal and a date of May 11, 1988, was set for Leeds United to take on a Revie All-Stars XI.

Invitations were sent out to a host of players and the response was heart-warming. Among those who agreed to play for the All-Stars XI were England duo Chris Woods and Mark Wright. Paul Gascoigne, English football's new brightest star, also accepted the invitation along with Graeme Souness, who would be making his final appearance before retiring as a player. Kevin Keegan flew in from his home in Spain to take part. The Leeds side was, effectively, Billy Bremner's first-choice team plus Peter Shilton, Revie revealing on the day of the game how he had wanted to sign the England goalkeeper when in charge at Elland Road. Before the game, the team Revie had built and nurtured enjoyed an emotional reunion in the players' lounge. John Reynolds, the club's groundsman and a good friend of Revie, recalls: "Don came into the lounge and called me over. He then pulled £20 out of his pocket and said, 'Make sure all my lads get a drink'. For that moment, it was the Don of old. I felt very emotional at the time and I still feel the same thinking about it now. It is the saddest memory I have of Don but also, in a funny way, one of the best." As his former players reminisced about their shared memories, Revie looked on with pride from his wheelchair. After all these years, they were still a team and still devoted to one another. As kick-off approached, Revie was pushed down the tunnel to receive the acclaim of the 7,305 crowd. As the chant of 'There's only one Don Revie' rang out one last time, his top lip trembled. The Earl of Harewood recalls: "It was a sad night in many ways because seeing someone who had always been a wonderful friend suffering like that was awful. But it was also a happy night. I helped push Don down the tunnel and I could see he was very moved to be back with all his old players again. He was very emotional."

The emotion of the occasion meant Revie had to return to his hotel in Leeds before the game got underway. Before leaving, however, he found time to tell the *Yorkshire Evening Post*: 'I am so grateful. I knew my lads would respond. They are always in my thoughts and my heart. I owe them so much and I like to believe I contributed to their success.' Seeing Revie leave Elland Road for what, deep down, they knew would be the last time was an emotional moment for his players, too. Some had not seen their former manager for a couple of years and had been shocked at the sight of the powerful and active man they remembered so vividly being confined to a wheelchair. In Revie's absence, his All-Stars XI, who were minus George Best following the wayward former Manchester United star's failure to turn up, went a goal up through a cheeky back-heel by Paul Gascoigne. Leeds equalised through Ian Baird shortly after half-time before the striker was replaced by Norman Hunter to elicit the biggest cheer of the night. John Sheridan then won the game for United with a 20-yard shot that flew past Chris Woods. The two charities benefited from gate receipts of £24,519.

Once back in Scotland, the muscle-wasting disease continued to rob Revie of more and more of his physical faculties. His mind, though, remained as active as ever - perhaps the cruellest of all the effects of motor neurone as it means sufferers are acutely aware of how their body is failing them. Revie's son Duncan recalls: "He started to go downhill really fast and it became horrendous. His body was dying all around him and there was nothing we could do." By now, even the most straight-forward of tasks was beyond Revie. The disease with no known cause was proving particularly unforgiving as his weight, which had once been 17 stone, plummeted to under nine stone. Visits from family and friends did perk up Revie, even though they often proved exhausting. Jack Charlton recalls: "I would always pop in when I was in Scotland. If I had caught anything fishing or had shot a pheasant, I would hand it over. It was horrible seeing Don stuck in the wheelchair like that, absolutely horrible. I once read an article about motor neurone and it said the disease was caused by stress. I could believe that with Don because he would get quite stressed when working so hard for Leeds United." Such a theory has particular support among doctors in America but, whatever the true cause, by 1989 it was clear Revie's life was drawing to a close. He had tried to remain defiantly optimistic for the sake of his family but, when his speech went, even he had to accept the inevitable. Son Duncan recalls: "When Dad could no longer talk, it became a case of him blinking once for yes and twice for no. That is what motor neurone does to someone and it was a diabolical time for the family. This may sound strange, but in the end I was glad when he passed away because it meant his suffering was finally over."

Revie died on May 26, 1989, in an Edinburgh hospital. Two hundred miles away, the gates at Elland Road were soon covered in scarves and flags. Some contained personal tributes, while others just had simple messages of 'thanks' scrawled across them. The players, despite having seen for themselves 12 months earlier how ill Revie had become, were stunned to lose a man who had been a surrogate father to so many. Gordon McQueen recalls: "I remember being tremendously sad when I heard the news. I had been at Elland Road the previous year for Don's testimonial and it was hard seeing him like that. I owe him so much and I am sure all the other lads will say the same about their own careers. In terms of the managers I played under during my career, Don was the best by a million miles. I doubt any of the players would have said any different. No-one came close. Don was old school in the same way as Matt Busby, Bill Shankly and Jock Stein. He deserves mentioning in the same breath as all those great men."

It was not just in Leeds where Revie's passing was mourned. His Leeds team may never have been loved outside their own city but, 15 years on from his Elland Road departure, there was a grudging respect evident for what Revie had achieved. Many of his former players had become managers themselves by 1989 and were putting into practice lessons learned under Revie. Joe Royle, who went on to lift the FA Cup with Everton in 1995, says: "I only have good words to say about Don Revie. I had a great deal of respect for him and what he achieved with Leeds. I played with Norman Hunter and Terry Cooper at Bristol City, and those two absolutely adored him. After just a short time playing for Don with England, I could see why." Revie's influence is still being felt today with former England Under-21s manager Peter Taylor still using lessons learned when making four appearances for the senior side in 1976. "I picked up a lot from Don," says the man who handed David Beckham the England captaincy for the first time when temporarily handed the reins of the senior side in 2000. "Probably the biggest lesson I took into my own managerial career was to be hands on. Nothing was too small a task for Don to get involved in and I have always admired that. I stopped short of giving the players a massage every Thursday, but I have tried to be close to my players in the way Don tried to be. It is also amazing how many of the ideas he came up with are standard practice today, such as the ice baths after training and the dossiers. I remain a big fan of Don Revie."

Four days after Revie had passed away, his funeral took place at Warriston Crematorium, near Edinburgh. It was a quiet, simple affair at which all aspects of his life were represented – bar one. As expected, his Leeds players were out in force and joined by Syd Owen and John Reynolds. The United board were also represented by Rayner Barker, Jack Marjason and Eric Carlile, while one group of supporters led by Gary Edwards hired a van and drove up to Scotland from West Yorkshire to pay their respects. It was a gesture that prompted Revie's widow Elsie, who would later succeed her late husband as president of the Leeds United Supporters' Club and hold the post until her own death in 2005, to later invite them to the reception. From his England days, Kevin Keegan was at the funeral after again jetting in from Spain to join Revie's old friends from Manchester City and all the other clubs he had represented as a player. Lawrie McMenemy, who would later give Revie's daughter Kim away at her wedding, was also present along with television commentator Brian Moore. Even the refereeing world, who if United's critics were to be believed would have more cause than most to stay away, was represented through Jack Taylor, who had officiated at more Leeds games during Revie's reign than anyone else. Everyone, it seemed, was there to pay their respects with one notable exception as the Football Association delivered one last snub. And no-one in Leeds was surprised one iota.

Statistics

PLAYER

Honours
FA Cup: Winners medal 1956, Runners-up medal 1955.
Footballer of the Year: 1955.

Debut: August 31, 1946   Leicester City 0 Manchester City 3
Last game: March 3, 1962   Huddersfield Town 2 Leeds United 1

		League		FA Cup		League Cup	
		App	*Gls*	*App*	*Gls*	*App*	*Gls*
1946-47	Leicester City	32	7	6	0		
1947-48	Leicester City	15	2	-	-		
1948-49	Leicester City	36	16	8	4		
1949-50	Leicester City	13	0	-	-		
	Hull City	22	0	3	1		
1950-51	Hull City	41	8	3	0		
1951-52	Hull City	13	4	-	-		
	Manchester City	26	5	2	1		
1952-53	Manchester City	32	6	3	0		
1953-54	Manchester City	37	12	2	1		
1954-55	Manchester City	32	8	6	2		
1955-56	Manchester City	21	4	2	0		
1956-57	Sunderland	16	2	-	-		
1957-58	Sunderland	39	12	2	0		
1958-59	Sunderland	9	1	-	-		
	Leeds United	20	2	1	0		
1959-60	Leeds United	35	7	-	-		
1960-61	Leeds United	14	1	-	-	3	1
1961-62	Leeds United	7	1	-	-	-	-

England
Caps six, four goals.

1954
October 2   Northern Ireland W 2-0 (Haynes, Revie)   Belfast
Home International
Wood, Foulkes, R Byrne, Wheeler, Wright, Barlow, S Matthews, Revie, Lofthouse, Haynes, Pilkington.
Attendance: 59,000.

1955
April 2   Scotland W 7-2 (Wilshaw 4, Lofthouse 2, Revie)   Wembley
Home International
Williams, Meadows, R Byrne, Armstrong, Wright, Edwards, S Matthews, Revie, Lofthouse, Wilshaw, Blunstone.
Attendance: 96,847.

May 15   France L 0-1   Paris
Friendly
Williams, P Sillett. R Byrne, Flowers, Wright, Edwards, S Matthews, Revie, Lofthouse, Wilshaw, Blunstone.
Attendance: 54,696.

October 2   Denmark W 5-1 (Revie 2, Lofthouse 2, Bradford)   Copenhagen
Baynham, Hall, R Byrne, McGarry, Wright, Dickinson, Milburn, Revie, Lofthouse, Bradford, Finney.
Attendance: 53,000.

October 22   Wales L 1-2 (own goal)   Cardiff
Williams, Hall, R Byrne, McGarry, Wright, Dickinson, S Matthews, Revie, Lofthouse, Wilshaw, Finney.
Attendance: 60,000.

1956
October 6   Northern Ireland D 1-1 (S Matthews)   Belfast
R Matthews, Hall, R Byrne, Clayton, Wright, Edwards, S Matthews, Revie, T Taylor, Wilshaw, Grainger.
Attendance: 58,420.

MANAGEMENT

Leeds United manager
Appointed: March 16, 1961.
Resigned: July 3, 1974.

Football League
Honours
Division One: Champions 1969, 1974. Runners-up 1965, 1966, 1970, 1971, 1972.
Division Two: Champions 1964.

	Comp	*Pos*	*Pl*	*W*	*D*	*L*	*F*	*A*	*W*	*D*	*L*	*F*	*A*	*Pts*
1960-61	Div 2	14th	9	1	2	1	12	6	0	2	3	4	9	6
1961-62	Div 2	19th	42	9	6	6	24	19	3	6	12	26	42	36
1962-63	Div 2	5th	42	15	2	4	55	19	4	8	9	24	34	48
1963-64	Div 2	1st	42	12	9	0	35	16	12	6	3	36	18	63
1964-65	Div 1	2nd	42	16	3	2	53	23	10	6	5	30	29	61
1965-66	Div 1	2nd	42	14	4	3	49	15	9	5	7	30	23	55
1966-67	Div 1	4th	42	15	4	2	41	17	7	7	7	21	25	55
1967-68	Div 1	4th	42	17	3	1	49	14	5	6	10	22	27	53
1968-69	Div 1	1st	42	18	3	0	41	9	9	10	2	25	17	67
1969-70	Div 1	2nd	42	15	4	2	50	19	6	11	4	34	30	57
1970-71	Div 1	2nd	42	16	2	3	40	12	11	8	2	32	18	64
1971-72	Div 1	2nd	42	17	4	0	54	10	7	5	9	19	21	57
1972-73	Div 1	3rd	42	15	4	2	45	13	6	7	8	26	32	53
1973-74	Div 1	1st	42	12	8	1	38	18	12	6	3	28	13	62

Domestic Cup Competitions
Honours
FA Cup: Winners 1972, Runners-up 1965, 1970, 1973.
League Cup: Winners 1968.

	FA Cup	League Cup
1960-61	-	-
1961-62	R3r Derby (a) 1-3	R4r Rotherham United (h) 1-2
1962-63	R5 Nottingham Forest (a) 0-3	R3 Blackburn Rovers (a) 0-4
1963-64	R4r Everton (a) 0-2	R4 Manchester City (a) 1-3
1964-65	F Liverpool (Wembley) 1-2 AET	R3 Aston Villa (h) 2-3

...

Domestic Cup Competions, continued...

1966-67	SF Chelsea (Villa Park) 0-1	R4 West Ham (a) 0-7
1967-68	SF Everton (Old Trafford) 0-1	F Arsenal (Wembley) W 1-0
1968-69	R3r Sheffield Wednesday (h) 1-3	R4 Crystal Palace (a) 1-2
1969-70	Fr Chelsea (Old Trafford) 1-2 AET	R3r Chelsea (a) 0-2
1970-71	R5 Colchester United (a) 2-3	R2 Sheffield United (a) 0-1
1971-72	F Arsenal (Wembley) W1-0	R3r West Ham (h) 0-1 AET
1972-73	F Sunderland (Wembley) 0-1	R4r Liverpol (h) 0-1
1973-74	R5r Bristol City (h) 0-1	R2 Ipswich Town (a) 0-2

Domestic final appearances

FA Cup

1965
May 1   Liverpool L 1-2 (Bremner)   Wembley
Sprake, Reaney, Charlton, Hunter, Bell, Bremner, Collins, Giles, Johanesson, Storrie, Peacock.
Attendance: 100,000.

1970
April 11   Chelsea D 2-2 (Charlton, Jones) AET   Wembley
Sprake, Madeley, Charlton, Hunter, Cooper, Lorimer, Bremner, Giles, Gray, Clarke, Jones.
Attendance: 100,000.

April 29 Replay   Chelsea L 1-2 (Jones) AET   Old Trafford
Harvey, Madeley, Charlton, Hunter, Cooper, Lorimer, Bremner, Giles, Gray, Clarke, Jones.
Attendance: 62,078.

1972
May 6   Arsenal W 1-0 (Clarke)   Wembley
Harvey, Reaney, Charlton, Hunter, Madeley, Lorimer, Bremner, Giles, Gray, Clarke, Jones.
Attendance: 100,000.

1973
May 5   Sunderland L 0-1   Wembley
Harvey, Reaney, Madeley, Hunter, Cherry, Lorimer, Bremner, Giles, E Gray (Yorath), Clarke, Jones.
Attendance: 100,000.

League Cup
1968
March 2   Arsenal W 1-0 (Cooper)   Wembley
Sprake, Reaney, Charlton, Hunter, Cooper, Lorimer, Bremner, Giles, Gray (Belfitt), Greenhoff, Madeley.
Attendance: 97,887.

Charity Shield
1969
August 2   Manchester City W 2-1 (Gray, Charlton)   Elland Road
Sprake, Reaney, Charlton, Hunter, Cooper, Madeley, Bremner, Giles, Gray, Clarke, Jones (Lorimer).
Attendance: 39,835.

European Competition

Honours

Inter-Cities Fairs Cup: Winners 1968, 1971. Runners-up: 1967.
European Cup Winners' Cup: Runners-up 1973.

1965-66	Inter-Cities Fairs Cup	SFr	Real Zaragoza 1-3 H
1966-67	Inter-Cities Fairs Cup	F	Dinamo Zagreb 0-2 (on agg) H 0-0 A 0-2
1967-68	Inter-Cities Fairs Cup	F	Ferencvaros W 1-0 (on agg) H 1-0 A 0-0
1968-69	Inter-Cities Fairs Cup	QF	Ujpesti Dozsa 0-3 (on agg) H 0-1 A 0-2
1969-70	European Cup	SF	Celtic 1-3 (on agg) H 0-1 A 1-2
1970-71	Inter-Cities Fairs Cup	F	Juventus 3-3
			(on agg, Leeds win on away goals) H 1-1 A 2-2
1971-72	Inter-Cities Fairs Cup	R1	Lierse SK 2-4 (on agg) H 0-4 A 2-0
1972-73	European Cup Winners' Cup	F	AC Milan 0-1 (Salonika)
1973-74	UEFA Cup	R3	Vitoria Setubal 1-3 (on agg) H 1-0 A 1-3

European finals/play-offs

1967 Inter-Cities Fairs Cup
August 30   1st Leg   Dinamo Zagreb (a) L 0-2
Sprake; Reaney, Charlton, Hunter, Cooper; O'Grady, Bremner, Bates, E Gray; Lorimer, Belfitt.
Attendance: 40,000

September 6   2nd Leg   Dinamo Zagreb (H) D 0-0 Lost 0-2 on aggregate
Sprake; Bell, Charlton, Hunter, Cooper; Reaney, Bremner, Giles, O'Grady; Greenhoff, Belfitt.
Attendance: 35,604.

1968 Inter-Cities Fairs Cup
August 7   1st Leg   Ferencvaros (H) W 1-0 (Jones)
Sprake; Reaney, Charlton, Hunter, Cooper; Madeley, Bremner, Giles (Greenhoff), E Gray; Lorimer, Jones (Belfitt).
Attendance: 25,268.

September 11   2nd Leg   Ferencvaros (a) 0-0 Won 1-0 on aggregate
Sprake; Reaney, Charlton, Hunter, Cooper; Lorimer, Bremner, Madeley, O'Grady; Jones, Hibbitt (Bates).
Attendance: 76,000.

1971 Inter-Cities Fairs Cup
May 28   1st Leg   Juventus (a) 2-2 (Madeley, Bates)
Sprake; Reaney, Charlton, Hunter, Cooper; Lorimer, Bremner, Giles, Madeley; Clarke, Jones (Bates).
Attendance: 45,000.

June 2   2nd Leg   Juventus (H) 1-1 (Clarke) 3-3 on aggregate, won on away goals
Sprake; Reaney, Charlton, Hunter, Cooper; Lorimer, Bremner, Giles, Madeley (Bates); Clarke, Jones.
Attendance: 42,483.

1971 Play-off between first and last winners of Inter-Cities Fairs Cup
September 22   Barcelona (a) L 1-2 (Jordan)
Sprake; Reaney, Charlton, Hunter, Davey; Lorimer, Bremner, Giles, Galvin; Belfitt, Jordan.
Attendance: 35,000.

1973 European Cup Winners' Cup
May 16   AC Milan (Salonika) L 0-1
Harvey; Reaney, Yorath, Hunter, Cherry; Lorimer, Bates, F Gray (McQueen), Madeley; Jordan, Jones.
Attendance: 45,000.

ENGLAND
Appointed: July 4, 1974.
Resigned: July 11, 1977.

	Pl	W	D	L	F	A
Home	13	7	3	3	30	10
Away	14	6	5	3	16	12
Neutral	2	1	0	1	3	3
TOTAL	29	14	8	7	49	25

(Game v Team America in 1976 was not classified as full international – England won 3-1)

1974

October 30   Czechoslovakia W 3-0 (Channon, Bell 2)   Wembley
European Championships qualifier
Clemence, Madeley, Watson, Hunter, Hughes, G Francis, Dobson (Brooking), Bell, Keegan, Channon,
Worthington (Thomas).
Attendance: 83,858.

November 20   Portugal D 0-0   Wembley
European Championships qualifier
Clemence, Madeley, Watson, Hughes, Cooper (Todd), Brooking, G Francis, Bell, Thomas, Channon, Clarke
(Worthington).
Attendance: 84,461.

1975

March 12   West Germany W 2-0 (Bell, Macdonald)   Wembley
Friendly
Clemence, Whitworth, Watson, Todd, Gillard, Bell, Ball, Hudson, Channon, Macdonald, Keegan.
Attendance: 100,000.

April 16   Cyprus W 5-0 (Macdonald 5)   Wembley
European Championships qualifier
Shilton, Madeley, Watson, Todd, Beattie, Bell, Ball, Hudson, Channon (Thomas), Macdonald, Keegan.
Attendance: 68,245

May 11   Cyprus W 1-0 (Keegan)   Limassol
European Championships qualifier
Clemence, Whitworth, Watson, Todd, Beattie (Hughes), Bell, Ball, Thomas (Tueart), Channon, Macdonald,
Keegan.
Attendance: 16,200.

May 17   Northern Ireland D 0-0   Belfast
Home International
Clemence, Whitworth, Watson, Todd, Hughes, Ball, Bell, Viljoen, Keegan, Macdonald (Channon), Tueart.
Attendance: 36,500.

May 21   Wales D 2-2 (Johnson 2)   Wembley
Home International
Clemence, Whitworth, Watson, Todd, Gillard, Ball, G Francis, Viljoen, Thomas, Channon (Little), Johnson.
Attendance: 53,000.

May 24   Scotland W 5-1 (G Francis 2, Beattie, Bell, Johnson)   Wembley
Home International
Clemence, Whitworth, Watson, Todd, Beattie, Ball, Bell, G Francis, Channon, Johnson, Keegan (Thomas).
Attendance: 98,241.

September 3   Switzerland W 2-1 (Keegan, Channon)   Basle
Friendly
Clemence, Whitworth, Watson, Todd, Beattie, Currie, Bell, G Francis, Channon, Johnson (Macdonald), Keegan.
Attendance: 30,000.

October 30   Czechoslovakia L 1-2 (Channon)   Bratislava
European Championships qualifier
Clemence, Madeley, McFarland (Watson), Todd, Gillard, Keegan, G Francis, Bell, Channon (Thomas), Macdonald, Clarke.
Attendance: 50,651.

November 19   Portugal D 1-1 (Channon)   Lisbon
European Championships qualifier
Clemence, Whitworth, Watson, Todd, Beattie, Keegan, G Francis, Brooking, Madeley (Clarke), Macdonald (Thomas), Channon.
Attendance: 60,000.

1976

March 24   Wales W 2-1 (Kennedy, Taylor)   Wrexham
Friendly
Clemence, Neal, Thompson, Doyle, Mills, Cherry (Clement), Kennedy, Boyer, Brooking, Keegan, Channon (Taylor).
Attendance: 20,927.

May 8   Wales W 1-0 (Taylor)   Cardiff
Home International
Clemence, Clement, Thompson, Greenhoff, Mills, G Francis, Kennedy, Towers, Keegan, Pearson, Taylor.
Attendance: 24,592.

May 11   Northern Ireland W 4-0 (G Francis, Channon 2, Pearson)   Wembley
Home international
Clemence, Todd, Greenhoff, Thompson, Mills, Kennedy, G Francis, Taylor (Towers), Keegan (Royle), Pearson, Channon.
Attendance: 48,000.

May 15   Scotland L 1-2 (Channon)   Glasgow
Home international
Clemence, Todd, Thompson, McFarland (Doyle), Mills, Kennedy, G Francis, Taylor, Keegan, Pearson (Cherry), Channon.
Attendance: 85,165.

May 23   Brazil L 0-1   Los Angeles
US Bicentennial Tournament
Clemence; Todd, Doyle, Thompson, Mills; G Francis, Cherry, Brooking; Keegan, Pearson, Channon.
Attendance: 32,900.

May 28   Italy W 3-2 (Channon 2, Thompson)   New York
US Bicentennial Tournament
Rimmer (Corrigan), Clement, Thompson, Doyle, Neal (Mills), Towers, Wilkins, Brooking, Hill, Royle, Channon.
Attendance: 40,650.

June 13   Finland W 4-1 (Keegan 2, Channon, Pearson)   Helsinki
World Cup qualifier
Clemence, Todd, Thompson, Madeley, Mills, G Francis, Cherry, Brooking, Keegan, Channon, Pearson.
Attendance: 24,336.

September 8   Republic of Ireland D 1-1 (Pearson)   Wembley
Friendly
Clemence, Todd, McFarland, Greenhoff, Madeley, Cherry, Wilkins, Brooking, George (Hill); Keegan, Pearson.
Attendance: 51,000.

October 13   Finland W 2-1 (Tueart, Royle)   Wembley
World Cup qualifier
Clemence, Todd, Thompson, Greenhoff, Beattie, Wilkins, Brooking (Mills), Keegan, Channon, Royle, Tueart (Hill).
Attendance: 92,000.

November 17   Italy L 0-2   Rome
World Cup qualifier
Clemence, Clement (Beattie), Greenhoff, McFarland, Mills, Cherry, Brooking, Hughes, Keegan, Bowles, Channon.
Attendance: 70,718.

1977

February 9   Holland L 0-2   Wembley
Friendly
Clemence, Clement, Doyle, Watson, Beattie, Greenhoff (Todd), Madeley (Pearson), Brooking, Keegan, Bowles, T Francis.
Attendance: 90,260.

March 30   Luxembourg W 5-0 (Channon 2, Keegan, T Francis, Kennedy)   Wembley
World Cup qualifier
Clemence, Gidman, Watson, Hughes, Cherry, Kennedy, Keegan, Hill, Channon, Royle (Mariner), T Francis.
Attendance: 81,718.

May 28   Northern Ireland W 2-1 (Channon, Tueart)   Belfast
Home International
Shilton, Cherry, Watson, Todd, Mills, Wilkins (Talbot), Greenhoff, Brooking, Tueart, Channon, Mariner.
Attendance: 35,000.

May 31   Wales L 0-1   Wembley
Home International
Shilton, Neal, Watson, Hughes, Mills, Greenhoff, Kennedy, Brooking (Tueart), Keegan, Channon, Pearson.
Attendance: 48,000.

| June 4 | Scotland L 1-2 (Channon) | Wembley |

Home International
Clemence, Neal, Watson, Hughes, Mills, Talbot, Kennedy (Tueart), Greenhoff (Cherry), T Francis, Channon, Pearson.
Attendance: 98,103.

| June 8 | Brazil D 0-0 | Rio |

Friendly
Clemence, Neal, Watson, Hughes, Cherry, Wilkins (Kennedy), Greenhoff, Talbot, Keegan, T Francis, Pearson (Channon).
Attendance: 77,000.

| June 12 | Argentina D 1-1 (Pearson) | Buenos Aires |

Friendly
Clemence, Neal, Watson, Hughes, Cherry, Wilkins, Greenhoff (Kennedy), Talbot, Keegan, Channon, Pearson.
Attendance: 60,000.

| June 15 | Uruguay D 0-0 | Montevideo |

Friendly
Clemence, Neal, Watson, Hughes, Cherry, Wilkins, Greenhoff, Talbot, Keegan, Channon, Pearson.
Attendance: 25,000.

Bibliography

Charles Buchan's Soccer Gift Book 1957-58, Charles Buchan (Charles Buchan's Publications, 1957
Cup Final Story 1946-1965, David Prole (Robert Hale, 1966).
Don't Shoot The Manager, Jimmy Greaves and Norman Giller (Boxtree, 1993).
Don Revie – Portrait of a Footballing Enigma, Andrew Mourant (Mainstream Publishing, 1990).
England Managers – The Toughest Job in Football, Brian Glanville (Headline, 2008).
English Football – Rough Guide, Dan Goldstein (Rough Guides, 1999).
Jack Charlton – The Autobiography, Jack Charlton with Peter Byrne (Partridge Press, 1996).
Leeds United and a Life in the Press Box, John Wray (Vertical Editions, 2008).
Leeds United and Don Revie, Eric Thornton (Rober Hale & Company, 1970).
Leeds United – A Complete Record, Martin Jarred and Malcolm Macdonald (Breedon Books, 1996).
Leeds United in Europe, Richard Sutcliffe, John Wray & Richard Coomber (Leeds United Publishing, 2000).
Leeds United Book of Football No 1 (Souvenir Press, 1969).
Leeds United Book of Football No 2 (Souvenir Press, 1970).
Leeds United Book of Football No 3 (Souvenir Press, 1971).
Leeds United Internationals, Martin Jarred (Breedon Books, 2009).
Leeds United – The Complete European Record, Martin Jarred and Malcolm Macdonald (Breedon Books, 2003).
Marching On Together – My Life With Leeds United, by Eddie Gray & Jason Tomas (Headline, 2001).
Paint It White, Gary Edwards (Mainstream Publishing, 2003).
Peter Lorimer – Leeds and Scotland Hero, Peter Lorimer and Phil Rostron (Mainstream Publishing, 2005).
Rothmans Football Year Book 1972-73, Jack Rollin & Leslie Vernon (Queen Anne Press, 1972).
Rothmans Football Year Book 1974-75, Jack Rollin & Leslie Vernon (Queen Anne Press, 1974).
Rothmans Football Year Book 1975-76, Jack Rollin & Leslie Vernon (Queen Anne Press, 1975).
Sir Alf, Leo McKinstry (Harper Sport, 2006).
The Boys of '72, David Saffer (Tempus, 2005).
The FA Cup Final – A Post-War History, Ivan Ponting (Tony Williams Productions, 1993).
The Football Grounds of Great Britain, Simon Inglis (Willow Books, 1987).
The Leeds United Story, Martin Jarred and Malcolm Macdonald (Breedon Books, 2002).
The Second Most Important Job in the Country (Virgin Publishing, 2000).
The Unforgiven, Rob Bagchi & Paul Rogerson (Aurum Press, 2002).

Acknowledgements

It all started one Saturday afternoon in the press room at Elland Road and a conversation with Eddie Gray.

Eddie had been, along with John Sheridan, my hero when Leeds United was the beginning and end of my world as a spotty adolescent. Yet here I was, almost a quarter-of-a-century on from the day I had joined hundreds of fans to protest at his sacking as manager in 1985, talking football with the club's greatest servant. He had just read the book, *The Damned United*, and was asking how anyone could get away with the merging of fact and fiction to produce an account that many would believe to be the gospel truth. Eddie was, in common with those who knew Don Revie from his time at Leeds, particularly upset with the depiction of his former manager. I mumbled something back about it being impossible to libel the dead and we left it at that. But the gnawing feeling of annoyance would not go away and, a couple of days later, I decided to try and do something about it. The idea for a Don Revie biography had been born.

Approaching Don's family, I was initially nervous. I had once interviewed Don's widow, Elsie, when I contributed to the matchday programme at Elland Road but did not know the couple's two children, Duncan and Kim. Would they really want their Dad's life raked up again? I needn't have worried. Duncan and Kim have both been hugely encouraging throughout, particularly in providing a phone number here or a contact there when I seemed to have hit a brick wall. Don was hugely devoted to his family, and I hope they feel this book is worthy of his memory.

I am also indebted to the dozens of Don's friends, former team-mates, former players, officials and journalists who gave up their time so freely. There are too many to list here but readers will be able to see for themselves just how invaluable the reminisces of those who knew Don the best have been. It was fascinating to speak to every single one of you. Some memories were, understandably after 50 or 60 years in some cases, hazy in parts. In that respect, I would like to thank several people for helping fill in the gaps at Don's former clubs. Namely, Alan Bennett of the Leicester City Ex-Players' Association, David Bond of the Hull City Ex-Players' Association and Winston Young of the Sunderland Ex-Players' Association. Not only did all three help with details about games that had long since been forgotten by most and provide career statistics, they also provided invaluable contact numbers and background information at their respective clubs.

The reading skills of Robert Gledhill and John Wray are also greatly appreciated, both having given up precious time away from their own work as journalists to sit in a darkened room and read early drafts.

Duncan Hamilton, a former colleague at the *Yorkshire Post*, is another I am indebted to for not only his reading skills, but also his encouragement and counsel. This book could not have been written without Duncan's help, not least because it was he who initially pointed me in the direction of Great Northern. Great Northern's Barry Cox was, thankfully for me, very receptive to the idea and his belief and support has never wavered. David Burrill has also been a tremendous help in turning my initial idea into reality, while equally invaluable was Andrew Collomosse's editing of the final draft. Likewise, David Clay for his tremendous help in scouring the *Yorkshire Post* photographic archive.

Last, but by no means least, I would like to thank my wife Anne. Your support, love and encouragement has helped me immeasurably throughout the writing of this book. I particularly appreciate the patience you showed as I spent my days off from the *Yorkshire Post* travelling the country for interviews and research work in libraries, rather than doing the household chores! Thank you, darling.

Richard Sutcliffe
September, 2010